DYNAMICS OF ELECTRONIC COMMERCE

DYNAMICS OF ELECTRONIC COMMERCE

Edited by

S.B. VERMA

Faculty of Commerce,
SNS College, Muzaffarpur,
BRA Bihar University, Muzaffarpur
Former Reader
Nagaland (Central) University, Kohima

R.K. SHRIVASTAWA

Faculty Member,
University Department of Commerce,
BRA Bihar University, Muzaffarpur

S.K. SINGH

Reader-cum-Coordinator,
Institute of Commerce and Management,
Jiwaji University, Gwalior

DEEP & DEEP PUBLICATIONS PVT. LTD.

F-159, Rajouri Garden, New Delhi - 110 027

DYNAMICS OF ELECTRONIC COMMERCE

ISBN 978-81-8450-028-8

Typeset by VERONICA GRAFIC ARTS
VP-216A, Pitampura, Maurya Enclave, Delhi - 110 088

Printed in India at NEW ELEGANT PRINTERS
A-49/1, Mayapuri, Phase-I, New Delhi - 110 064

Published by DEEP & DEEP PUBLICATIONS PVT. LTD.
F-159, Rajouri Garden, New Delhi - 110 027
Phones : 25435369, 25440916
E-mails : deep98@del3.vsnl.net.in • ddpbooks@yahoo.co.in
Showroom :
2/13, Ansari Road, Daryaganj, New Delhi - 110 002 • Telefax : 23245122

Contents

PART II

INFORMATION TECHNOLOGY AND E-COMMERCE

Preface

Global E-commerce can create new opportunities for developing countries like India to take advantage of the benefit of open world trading system. Thus furthering the advent of E-commerce. Some of the issues need to be addressed on an urgent basis, such as development of infrastructure, protection to consumers, development of human resource, enactment of laws governing E-commerce.

The growing importance of E-commerce in the era of globalisation and liberalisation along with the membership of WTO has brought about significant changes in the business deals in Indian economy. It has opened new vistas to the entrepreneurs in India and the real success depends upon the efforts and attitude of business units as well as consumers to make use of opportunities by availing the protection and security measures provided in the IT Act. Let us hope that the electronics means of trading activities would pave the way to revolutionise the marketing system ensuring maximum benefits to the entrepreneurs and consumers in the time to come.

Electronic Commerce (E-commerce) is entirely a phenomenon of the technology revolutions of the late 20th century. It begins in computers and information systems in telecommunications also in banking systems and even in postal and delivery services.

E-commerce is the process of buying and selling goods and services electronically with computerised business transactions using the Internet networks and other digital technology. E-commerce is a new term for existing business opportunities in the market place, which is pressurising business operations all round the world to change traditional methods of conducting business. It replaces traditional business through new ways of transferring and processing the information which is the life-blood of any business. It is about taking benefit of revolutionary new technology to improve current business process and to improve operating efficiencies and maintain or extend the lead over competition.

E-commerce refers to the paperless exchange of business information using EDI, e-mail, EFT and other network-based technology. E-commerce is shrinking the world. Distance markets suddenly are within easy reach, saving business time, money and energy, prospecting and presenting new business opportunities for better and more thorough information. It creates value and enable new relationship between businessmen and customers. Areas of E-commerce services available are:

(a) Legacy application integration,
(b) Internet application integration,
(c) EDI – Electronic Data Interchange,
(d) Migration to web-based models,
(e) New IT framework,
(f) Integration with business strategies, and
(g) E-commerce training services.

The importance of e-commerce is high that it has been recognised by the international community. It is as a methodology to boost up the trade at international level. The global market is turning into a global village due to e-commerce. Advantages of e-commerce are as follows:

(a) No barrier of time and distance,
(b) Less marketing and distribution expenses,
(c) Eliminate the gap between big and small traders,
(d) Better customer satisfaction,
(e) Fewer middlemen in business,
(f) Paperless transaction,
(g) Better mode of payment,
(h) Global market,
(i) Save time and cost,
(j) E-entertainment,
(k) E-banking,
(l) E-shopping,
(m) New sales opportunities, and
(n) Optimum use of resources.

International organisations have started creating the necessary framework. Some of the prominent organisations which have made inroads on such issues include:

(a) World Trade Organisation (WTO),

(b) Organisation for Economic Co-operation and Development (OECD),
(c) United Nations Economic Commission for Africa (UNECA),
(d) Asia Pacific Economic Co-operation (APEC),
(e) World Intellectual Property Organisation (WIPO), and
(f) Global Information Infrastructure Commission (GIIC).

Soon with the coordinated efforts of these organisations, business communities and governments of various nations, a legal framework suitable for new medium of doing business will be in place keeping in view the efforts made in this direction. Some basic principles may be evolved to guide the formulation of rules and regulations governing e-commerce in various countries around the globe. This will facilitate building of a uniform foundation for the development of e-commerce.

This venture will be useful for researchers, academicians, electronic media and so on. The Editors-*cum*-anthologist are thankful to *Yojana, Kurukshetra, Employment News, Chartered Accountant, Chartered Secretary* and so on for giving their permission to reprint the articles published by them.

I, Dr. S.B. Verma am highly obliged to the contributors, authors and journalists for giving their co-operation in completing the venture. I would like to articulate my deep sense of gratitude to my father Late Shri Baban Pd. Srivastawa, Additional District Magistrate, my mother Late Mrs. Lalmuni and my wife Late Dr. Hema Verma, Deputy Collector, whose invisible soul inspired me to arrive at the venture. I am also obliged to Binay Kumar Sinha and his son Nitesh Kumar Sinha, Kalambag Chauk, Muzaffarpur who encouraged me from time to time in shaping the venture.

Muzaffarpur EDITORS

List of Contributors

Ajai Tiwari: Statistical Supervisor, MONIRBA, Allahabad University.

Ajay Kumar Sah: Indian Institute of Sugarcane Research, Lucknow.

Alok Srivastava: Professor, MONIRBA, University of Allahabad.

Amita Sharma: Associate Professor, Deptt. of Statistics, University of Rajasthan, Jaipur.

Amit Neb: Deptt. of Commerce, Allahabad University, Allahabad.

Anju Agrawal: Education Officer, Directorate of Studies and Research, Institute of Company Secretary of India.

A. Ranga Reddy: Professor, Deptt. of Economics, Venkateswara University, Tirupati.

Archana Kaul: Education Officer, Directorate of Studies and Research, Institute of Company Secretary of India.

Arun Kumar: Reader, MONIRBA, University of Allahabad.

A. Saravanan: DESIDOIC, Defence Research and Development Organisation, Ministry of Defence, New Delhi.

Ashok Agarwal: Associate Professor, Deptt. of ABST, University of Rajasthan, Jaipur.

B.B. Mansuri: Faculty, Deptt. of Commerce, Govt. P.G. College, Jalaun.

Bucheshwar Mandal: Teacher, B.N. College, T.M. Bhagalpur University, Bhagalpur.

Don Richardson: Specialist in Internet.

D. Ravi: Faculty Member, Alluri Institute of Management Science, Warangal, Andhra Pradesh.

Himanshu Sekhar Singh: Reader, DBME, Dr. R.M.L. Awadh University, Faizabad, U.P.

J.V. Vilanilam: Ex. Vice-Chancellor, University of Kerala, Thiruvananthapuram, Kerala.

K. Pandyan: Expert in Information Technology, New Delhi.

K. Rajeshwar Rao: Professor, Deptt. of Commerce and Business Administration, Kakatiya University, Warangal, Andhra Pradesh.

Lal C. Morani: Assistant Professor, Deptt. of Accountancy and Business Statistics, University of Rajasthan, Jaipur.

Leeba Babu: Research Scholar in Commerce, University of Kerala.

Madhu: Deptt. of Commerce, Allahabad University, Allahabad.

M. Sarngadharan: Professor and Head, Deptt. of Commerce, University of Kerala, Thiruvananthapuram.

Navin Prakash: IAS, Director, NCZCC, Allahabad.

Panchali Singh: Lecturer, KNIPSS, Sultanpur, U.P.

Patrick Kommu: Consultant with NABARD, New Delhi.

Peeyush Kr. Pandey: Lecturer, KNIPSS, Sultanpur, U.P.

P.V. Jayakumar: Officer, Branch Computerisation Cell, RO Thrissur.

Rahul Ganguli: Deptt. of Commerce, Allahabad University, Allahabad.

Rajendra P. Srivastava: Director, Ernst and Young Centre for Auditing Research and Advanced Technology, School of Business, The University of Kansas, Lawrence, U.S.A.

Ravi Kumar Shrivastawa: Senior Faculty, University Department of Commerce, BRA Bihar University, Muzaffarpur.

Satyanarayana Patnaik: DESIDOIC, Defence Research and Development Organisation, Ministry of Defence, New Delhi.

Sawalia Bihari Verma: Professor, Faculty of Commerce, S.N.S. College, Muzaffarpur, Former Reader, Nagaland (Central) University, Kohima.

Shantanu Kumar: Scientist, Central Potato Research Station, Upper Shillong, Meghalaya.

Shiv Kumar Jiloka: Reader in Commerce, B.N. College, T.M. Bhagalpur University, Bhagalpur.

Shiv Kumar Singh: Reader, Institute of Commerce and Management, Jiwaji University, Gwalior.

Sitaram Sharma: University Professor of Commerce, Marwari College, T.M. Bhagalpur University, Bhagalpur.

S.K. Gupta: Researcher, University of Rajasthan, Jaipur.

S.K. Mangal: Associate Professor, Deptt. of ABST, University of Rajasthan, Jaipur

Sonal Mishra: Research Scholar, MONIRBA, Allahabad University, Allahabad.

Subhashis Datta: Specialist in Information Technology, Kolkata.

Subodh Kesharwani: Researcher, MOBIRBA, Allahabad University, Allahabad.

Sunil Kr. Pandey: Lecturer, KNIPSS, Sultanpur, U.P.

Sunnykutty Thomas: Lecturer, St. Dominic's College, Kanjirapally, Kottayam, Kerala.

Tripti Singh: Research, MONIRBA, University of Allahabad.

Uma Sah: Scientist, CPRS, Shillong, Meghalaya.

Vijay Mukhi: Expert in Information Technology, New Delhi.

V.K. Agarwal: Director, Directorate of Studies and Research, Institute of Company Secretary of India, New Delhi.

V.K. Vasal: Reader in Financial Studies, University of Delhi.

Yogesh Upadhyay: Reader in Management, Institute of Commerce and Management, Jiwaji University, Gwalior. Ex-Dean, Faculty of Commerce, M.G. Chitrakoot Gramodaya University, Chitrakoot, Satna, Participant, FDP Programme, IIM Ahmedabad. Ex-Faculty Member, Prestige Institute of Management, Gwalior.

PART I

E-COMMERCE: CONCEPTUAL FRAME

1

E-Commerce: An Overview in the Indian Context

SUBHASHIS DATTA

There was a time when resources and markets were generally co-related. A company would set-up business where four main resources (men, machines, material and money) were readily available. It would use these resources to manufacture a product. It would then build up and serve a local (sometimes national) customer-base. Progressively, 'the national' market became saturated and the companies began to look beyond these horizons. Thus, the companies began to export excess production to overseas markets. Growing demand from these markets sometimes warranted establishing a local sales office or manufacturing operation. Occasionally, it even led to a token R&D presence, to adapt the offering to local tastes.

Alongside the dispersal of markets, came the dispersal of resources. Initially, it was just a question of capitalising on cheaper sources of material or labour in remote locations — while the strategic competencies remained buried in-house. But over time, many of the overseas producers used the low-cost platform to build up real expertise in a particular domain with the result that pockets of excellence have sprung up around the world. Finally, companies themselves have grown increasingly dispersed and decentralised in order to get close to these emerging markets and technologies. Global coverage allows companies to be responsive to market needs and gives them rapid access to far-flung strategic resources. At the same time, however, it impedes the internal flow of communication.

Dispersion on all fronts has, therefore, dramatically changed some of the rules of business competition. Companies no longer own all the key resources but must locate and access them first. The attractive growth opportunities have to be actively identified as the domestic market is not necessarily the lead market and corporate competencies are not all co-located at the headquarters. They have to be pooled from distant nodes.

All this puts a premium on the movement of information—internally and externally—as a competence. This is where the strategic value of the Internet lies. It can significantly enhance the quality of a company's linkages. Externally, it helps the company to sense new markets and to access new knowledge as it emerges. Internally, it allows information acquired or generated on the periphery to circulate throughout the group. The Internet is a basic driving force for the conduct of e-commerce. E-commerce provides an environment where time differences and location do not matter.

INTERNET

The Internet and its related basic services such as electronic mail (e-mail) and the world wide web (WWW) have created a new space in which any individual or company can exchange information, sell or purchase different products and services and initiate formal business transactions. In simple terms, the Internet is a world-wide network of thousands of computer networks. The Internet was developed in the late 1960s, but the Internet revolution is a phenomenon of 1990, when it moved out of the research institute and started to be used as an organisational tool for business across the world. According to a survey by ICRA, which published *The Indian Internet Business Report,* the Internet subscribers in the country grew from a mere 0.05 million in 1996 to six million in March 2000. During the same period, the number of Internet users went up from 0.25 million to 16 million.

E-commerce

E-commerce (electronic commerce) is the buying and selling of goods and services on the Internet. It helps in conducting traditional commerce through new ways of transferring and processing the information which is the life blood of any business. It is about taking advantage of revolutionary new technology to improve current business processes and to improve operating efficiencies and maintain or extend the lead over competition. It refers to the paperless exchange of business information using EDI, e-mail, EFT and other network-based technology. E-commerce is shrinking the world. Distant markets suddenly are within easy reach, saving business time, money and energy, prospecting and presenting new business opportunities for better and more thorough information.

Today a person just needs a computer, a browser and access to the Internet and he can buy anything from a pin to a plane. E-commerce success stories are many. To name a few – Intel, the No. 1 company in computer processor manufacturing, generated an estimated $ 10 billion of its $ 27 billion overall revenue through its online operations. Dell, America's No. 1 PC-maker, brings in roughly $ 6.1 billion through online sales against its overall revenue of $ 21.67 billion.

Online business purchasing was around $ 406 billion in 2000 and will be $ 2.7 trillion in 2004. More than half of this trade will go through e-marketplaces (as per the *Forester Research Report*).

E-business

E-business (electronic business) is the conduct of business on the Internet, not only buying and selling, but also servicing consumers and collaborating with business partners. E-business is the future of all business; it encompasses the use of technologies and processes and management practices that enhance organisational competitiveness through strategic use of electronic information. It goes beyond e-commerce by integrating e-commerce tightly with business operations to improve performance, create value and enable new relationships between businessmen and customers.

Electronic Data Interchange (EDI)

EDI is computer-to-computer communication of business messages in standard codes and formats. This system allows the direct, automatic and instantaneous input of messages into the transaction processing system without human re-keying. This system, used extensively for contracts, invoices and order-placing between component suppliers and manufacturers, is being extensively integrated within the electronic commerce models converging around the Internet.

Search Engine

A search engine is a type of software that creates indices of databases or Internet sites based on file titles, key words or the full text of the files. The search engine has an interface allowing users to type their requests into a blank field. It then lists the search results. Search engines on the web return the results in hypertext so that users can click on any item in the list to get the actual file.

Internet Service Provider (ISP)

An Internet service provider is the computer system providing the Internet connection. ISPs are accessed by modem and telephone line which are called dial-up services. The State-owned Videsh Sanchar Nigam Limited has the maximum number of Internet subscribers in the country (344,000 subscribers in April 2000) followed by Satyam Infoway (151,000 subscribers in the same period). Some of the other ISPs are Department of Telecom, Caltiger, MTNL, Dishnet, etc.

Benefits of E-commerce

E-commerce leads to a win-win situation for both companies and customers. The companies can reach more customers all over the world, gather better information about them, target them more effectively and thus serve them better. The companies can also reduce cost considerably by reducing cycle times, sales and marketing costs, document processing costs and, therefore, improve their working capital and productivity.

The market places also create value for third party intermediaries which can earn transaction commissions and fees for value-added services such as information and analysis, order and payment processing, integration of buyer and seller IT systems and consultancy services.

However, the best rewards go to the customers. They are able to compare products and prices early, demand a better quality of service at a lower cost and, in turn, compel suppliers to compete more fiercely than ever.

E-commerce Business Models

Business to Business (B2B)

Commercial transactions take place between different business organisations. It forms a major portion of total e-commerce volume. Value per transaction is high when compared with other models. B2B in India – Maruti Udyog, Telco, Bajaj Auto and Thermex. According to ICRA in *The Indian Internet Business Report*. B2B e-commerce turnover will increase from Rs. 4.1 billion in the financial year 2000 to Rs. 232.8 billion in the financial year 2005, representing over 90 per cent of the total e-commerce activity in the country.

Business to Consumer (B2C)

Commercial transactions take place between a business and its consumers. Each transaction in B2C mode represents an individual buying online, for example, Amazon.com – books and CDs, Amul.com – products of Amul.

The total worth of B2C e-commerce activities in India is expected to increase from Rs. 0.5 billion in the financial year 2000 to Rs. 18.82 billion in 2005.

The difference between business to business (B2B) and business to consumer (B2C) models are given below:

Business to Consumer (B2C)	*Business to Business (B2B)*
Transaction-driven	Relationship-based
Short-term	Long-term
Casual	Mission-control
Differentiation based on price and image	Differentiation based on reliability and service
Many vendors	Few partners
Time insensitive	Time sensitive
No vendor loyalty, no switching cost	Very high switching cost

Consumer to Consumer (C2C)

Commercial transactions taking place between individual customers and buyers. The important differentiation is that no business organisation is involved, for example, Automartindia.com – focussing on automobiles, Propertymartindia.com – focussing on real estate.

Barriers in Progress of E-commerce

Perceived barriers to selling over the Internet:

- High costs of setting up of e-commerce enabled sales platform on the Internet and even higher cost to maintain it.
- Do not know where to start from as most of the companies do not have a full-fledged EDP/IT department.
- Customers/buyers are less sophisticated. Lack of trust among trading partners.
- Have only customised products. No readymade products.
- Differential pricing—every buyer has to negotiate contract price. Lack of standard payment infrastructure.
- Does not have a catalogue.

Factors Influencing E-commerce in India

Low PC Penetration

The entire e-commerce activity depends heavily on the availability of high speed data communication networks and availability of personal computers to a large segment of the population. At present, the penetration of personal computers is extremely poor in India—about 2.1 PCs per 1,000 people as against 407 PCs per 1,000 people in the U.S.A. Till the usage of computers becomes widespread, e-commerce cannot flourish.

Internet Access

The problem of low PC penetration is compounded by the low telephone connections. At present, there are 19.1 million telephone connections in India. The number of telephone lines has to increase further to facilitate the spread of Internet services. The number of hosts which provide the facility of web pages and website hosting/launching in India is only 16,253 as against over three million in the U.S.A. and 1.8 million in Japan. The situation will not improve further unless we explore other Internet access modes like cable connections or mobile phones. The Internet through cable system has been implemented successfully in Orissa.

Cyber and Tax Laws

The major legal barriers for e-commerce implementation are the admissibility of EDI-generated documents and their acceptability as evidence in court. Though the Government has passed the Information Technology Act, 2000 to resolve most of the issues associated in the implementation of e-commerce, the ordinary people are not fully aware of this legislation. Therefore, the government and professional bodies have to take the initiative to create awareness among the people about the cyber laws.

The mode of transacting business through e-commerce has posed varied problems concerning income tax. The complications that arise in taxing e-commerce transactions relate to jurisdiction, establishing the identity of the taxpayers, absence of tangible documents, electronic manipulation, etc. Proper solutions have to be worked out in co-operation with other countries keeping in mind that the growth of e-commerce is not checked.

Credit Card Mindset and Personal Information

Most people are very reluctant to give credit card information over the Internet as they feel that once they give this information it can be misused. Thus, every effort should be made by the Government to remove the fear psychosis among the people. Moreover, severe penal action can be initiated against those who violate laws in connection with collection, use and dissemination of personal information.

Set-up Cost

Most companies, other than the big-sized ones, are reluctant to do business through e-commerce as it involves a lot of expenditure in setting up a system to support e-commerce activity, design and development of web pages and its regular maintenance.

CONCLUSION

E-business, Yes or No

Although still in its infancy, e-commerce has a very big potential world-wide in the business-to-business and business-to-consumer sectors and this is true for India, too. Thus, the new economies of doing business in a virtual marketplace create new business opportunities but, at the same time, most of the conventional methods of business are threatened. Companies hoping to leverage the potential of the

Internet will have to create new rules or even new functions; a scanning function to monitor and influence Internet opinion, a new service development function to think up new ways of creating value for customers, liaison roles to support networks of remote members, usage analysts to perform market research on the web and archivists for keeping track of content generated on the company's website.

The winners will be those companies that organise themselves to capitalise on the Internet's capacity to increase sensitivity to resource and market opportunities world-wide and to share knowledge and experience internally. Thus, a company that incorporates electronic commerce as a major component of its marketing strategy stays at least in line with, if not ahead, of the competition. The others will die within a short span of time, thus proving that the Darwinian law – survival of the fittest – still prevails.

2

E-Commerce: Indian Perspective

AJAI TIWARI AND SONAL MISHRA

India is currently in the midst of an e-commerce revolution. The arrival of the internet followed by the escalating growth of Web-based businesses is leading to e-commerce both on the B2B and the B2C sides. The e-commerce trends in India are in perfect accordance with the sweeping changes taking place in the global markets. The government itself has proved to be IT friendly and has initiated significant steps in the past few months to ensure that the economic climate is ripe for e-business.

Today, everywhere one looks, the signs of Internet's arrival and adoption loom large. And as the Internet proliferates, so will e-commerce and e-business – this is now a universally recognized fact. Therefore, a boost in the expansion of the Internet in the country will not only help India become a vital part of the emerging global economy, it will also enable its citizens to avail the benefits of the web enabling experience.

The internet has existed since the 1970s. But 99% of the internet-cognizant population has become familiar with it only as recently as the past six years – driven entirely by the advent of the world-wide web (WWW). The web is probably one of the most exciting phenomena in recent times and has the potential to change how we lead our day-to-day lives, through the much-hyped business to consumer (B2C) e-commerce wave. The deployment of e-commerce applications can provide an organization with significant benefits in reaching new markets, reducing cost, improving cycle times and enhancing service levels. In fact in many parts of the western world this is already happening. However, in India, though the promise and capabilities of the technology are already in evidence it is still a long way to go before these become common-place for a number of reasons.

HELICOPTER VIEW OF VARIOUS PARTICIPANTS AND VARIOUS CONSUMERS ON THE WEB

Business to Business (B2B)

This is supposed to be a huge opportunity area in the web. Companies have by and large computerized all the operations world-wide and now they need to go into the next stage by linking their customers and vendors. This is done by supply chain software which is an integral part of our ERP application. Companies need to set-up a backbone of B2B applications which will support the final customer requirements at the web. Many B2B sites are company and industry specific catering to a community of users or a combination of forward and backward integration. Companies have achieved huge savings in distribution-related costs due to their B2B applications. The example which comes to mind immediately is that of CISCO systems, who sell the networking equipment which powers the Internet.

Business to Consumer (B2C)

This is a direct application from a seller of products to an end consumer of those products particularly the retail products. Amazon.com is typical example.

Consumer to Business (C2B)

These refer to the applications emanating from a consumer to a business which are actually consumer items but need a business intermediary. Most of the search engines are operating C to B models. Priceline.com offers named price product offerings in travel, tickets holidays, etc. is another example. The site asks for a price from the customer and goes and finds out the best match for that given price.

Consumer to Consumer (C2C)

C to C applications are the ones involving consumers who deal with each other on the web. They need a site like an online auction site for example to transact with each other. E Bay is an example. Message boards, community sites, chat forums are also C to C applications.

It doesn't mean that the Internet is all about buying and selling goods or services or information. The internet works because of a whole industry works painstakingly to make it happen.

There are probably already a dozen or so B2C e-commerce sites in India at present. Ranging from general purpose sites (www.rediff.com) to specific sites that will let us order our groceries (www.homeland.com, www.bababazaar.com) buy cinema tickets (www clicktickets.com) real estate property listing services (www.indiaproperties.com), to a site that will even (supposedly) enable us to buy an automobile *via* the internet! However a number of things have to happen before it can be heralded as the dawn of a new era in India.

REASONS FOR ADOPTING E-BUSINESS BY INDIAN COMPANIES

Direct Interaction with Customers

This is the greatest advantage of e-business. The unknown and faceless customer buying the products of a large MNC like say HLL or Proctor & Gamble through distributors, channels, shops, etc., now he has a name, face and a profile. Large MNC's pay a fortune for this information on customer buying patterns.

Focussed Sales Promotion

This information gives authentic data about client likes, dislikes and preferences and thus help the company bring out focussed sales promotion drives which are aimed at the right audience.

Building Customer Loyalty

It has been observed that on line customers can be more loyal than other customers if they are made to feel special and their distinct identity is recognised and concerns about privacy are respected. It has also been seen that once customers develop a binding relationship with a site! product on the web they don't like to shift loyalties to another site/product and re-enter their profile information all over again.

Scalability

The web is open 24 hours a day and seven days a week. Thus provides an access never known before to the customer. This access is across locations and time zones. Thus a company is able to handle much more customers on much wider geographical spread if it uses an e-business model. The company can set lip a generic parent site for all locations and make regional domains to suit such requirements. This model is being used by Microsoft very successfully. The additional cost of servicing additional customers comes down drastically once a critical mass is reached.

Savings in Distribution Costs

A company can huge savings in distribution, logistical and after sales support costs by using a business models. Typical examples are of computer companies, airlines, and telecom companies. This is because the e-business models involve the customer in the business interaction to such a level that they are able to avoid setting up the huge backbone of sales and support force which ordinarily would have to set-up.

E-commerce revenues in India are expected to increase dramatically over the next three years. Though we still lag behind stalwarts like China, Japan and Taiwan in terms of internet usage yet the gradual quickening in the pace of India's Internet growth can be judged by the India Internet Log Book 2000, which reports over 1.8 million subscribers (and more than 55 million users). And the estimated figure by 31 December, 2003 is a whopping 50 million. According to a 1999 report by International Data Corporation (IDC), e-commerce will account for $ 575 million by financial year 2002-03, making India the fourth largest Internet market in Asia.

Experts have argued that the low cost of personal computers, a growing installed base for internet use, and an increasingly competitive Internet Service Provider (ISP) market will help fuel e-commerce growth in Asia's second most populous nation. Dataquest an Indian computer magazine, has found that the rise of Indian Internet subscribers will ultimately depend on the proliferation of network computers and Internet cable. Cyber cafes will also continue to provide low cost access.

As per a Nasscom-McKinsey study 1999, India has the potential to earn revenues worth US $ 10 billion by 2008 from e-business solutions. (Both the domestic and export markets put together.)

And the Indian players can achieve this goal by increasing their reach, establishing deep relationships, and expanding the scope of businesses covered. As part of its survey on e-commerce Nasscom also conducted a study on the plans and capabilities of software companies in India. Some of the preliminary findings on e-commerce/e-business software exports potential are as follows:

- The study revealed that Supply Chain Management optimisation and Customer Relation Management are going to be one of the strongest drivers of the global e-commerce solution market. And more than 72 percent of Indian software houses were found to possess strong expertise in Supply Chain Management and CRM.
- Some of the areas of e-commerce services available are:
  1. Legacy application integration,
  2. Internet application integration,
  3. EDI,
  4. Migration to Web-based models,
  5. New IT frameworks,
  6. Integration with business strategies, and
  7. E-commerce training services.

There are still enormous challenges facing e-commerce sites in India. The relatively small credit card population and lack of uniform credit agencies creates a variety of payment challenges unknown in the United States. Increased distribution of online purchases could be complicated by India's complex postal system and an uncertain regulatory environment. Nonetheless, everyone from Yahoo, Microsoft, and IBM to local carpet vendors, hotels, and some Indian ISP's are trying to claim a slice of the rapidly emerging Indian e-commerce market.

The past two years have seen a rise in the number of companies's embracing e-commerce technologies and the Internet in India. Major Indian portal sites have also shifted towards e-commerce instead of depending on advertising revenue. The major in this services being Rediff on the net (www.rediff.com) and India plaza which started a shopping section after their highly successful content site generated WEB visitors. In spite of RBI regulation, low Internet usage e-commerce sites have popped up everywhere hawking things like groceries, bakery items, gifts, books, audio and videocassettes, computer, etc. None of the major players have been deterred by the low PC penetration and credit card usage in India and have tried to close the success world-wide of online commerce. BPB publication went online selling its complete range of computer books about 2 years ago, it might not have the success like Amazon.com, but they definitely have promised the cause of e-commerce in India with at least 1 to 5 web sites like Indiabookshop coming online.

This is not to say that the e-commerce scenario has been bad in India as highly successful e-business like baba bazaar and India mart have proved. Indian banks too have been very successful in adapting EDI Technologies to provide customers with real time account status, transfer of funds between current and checking accounts, stop payment facilities ICICI Bank, Global TRUST BANK and UTI-Bank also have put their electronic banking over the internet facilities in place for the upcoming e-commerce market. The future does look very bright for e-commerce in India with even the stock exchanges coming online providing an online stock portfolio and status with a fifteen minute delay in prices. The day cannot be far when with RBI regulations we will be able to see stock transfer and sale over the Net.

Though with security and encryption being proven Technologies for transfer of funds over the Internet, the Indian Government still has problems with 'Digital signatures' and verification processes over the Internet. This combined with RBI norms and regulations has proved to a major hurdle for e-commerce even though VSNL India's monopolistic ISP does want to jump on to the electronic transaction bandwagon with the advent of private ISP's and India new and positive attitude towards IT and prime ministers new "IT policy". The future is very positive in India for doing commerce with a-e.

INTERNET TRENDS IN INDIA (2001)

- The number of active Internet subscribers is forecast at 1.5 million in March 2002, an increase of only 30 percent, compared to 1.1 million in March 2001, or a growth of 74 percent. (These figures exclude users of free ISPs as well as inactive accounts.)
- The total investments made by all ISPs are estimated at around Rs. 5500 crore. The industry revenues are likely to be only a fifth of that Rs. 1,000 crore.

  The number of licensed ISPs during 2001 was 470. Only 130 licensees are operational today, and only one, the oldest player, VSNL is reportedly profitable.

- A shakeout is underway, with some players exiting the business completely, or selling out to larger players.
- Most B2C dot coms were unable to sustain operations: a few leading ones continue to survive, well funded, they lowered costs and honed their value proposition and also introduced offline business models.

Most B2B initiatives have gone unnoticed in the general gloom surrounding dot coms. The automotive sector continues to take significant steps in wiring up their supply chain; while Internet usage in the banking and financial sector is on the upswing.

SOURCE: NASSCOM

The forces that determine the web's winners and losers are just taking shape and technological advances could add even more uncertainty. On the downside, some experts predict that it will be increasingly difficult for smaller companies to establish their presence. Public companies and traditional brand name retailers have deep pockets and a name recognition that will make it difficult for smaller sites and mom-and-pop shops to attract customers, thereby forcing them to complete with the big boys. On the Net, it's one big neighbourhood. On the upside, nearly all experts believe that overall e-commerce will increase exponentially in coming years. Business to business transactions will represent the largest revenue. Online retailing will also enjoy a drastic growth. Areas expected to go include financial services, travel, entertainment and groceries. And for those considering opening a virtual storefront, forthcoming technology and standards agreements will make it easier to create a site, to protect it against payment fraud, and to share information with suppliers and business partners.

REFERENCES

Deloitee Research, 'The Future of B2B—A New Genesis', 2002.

Hanson W., 'Principles of Internet Marketing', South-Western College Publishing, USA.

Trombly: 'E-Business Model', Computer World, 2001.

Wilson, R.F., 'Business Models on the Web', Web Marketing Today.

Website References

Altavista.com
Amazon.com
Automartindia.com
Expressindia.com
Indiatimes.com
Itsgzb.com
Nasscom.org
Rediff.com
Yahoo.com

3

E-Commerce—An Overview

SAWALIA BIHARI VERMA AND
RAVI KUMAR SHRIVASTAVA

Electronic Commerce (e-commerce), buzz word of the decade, is entirely a phenomenon of the technology revolutions of the late 20th century. It begins in computers and information systems, in telecommunications and also in banking systems and even in postal and delivery services.

E-commerce is the process of buying and selling goods and services electronically with computerised business transactions using the Internet, networks and other digital technologies. E-commerce is a new term for existing business opportunities in the market place, which is pressurising business operations all round the world to change traditional methods of conducting business. It replaces traditional business through new ways of transferring and processing the information which is the lifeblood of any business. It is about taking benefit of revolutionary new technology to improve current business processes and to improve operating efficiencies and maintain or extend the lead over competition.

E-commerce refers to the paperless exchange of business information using EDI, e-mail, EFT and other network-based technology. E-commerce is shrinking the world. Distance Markets suddenly are within easy reach. Saving business time, money and energy, prospecting and presenting new business opportunities for better and more through information. It creates value and enable new relationship between businessmen and customers.

MODELS/TYPES OF E-COMMERCE

There are three parties involved in e-commerce—(1) Business (B),

(2) Consumers (C), and (3) Government. E-banking, E-shopping and E-business are different forms of E-commerce but generally following types of E-commerce are recognised as major models—

B2B (Business to Business)	Transactions between two companies.
B2C (Business to Consumer)	Transactions between company and a consumer.
C2C (Consumer to Consumer)	Transactions between two consumers.
C2B (Consumer to Business)	Transactions between consumer and business enterprise.

There are transactions between two businesses or corporations where the product branded is for business use. This category is characterised by a limited number of transactions. Where each transaction is typically of larger volume. The end-customer is typically a previously approved or registered customer or at least known to the merchant. Many B2B sites are company and industry specific catering to a community of users or a combination of forward and backward integration. Companies have achieved huge saving in distribution-related costs due to their B2B applications. The example which comes to mind immediately is that of CISCO Systems, who sell the networking equipment which powers the Internet.

There are the transactions that most of us are familiar with today, with individual customers buying books and music CDs over the web or surfing the web to find the best deal for particular item. Merchants setting up shop on the web deal directly with the end customer. This category is characterised by a large number of transactions, where each transaction is typically small in volume. The end-customer could be totally unknown to the merchant or might be visiting the shop for a few occasional purchases. Thus, this is a direct application from a seller of products to an end consumer of those products particularly the retail products. Amazon.com is typical example.

C2C applications are the ones involving consumers who deal with each other on the web. They need a site like an online auction site for example to transact with each other. E Bay is an example. Message boards, community sites, chart forums are also C to C applications.

C2B refer to the applications emanating from a consumer to a business which are actually consumer items but need a business intermediary. Most of the search engines are operating C to B models. Priceline.com offers named price product offerings in travel, tickets, holidays, etc. is another example. The site asks for a price from the customer and goes and finds out the best match for that given price.

Besides, some other models are recognised which are – Business to Government (B2G), Consumer to Government (C2G).

It does not mean that the Internet is all about buying and selling goods or services or information. The Internet works because of a whole industry works painstakingly to make it happen.

ACTIVITIES OF E-COMMERCE

The different activities that could be carried on electronically include –

- **Electronic Presentation of Goods and Services** – This would include making e-catalogue on the site through which the customer could browse to select his/her purchase. It could also include search facilities, where the user could search for items based on its attributes.
- **Online Order Taking and Bill Presentation** – This would include provision for the user to specify the items he wishes to order, define the terms of payment and delivery and an automated billing system for the users.
- **Automated Customer Account Inquiries** – This could function independent of how the other activities were finalised, online or offline. This would be an integral part of customer support.
- **Online Payment and Transaction Handling** – The merchant may provide or tie up with some third party for the payment verification and special payment methods must be defined and the back and connectivity for these established.
- **Automated Supply – Chain Management Solutions** – This is a collaboration between a company, its business partners and its customers where various applications talk to each other. One of the benefits of e-commerce is that it is much simpler to integrate supply chain solutions fully to the system.

Some of the areas of e-commerce services available are –

1. Legacy application integration.
2. Internet application integration.
3. EDI – Electronic Data Interchange.
4. Migration to web-based models.
5. New IT frameworks.

6. Integration with business strategies, and
7. E-commerce training services.

Increased distribution of online purchases could be complicated by India's complex postal system and an uncertain regulatory environment. Nonetheless, everyone from Yahoo, Microsoft, and IBM to local carpet vendors, hotels, and some Indian ISPs are trying to claim a slice of the rapidly emerging Indian e-commerce market.

FRAMEWORK FOR GLOBAL E-COMMERCE

As per a report 'A Framework for Global Electronic Commerce' released by the President of U.S.A. in 1997, five principles have been enunciated to guide government action and to give an impetus to the growth of e-commerce. The five principles are—

1. *The private sector should lead.* Internet should develop in a market driven arena where government should encourage industry self-regulation.
2. *The government should avoid undue restriction on e-commerce.* The government should refrain from imposing new and unnecessary regulations, bureaucratic procedures or new taxes and tariffs on commercial activities taking place *via* the Internet.
3. ***Where government involvement is needed, its aim should be to support and enforce a predictable minimalist consistent and simple legal environment for e-commerce.*** Government intervention should be to ensure competition, protest intellectual property and privacy, prevent fraud, faster transparency and to facilitate dispute resolution.
4. Government should recognise the unique qualities of the Internet and review and revise existing laws and regulations to fit the new electronic age.
5. Electronic commerce on the Internet should be facilitated on a global basis. The legal framework supporting commercial transactions should be consistent and predictable, regardless of the jurisdiction in which particular buyer and seller reside.

Similarly, some basic principles may be evolved to guide the formulation in various countries around the globe. This will facilitate building of a uniform foundation for the development of e-commerce.

FUNCTIONS OF E-COMMERCE

Functions of E-commerce are the following—

1. Communication function aiming at providing information to facilitate the business transaction (e.g. e-mail).
2. Process management function covering the automation and improvisation of business process (e.g. networking of computers).
3. Service management function for improving the qualities of service with the application of technology (e.g. racking shipments and scheduling pick-up).
4. Transaction capabilities function expending, buying and selling (e.g. varies online services).

IMPORTANCE OF E-COMMERCE

The importance of e-commerce is high that it has been recognised by the international business community. It is as a methodology to boost the trade at international level. The global market is turning into a global village due to e-commerce. Advantages or importance of e-commerce are as follows—

1. No Barrier of Time and Distance

On the Internet shopping open for 24 hours and seven days a week. Which makes it attractive. It allows people to transcend the barriers of time and distance as well as advantage of global markets and business opportunities.

2. Less Marketing and Distribution Expenses

Expensive and large showrooms have been replaced by web sites which show the details of the products and their manufacturers. This provides the opportunities to small traders to compete with big traders. Marketing expenses have become quite low as compared to traditional business. The over-all business expenses are reduced. As it provides the global market and hence the consumer gets the goods and services at a lower cost.

3. Eliminate the Gap Between Big and Small Traders

E-commerce has eliminated the gap between big and small manufacturers and traders. As both can contact the customers world-wide.

4. Better Customer Satisfaction

E-commerce provides various opinions for consumer and buyers. They can compare the quality and prices of various products and services before making a purchase. So, in this way one can buy the best product at the best available price.

5. Fewer Middlemen in Business

E-commerce has opened a new channel of distribution where middlemen are eliminated. It is in the benefit of businessman as well as customer as profit of middlemen. It will be either enjoyed by seller or it will be passed on to the customer.

6. Paperless Transaction

E-commerce has a reduced paper cost to a great extent. Thus, in addition to saving in cost of paper, it is environment friendly as many trees are saved which will be used otherwise for manufacturing of paper.

7. Better Mode of Payment

After e-shopping seller tells the purchaser to select a payment instrument. He may opt for any kind of e-money including credit card. In case of credit card, the consumer has to give his credit card number for making the payment. The purchaser fills in the credit card and address information on the screen and sends the information to the merchant over the Internet. At the merchant's site, Electronic payment systems validate and confirm the transaction. On realisation of money seller may dispatch the product to the customer either online or through courier depending on nature of the products.

8. Global Market

E-commerce has provided a global market for manufacturers and sellers for their products and services. The biggest advantage is its extensive reach, through which the manufacturers at a mass scale at low cost.

9. Save Time and Cost

E-commerce saves time and the cost of the exchange of business information. A customer can contact many businessmen in few minutes that too at a very low cost.

10. E-entertainment

Now-a-days, a housewife can buy household goods, cinema tickets, market, hotel and ticket reservation through Internet while sitting at home.

11. E-banking

An account holder can view his bank balance, transfer the amount and funds from one account to another, apply for cheque books or stop the payment of a particular cheque through Internet.

12. E-shopping

There are several sites for e-commerce, which have the retail shops for all types of goods. An E-commerce site is like a catalogue page from where a user can buy the goods and can make the payment for those goods through credit card.

13. Benefit to Business

E-commerce provides electronic communication between factories, marketing and purchasing departments. This results in lower inventory, carrying costs and better service to customers.

14. New Sales Opportunities

The Internet operates world over round the clock. As a result, business on the web can reach new markets they could not reach effectively with traditional sales force or advertising campaigns.

15. Optimum Use of Resource

E-commerce checks the misuse of resource due to market imperfections specially in developing and underdeveloped countries.

16. Other Benefits

Use of this medium to supplement traditional distribution by replacing it as education for the target audience. Maintenance of direct and regular contract with consumers resulting in better monitoring of changes in consumer behaviour and the possibility of micro-transactions, for example, purchasing a chapter of a book rather than the whole book.

BARRIERS/PROBLEMS IN PROGRESS OF E-COMMERCE

E-commerce suffers from the following barriers to selling over the Internet—

1. High cost of setting up of e-commerce enabled sales platform on the Internet and even higher cost to maintain it.
2. Do not know where to start from a most of the companies do not have a full-fledged EDP/IT department.
3. Customers/buyers are less sophisticated. Lack of trust among trading partners.
4. Have only customised products. No readymade products.
5. Differential pricing—Every buyer has to negotiate contract price. Lack of standard payment infrastructure.
6. Does not have a catalogue.
7. The communication infrastructure facilities play a crucial role—It is the base for the interaction of customers with world-wide web. These fàcilities and their awareness among the society are restricted and limited.
8. The computer literacy continues to be awfully poor in India. Without an improvement to this sad state of affairs, computer in India is mainly attributed to the Internet connections available at present even in the remote areas.
9. Economic transactions on the Internet are singularly abstract. Miscreants cannot be readily identified or physically handcuffed. It is not always clear who stands behind an electronic store front.

ORGANISATIONS WORKING ON E-COMMERCE ISSUES

International organisations have started creating the necessary framework. Some of the prominent organisations which have made inroads on such issues include—

1. World Trade Organisation (WTO).
2. Organisation for Economic Co-operation and Development (OECD).
3. United Nations Economic Commission for Africa (UNECA).
4. Asia Pacific Economic Commission (APEC).
5. World Intellectual Property Organisation (WIPO).
6. Global Information Infrastructure Commission (GIIC).

Soon with the co-ordinated efforts of these organisations, business communities and governments of various nations, a legal framework suitable for new medium of doing business will be in place keeping in view the efforts made in this direction.

E-COMMERCE IN INDIAN SCENARIO

Global e-commerce can create new opportunities for developing countries like India to take advantage of the benefit of development. However, there is widespread concern on issues arising due to the advent of e-commerce. Some of the issues need to be addressed on an urgent basis, such as development of infrastructure, protection to consumers, development of human resource enactment of laws governing e-commerce.

The growing importance of e-commerce in the era of globalisation and liberalisation along with the membership of WTO has brought about significant changes in the business deals in Indian economy. It has opened new vistas to the entrepreneurs in India and the real success depends upon the efforts and attitude of business units as well as consumers to make use of opportunities by availing the protection and security measures provided in the IT Act. Let us hope that the electronic means of trading activities would pave the way to revolutionise the marketing system ensuring maximum benefits to the entrepreneurs and consumers in the time to come.

4

E-Commerce in India—Legal Framework and Problems

M. SARNGADHARAN AND LEEBA BABU

Exchange of goods and services between individuals and groups has been in existence since time immemorial. A wide rangé of methods, devices, techniques and tools developed by technocrats and traders have made the process more dynamic. E-commerce, the latest addition to this area, denotes the exchange of goods and services with the help of electronic devices and internet. It covers any business deal that generates commerce and leads to payment on the net.

E-commerce, in such a context, can be referred to as 'any process of delivery of information, products or services and payments by telephone lines, computer networks or other similar means'. The internet's two-way flow of information—from, as well as to, the customers facilitates business houses with a powerful means to expand the richness of their offerings. Electronic commerce addresses the needs of organisations, merchants and customers to cut costs while improving the quality of products and enhancing the speed of delivery. It also covers the use of computer networks to search and retrieve information in support of human and corporate decision-making.

Usually e-commerce and i-commerce are referred to interchangeably. However, distinction of these two terms can be made that i-commerce is a subset of electronic commerce. E-commerce is business conducted exclusively through the electronic format, whereas, i-commerce is business conducted through electronic format on internet. There are three parties involved in e-commerce—Business (B), Consumer (C) and the Government (G). This leads to five major models in e-commerce deals – Business-to-Business (B2B); Business-to-Consumer (B2C); Consumer-to-Consumer (C2C); Business-to-Government (B2G); and Consumer-to-Government (C2G).

With the advent of IT revolution and adoption of globalisation, liberalisation and privatisation policies, e-commerce has been gaining popularity in India on a wide scale. In fact, the growth and development of e-commerce in India is directly related to the world-wide momentum already attained by this form of business deals, E-commerce has broken down the geographical barriers and brought together customers across the globe. Industrial units and business-houses in India are in the process of transition to electronic commerce. The noteworthy feature is that there has been a considerable change in the rule of doing business in accordance with the changed scenario of business dealings. Internet facilities established a link between information technology and business and the wide popularity already attained by the internet contributed a lot towards the growth of e-commerce.

Specific functions of e-commerce are:

- Communication function aiming at providing information to facilitate the business transaction. (e.g.: e-mail)
- Process management function covering the automation and improvisation of business processes. (e.g.: networking of computers)
- Service management function for improving the quality of service with the application of technology. (e.g.: racking shipments and scheduling pick up)
- Transaction capabilities function expediting buying.

E-COMMERCE IN INDIAN SCENARIO

As indicated earlier, in recent days, e-commerce has gained a vital positioning in the economic scenario of India. Most of the companies, which were till recently shying away from global competition, have started gearing up to cope with globalisation and liberalisation policies. It is quite obvious in the Indian situation that e-commerce has been accelerating new dimension to exchange of products by opening enormous opportunities to the corporate sector. It offers new places of marketing, new medium of communication, new forms of information and new means of distribution. The reason for the wide popularity of e-commerce enormously increased at present. There is at least one major site announcement per day and the nature and appearance of sites also have changed drastically.

E-commerce revenues in India rose dramatically over the last three years. During 2003-04, e-commerce is expected to generate 30 million dollars with an approximate user base of 1 million. In India, the major share of e-commerce revenue is being generated from B2C market than from B2B. It is estimated that there would be considerable increase both in B2B and B2C transactions with the infrastructure development of telecommunication by 2005.

E-commerce as a tool helps the business houses to enhance the access to, the consumers, irrespective of their places of residence throughout the world. In case of traditional commerce, the product needs to be transferred from the place of production to warehouse and is to be processed through various channels of distribution in order to reach the consumer. E-commerce performs the role of minimising the number of intermediaries in distribution process and thus, shortening the supply-chain process. It helps in enlarging customer service, reaching new market, improving productivity and enhancing product quality. In India, almost all the business houses have the chain of middlemen and inappropriate pricing mechanism. These shortcomings can be circumvented using internet. The model that works in such an Indian context is expected to be peaceful and complementary coexistence of both online and offline deals created a wide range of related issues like e-patents, e-advertising, e-marketing, e-banking, e-taxation, e-trademarks, supply chain management and e-litigation. Judicial bodies are now over-burdened with prayers to get varied e-squabbles resolved. The modern forms of communication and trading practices have warranted thorough revamping of the old set of rules and regulations. The mounting pressures of the situation have influenced the enactment of following legislative measures at the national level:

- to provide legal recognition to electronic documents and define the time and placement of exchange so that they can be admitted as evidence in the law;
- to define the procedure for affixing digital signature attending electronic documents, provide for non-repudiation of contracts besides ensuring data integrity and confidentiality in storage and transmission of data;

- to define cyber crimes and suggest penalties and punishments; and
- to set-up the required mechanism to administer non-delayed justice in cyber related claims.

To pave way for the development of e-commerce and internationally acceptable level of legal uniformity, the United Nations Commission on International Trade Law (UNCITRAL) established by the General Assembly adopted the model law of electronic commerce in 1996. It sought to facilitate the use of electronic data interchange, e-mail, or controlled by the appropriate government in the electronic form as may be prescribed by the government. Section 5 provides for legal recognition of digital signature states, where any law provides that information or any other document shall be authenticated by affixing the signature or any document shall be signed or bear the signature of any person then not withstanding anything contained in such law, such requirement shall be deemed to have been satisfied, if such information or matter is authenticated by means of digital signature affixed in such manner as may be prescribed by the Central Government.

The Information Technology Act has made suitable amendments to the Indian Evidence Act, the Indian Penal Code and the Banker's Books Evidence Act to provide for the use of electronic records as evidence before Court of Law. The RBI Act has also been amended to provide recognition for transfer of funds through electronic means.

PROBLEMS OF E-COMMERCE IN INDIA

Business houses have been experiencing several hurdles in the process of conducting trade through cyber way. For the growth of e-commerce, the communication infrastructure facilities play a crucial role. It is the base for the interaction of customers with World Wide Web. These facilities and their awareness among the society are restricted and limited. Most important drawback is that the computer literacy continues to be awfully poor in India. Without an improvement to this sad state of affairs, computer in India is mainly attributed to the internet connections available at present even in the remote areas.

On independence day of 1995, there were about 2,000 internet connections and 10,000 users in India. This has been increased to 60 lakh of internet connections and 16 million of net users in the beginning of 2003. Till recently, there were only a few websites for Indian business houses and this has the low cost of PCs growing installed base for internet use and increasingly competitive Internet Service Providers (ISP) market would help the acceptance and growth of e-commerce in India. The role of cyber cafes in providing low cost access to the common man requires special mention as well as attention.

LEGAL FRAMEWORK

E-commerce has become highly competitive and this has telegram, telex, etc. by ensuring standards.

The Information Technology Act passed by the Parliament of India in May 2000, is the second cyber law in the whole of South Asia, after Singapore. India has joined the select band of nations in the world that have legislated cyber laws. The IT Act 2000 promotes legal infrastructure to the cyber world. It facilitates electronic intercourse in trade and commerce, eliminating barriers that stand in the way of electronic commerce. It specially caters to the uncertainties relating to writing and signature requirements over the net. The Act makes e-mail as a valid and legal form of communication in India, which can be duly produced and applied before the law. Industrial and business houses are now in a position to carry out electronic commerce using the legal infrastructure provided by the Act. Legal entities can use digital signatures to carry out their transactions online. These digital signatures have been given legal validity and sanction in the Act.

With the growth of internet worldwide, cyber laws deals with numerous legal issues. This may vary from Domain names to Intellectual Property Rights; to Electronic Commerce; to Encryption, Electronic Contracts, Cyber Crimes; to Online Banking and so on.

The Act also provides for e-governance in India. The Chapter III of the Act deals with filling of any form, application or other document with any office, authority, body or agency owned facilities available throughout the country makes no sense. The common man's phobia to the computer and internet is something that requires serious attention of planners; policy-makers and administrators.

Another major barrier is the apathy of consumers in India towards plastic money available in varied forms like credit cards, debit cards and other similar smart cards. Though there are a large number of card-holders, the proportion of active card users is less than 20 percent.

This is likely to make plastic money an inappropriate device to provide support to e-commerce over the net especially among the common rural mass. Inadequate facilities for electronic payment make the situation worst.

Yet another obstacle to e-commerce is the security and privacy issues. E-commerce is unwittingly exposing private customer information including name, address and data related to plastic money. Owning to security concerns of credit and information, the consumers are afraid of effecting online purchases.

Absence of cyber laws was another major problem for e-commerce deals in India. The IT Act, 2000 was introduced with the intention of eliminating this hindrance. However, consumers are yet to gain confidence that cyber laws are effectively implemented.

Payment and delivery systems are the vital ingredients that determine the ultimate success of e-commerce. Delivery systems in India are mainly handled by courier network. Delayed delivery is one of the major issues confronted by the parties involved in e-commerce. Inadequate bandwidth that limits growth of web and e-commerce is a major issue that requires proper management. Other barriers include inadequate volume, non-availability of skills, high rate of technological obsolescence and increase in infrastructural costs.

CONCLUSION

The growing importance of e-commerce in the era of globalisation and liberalisation along with the membership of WTO has brought about significant changes in the business deals in Indian economy. It has opened new vistas to the entrepreneurs in India and the real success depends upon the efforts and attitude of business units as well as consumers to make use of opportunities by availing the protection and security measures provided in the IT Act. Let us hope that the electronic means of trading activities would pave the way to revolutionise the marketing system ensuring maximum benefits to the entrepreneurs and consumers in the coming days.

REFERENCES

Parag Diwan and Sunil Sharma, 2000, *Electronic Commerce—A Manager's Guide to E-Business*, Vanity Books International, New Delhi.

Sarngadharan, M., 2001, *E-Commerce* (Malayalam), State Language Institute, Trivandrum.

The Economist, 2000, "E-commerce—Shopping Around the Web", London, February and March.

The Indian Journal of Commerce, 2001, "Electronic Commerce, Potential and Challenges: An Indian Perspective", January-June.

5

E-Commerce—The True Picture

LAL C. MORANI

1. INTRODUCTION

The revolutionary changes in Information Technology in last decade has opened up a new chapter in every field, be it medical, engineering, or trading or many more. All of a sudden the world has become very small. A large chunk of society who is in the range of 40 to 50 years of age will vouch the nostalgic moments of waiting, may be for postman or news paper hawker for a magazine like *Dharmayug, Saptahic Hindustan, Sarita, Champak, Chandamama*, etc." The main 2 sources of entertainment were Radio/Transistor and Films out of which the most common in rural background was Radio/transistor. In late 80's computer came to our country and in the beginning was dedicated to data processing. In late 90's Internet became popular and revolutionized the entire scenario of the world.

A new era began and came the popular world e-commerce what it is, how does it work and what is the future.

2. BRIEF HISTORY OF BUSINESS

The methods of doing business was trading on carts in the old times, then with the change in the methods of transportation and communication the speed of doing business became fast. The popularization of INTERNET gave a new dimension to business where you can shop online without wasting even a minute you see a product you decide and you order. This all appears like a magic happening in front of you.

3. HISTORY OF INTERNET

To go into the depth of INTERNET let us find out the history of INTERNET. Internet evolved during days of cold war USA and USSR were in a constant race for technological supremacy. This resulted in the creation of vast scientific and military infrastructure across the United States. All these research projects had to be tightly coordinated and a lot of information sharing had to take place. This also meant the need for a command and control network, which could survive even a nuclear attack. Also the researchers needed a means for exchanging information, which was fast, reliable and secure, developing such a medium was inherently difficult for many reasons:

- The teams were across large distances, thousands of miles apart.
- The communication media were not very reliable and prone to losses and breakdown.
- The teams were using different kind of mutually incompatible computers.
- The information was highly sensitive, hence security was of paramount importance.
- Further, the network was to be functional even if some segments of it were damaged in war. A TCP/IP (Transmission Control Protocol/Internet Protocol) based network will continue to work even if a part of the network is damaged beyond repair. It does this through a clever mechanism of rerouting/retransmitting packets.

The Advanced Research Projects Agency (ARPA) of the Department of Defense of USA started developing a network to overcome the above difficulties. The result is now known as Internet (INTER + NET). INTERNET is a network of a large number of Local Area Networks (LAN).

This method is so powerful that it has taken only 4 years to achieve the same popularity for which TV took 13, Computer took 16 and radio took 38 years (See Chart 5.1).

4. BIRTH OF E-COMMERCE

Once internet became popular the computer engineers and business community of computer industry saw a great opportunity and a

CHART 5.1

Years taken to become popular

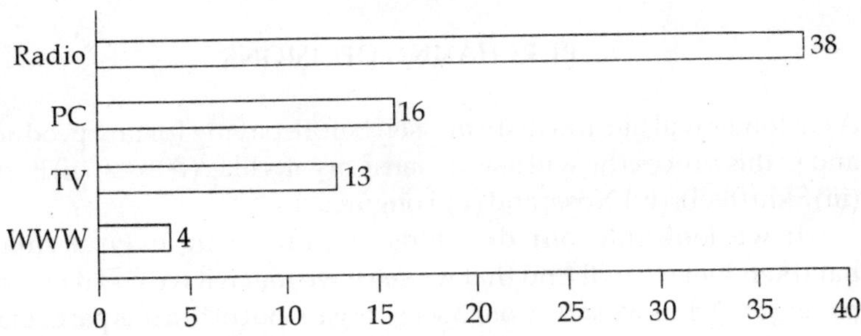

Source: Human Development Reports 1999.

method to revolutionize the entire business method and the modus operandi. This was discussed and agreed by computer professional that if a product is available through internet the customer will not bother to go to market as going to market involves transportation which it self is a curse nowadays due to rough traffic conditions and of course is time consuming. Moreover, the product will cost less, as Internet will become a direct link between the manufacturer and user. Hence, a lot of WebSites were developed lot of new InternetService Providers (ISP's) came into existence.

It was logical from the point of view of computer specialists that business through INTERNET will be an instant hit thus in anticipation the rates of Internet Connection were lowered down by ISP's, services like e-mail were offered for free and web hosting became almost free. More and more companies came into existence, a glaring example is skumar.com, which promised a lot to the general public if they become franchisee of skumar.com, and under the hype created through media lot of people invested their money into this.

5. PRESENT SCENARIO

Today most of the ISP's are on the verge of closure, some have already closed. The revenue generation did not match the projections of their project reports hence the profitability never came in sight. Why did it happen? Where did the computer industry go wrong and now what is the future of e-commerce. To address these questions we have to understand business and decision-making process of a customer or buyer.

6. PURCHASING DECISIONS

A customer will like to satisfy himself before paying for any product and in this process he will use his sense organs like: (i) Eyes, (ii) Ears, (iii) Skin (feel), (iv) Nose, and (v) Tongue.

If we look into our decisions of purchasing even a small handkerchief we will find that we see it we touch it we feel it before paying for it thus we satisfy our 3 sense organs out of 5 in this particular case. This is left to advertising or selling community to take care of this aspect in order to sell their product. We can inspect any advertising campaign and we will find that the above module is the core of advertising and selling. Internet was and is capable of satisfying only 1 sense organ, i.e. SEEING (visuals) may be in some cases hearing (EARS).

Let us ask very small questions to ourselves for buying a product from INTERNET will buy a PEN from NET? Will I buy a pair of shoes from NET? Will buy a shirt from NET? And so on. A random survey was conducted this and the excerpts are given below:

95% Respondents refused to buy even a ball point pen from NET.
98% Respondents refused to buy a shirt from NET.
100% Respondents refused to buy a pair of shoes from NET.
74% Respondents refused to buy a Music CD from NET.
86% Respondents refused to buy grocery items from NET.

If these are the feelings of public how e-commerce could have survived thus in my opinion the planning of the e-commerce modules was faulty right from the beginning. Hence within 2 to 3 years this hype of e-commerce has died a premature death survived by bankrupt companies and jobless computer professionals.

7. FUTURE OF E-COMMERCE

I do not intend to scare the readers of this article by showing the gloomy picture of the Net. There is a rosy picture of the same which will take at least 5 years from now to bring back the e-commerce at it's right place. The same survey also revealed that—

75% Respondents will like to buy Books from Net.
69% Respondents will like to buy Softwares from the Net.
59% Respondents will like to buy Travel Ticket from Net. (This figure will go up.)
86% Respondents will like to buy Movie Tickets from the Net. (Respondents complaint that small seats are being kept by the picture halls for these customers.)

Looking into these results I conclude that the business module of e-commerce have to undergo a change and some signs are seen as more and more ISP's have started charging for e-mail services which is the right product for Net. Net in coming times will be used for service-oriented product like –

1. Hotel Bookings.
2. Travel Tickets.
3. E-mails and other modes of communication.
4. Sex Service (At this point of time I will not like to go into the moral aspects of this, as this is beyond the scope of this article, but this a fact that as on today the only real business happening through NET is pornography and prostitution, given an alternative name of dating).
5. Purchase of Books.
6. Purchase of Cigarettes and Liquor (if supplied by depots of manufacturer).
7. After Sales Service Requests (wherein a user asks the dealer or company to provide a service by lodging his request and/or complaint).
8. Advertisement of the products which will generate the probable list of customers.

8. CONCLUSION

The Business community and more in focus computer industry will have to re-look in the viability aspects of product sales through NET, and only the viable segments of the same will feature remain on NET. This entire process will take some time may be a few years, as now no businessman will even look on this. This is a recovery period.

Another aspect which is not being discussed here relates to TAX issues as the entire business through NET will be TAX PAID, once again this is beyond the scope of this article to discuss the TAX structure and TAX evasion, but the fact remains that an hand some amount of TAX is being evaded by business class every year and this class will not start paying the TAX overnight just in order to popularize e-Commerce.

6

E-Commerce—Prospects and Challenges

ASHOK AGARWAL AND S.K. GUPTA

Apart from technological changes, with the fast pace of change in global market place, businesses also started looking for ways to expand their opportunities, customer base, and business partners while reducing the cost of business operation. The technological changes and changing market scenario was conceived which resulted in the birth and development of E-commerce. Internet has brought down the cost of E-commerce.

E-commerce or Electronic Commerce is on line and mainly internet based methodology, to address the need to business and consumers for cutting costs and improving the quality of goods and services. In common parlance it can be understood as business through Internet, i.e. buying or selling the goods and services through Internet. The process of purchasing a product electronically is conceptually very similar to the process of purchasing a product from a physical store. The purchaser only shifts his purchasing from a physical store to a vertical store on Internet. He browses an on-line catalogue over the Internet, selects the product, tells the merchant system that product is acceptable to him and he is ready to purchase it.

E-commerce is a vehicle to be used judiciously, to get competitive advantages and to make one's presence felt in national and international trade. Moving on-line is not just a matter of reducing costs, reaching out new efficiencies, performing tasks with greater speed and convenience, supplanting or replacing existing commercial transactions with electronic transactions to boost paperless concept of commerce and not doing any thing physically or manually; rather it is about establishing a presumptive dominance in the market place that will assure long-term competitive advantages. E-commerce removes the barriers of time and distance; it checks the misuse of resource due to market imperfections, especially in developing and underdeveloped countries.

TYPES OF E-COMMERCE

E-banking, E-shopping and E-business are different forms of E-commerce but generally following types of E-commerce are recognised –

B2B (Business to Business) Transactions between two companies.

B2C (Business to Consumer) Transactions between company and a consumer.

C2C (Consumer to Consumer) Transactions between two consumers.

ADVANTAGES OF E-COMMERCE

The advantages of E-commerce are so high that it has been recognised by the international business community as a methodology to boost up trade, especially international trade. The global market is turning into a global village due to e-commerce. Main advantages of e-commerce are as follows –

1. No Barrier of Time and Distance

On the Internet shopping open for 24 hours a day seven days a week, makes it attractive. It allows people to transcend the barriers of time and distance and take advantage of global markets and business opportunities.

2. Global Market

It has provided a global market for manufacturers and sellers for their products and services. The biggest advantage of e-commerce is its extensive reach, through which the manufacturers get the opportunity to highlight the special features of the products at a mass scale at low cost.

3. Saves Time and Cost

It saves the time and the cost of the exchange of business information. A customer can contact many businessmen in few minutes that to at a very low cost.

4. Better Mode of Payment

After e-shopping, seller tells the purchaser to select a payment instrument. He may opt for any kind of e-money including credit card. In case of credit card, the consumer has to give his credit card number for making the payment, the purchaser fills in the credit card and address information on the screen and sends the information to the merchant over the Internet. At the merchant's site, Electronic Payment Systems validate and confirm the transaction. On realisation of money seller may dispatch the product to the customer either on-line or through courier depending on nature of the products.

5. E-entertainment

Nowadays, a housewife can buy household goods, cinema tickets, make hotel and ticket reservation through Internet while sitting at home.

6. E-banking

An account holder can view his bank balance, transfer the amount and funds from one account to another, apply for cheque books or stop the payment of a particular cheque through Internet.

These all are example of E-commerce.

7. E-shopping

There are several sites for E-commerce, which have the retail shops for all types of goods. An E-commerce site is like a catalogue page from where a user can buy the goods and can make the payment for those goods through credit card.

8. It has Eliminated the Gap Between Big and Small Businessmen

E-commerce has eliminated the gap between big and small manufacturers and traders. As both can contact the customers world-wide.

9. Less Marketing and Distribution Expenses

Expensive and large showrooms have been replaced by web sites which show the details of the products and their manufacturer. This provides the opportunity to small traders to compete with big traders. Marketing expenses have become quite low as compared to traditional business. The overall business expenses are reduced as it provides the global market and hence the consumer gets the goods and services at a lower cost.

10. Better Choice and Better Customer Satisfaction

E-commerce provides various options for consumers and buyers. They can compare the quality and prices of various products and services before making a purchase. So, in this way one can buy the best product at the best available price.

11. Paper-less Transactions

E-Commerce has a reduced paper cost to a great extent. Thus, in addition to saving in cost of paper, it is environment friendly as many tress are saved which will be used otherwise for manufacturing of papers.

12. Fewer Middlemen in Business

E-commerce has opened a new channel of distribution where middlemen are eliminated. It is in the benefit of businessman as well as customer as profit of middlemen will be either enjoyed by seller or it will be passed on to the customer.

PROBLEMS, CAUTION AND RESCUE IN E-COMMERCE

Trust is one of the most important challenges facing E-commerce. The problem is particularly acute because economic transactions on the Internet are singularly abstract. Miscreants cannot be readily identified or physically handcuffed. It is not always clear who stands behind an electronic storefront.

Authenticating the identities of buyers and sellers; ensuring the reliability of payments and credits: preventing theft and security breaches, ensuring recourse for errors and fraud, these are some of the central issues that must be resolved if people are going to trust and use the new cyber market place.

E-commerce, as a vehicle to boost up trade, especially international trade, has already been recognised by international business community. At present, the industry is more concerned about finding the solutions for the issues related to policies, laws and legality of the E-commerce. These issues need to be addressed properly to implement E-commerce even on national basis.

A concrete effort in this line is introduction of Cyber Laws but due to inherent nature of E-commerce it is very difficult to implement the same. There is a need to see how it can be followed strictly. It is observed that internet is misused in many ways and virus is the main hurdle in day-to-day business and it looks there is no way out for the same except some precautions.

CONCLUSION

It is imperative to understand that though it appears that establishing E-commerce is a panacea for quick return on investment, however, in reality it is not so. Selling on-line-is not that easy. It needs aggressive pricing, and customer service; logistics infrastructure investments and marketing; thus, for those looking for short-term profits. It may be a big disappointment. Nevertheless, participation in E-commerce is certainly the key-words of success, especially in International trade.

7

Electronic Commerce—Some Emerging Issues

ANJU AGRAWAL

The Internet and the Web have revolutionised commerce and created new paradigms. They have given birth to electronic commerce, which uses the Internet as a vehicle. E-commerce is not a new form of trade but rather a new medium/ mode for conducting trade in goods and services.

This article is intended to address the issues emerging due to the advent of e-commerce. The issues have arisen in the areas of consumer protection, privacy laws, law on encryption and digital signatures and taxation. Emphasis has been given to the fact that to formulate laws on any of these areas, international consensus and co-operation is required as trading on the Internet can be based anywhere in the world and individual transactions may relate to more than one country. The laws of anyone country will not be applicable and may not be acceptable to all the constituents of an e-commerce transaction. Familiarity with the laws, due to their commonness, will lead to wide acceptability and less disputes. Besides, an international forum/ agency for consumer disputes redressal may be established for an easy and universality acceptable redressal system. Similarly, its basic provisions will also lead to better compliance as constituents of a transaction would not be required to learn the laws of different lands for each transaction.

E-COMMERCE TODAY

Earlier, computers were used for scientific and military purposes not commerce. They first made their way into commercial applications in the 1960s, and commercial use of computers quickly spread as companies in a variety of industries started using them to keep accounting ledgers, administer payrolls, create management reports and schedule production, etc. In the 1970s and 1980s, businesses extended their computing power beyond the company's walls, sending and receiving purchase orders, invoices and shipping notifications electronically *via* EDI (Electronic Data Interchange), thus giving birth to e-commerce. EDI is the earliest form of electronic commerce, which is used to electronically transmit business-related documents between trading partners. Electronic commerce today encompasses not only EDI but also other forms of communication, such as e-mail and the electronic bulletin board. It is the trading of goods and services for business, trade and general consumer purchasing through digital communication and transactions. It is a way of doing business better, faster and more effectively over open networks (like the Internet) or closed networks like America Online or Minitel that have a gateway onto the open network.

GROWTH OF E-COMMERCE

The usage of Internet and e-commerce is growing at a rapid pace. This is evident from a survey conducted by Price Waterhouse Coopers, revealing that business over the Internet in India crossed the Rs. 400 billion (Rs. 40,000 crore) mark in the financial year 2002-03.

Over time, three types of e-commerce, namely, consumer to business, business to business and consumer to consumer have emerged. Growth of business-to-business electronic commerce is being driven by lower purchasing costs, reduced inventory levels, lower product development cycle times, more efficient and effective customer service, lower sales and marketing costs and new sales opportunities.

E-commerce results in many advantages to a business such as:

- Reduced inventory by keeping the right products in stock, in turn lowering its operating cost. This is possible by having quick information of the estimated demand and fine tuning the production more frequently. Electronic communication between factories, marketing and purchasing departments have made this possible. Problems are communicated as they arise and appropriate adjustments are made. This results in lower inventory, carrying costs and better service to customers.

- Lower product development cycle time resulting in lower fixed cost.
- More efficient and effective customer service by providing customer service reports, order tracking and technical support information online. This saves money by freeing the company's own customer service staff to handle more complicated questions and manage customer relations leading to more satisfied customers.
- Lower sales and marketing costs as new customers are added with little or no additional cost. Since the sales/advertising function is housed in a computer server rather than physical store locations or sales people, its reach is bounded only by the capacity of the servers to respond to inquiries and orders. Also, electronic catalogues offer far more information and options than their paper counterparts. Direct marketing online can shorten purchase cycles and increase the ability to sell additional items.
- New sales opportunities. The Internet operates world-over round the clock. As a result, businesses on the Web can reach new markets they could not reach effectively with traditional sales force or advertising campaigns.

Other benefits due to e-commerce may be summarised as: use of this new medium to supplement traditional distribution by placing it as a preview channel (opportunity to try / preview before you buy), source of continuous information, education for the target audience, maintenance of direct and regular contact with consumers resulting in better monitoring of changes in consumer behaviour and the possibility of micro-transactions (for example, purchasing a chapter of a book rather than the whole book).

INFRASTRUCTURE REQUIREMENT FOR E-COMMERCE

Internet communications at present are generally established through the telephone network, which inherently is it little slow. In the expansion of electronic commerce, transfer of volume data at high speeds is an absolute necessity. At the same time, data transmission costs must come down to enable adequate penetration in the masses.

Speed in e-commerce is provided with high bandwidth, which may be realised through networks laid with optical fibre. Optical fibre is a cable made up of transparent material, such as glass or plastic, and is capable of transmitting large amounts of signals (or data) in the form of optical waves through very large distances without loss or interference. The other factor involved in lending speed to Internet communications is high-speed servers with large storage systems at international traffic gates, Internet service providers. LAN operators and client nodes. Additionally, software that can efficiently compress audio-visual signals for fast transmission and communications is a must.

Fortunately, hardware costs are coming down and technology is evolving at a fast pace. More recently, some private organisations have started providing Internet communications through the existing television cable network. This is expected to allow transmission of data round the clock reliably at lower cost in comparison to existing alternatives. Such innovations should lead to better penetration of internal services in the coming years. Still, laying optical fibre lines and building a high speed infrastructure are necessary and, looking at the high cost, both government and private organisations should pool resources for a shared network throughout the globe.

ISSUES PERTAINING TO E-COMMERCE

Lack of a predictable legal environment, concerns that governments will tax the Internet and uncertainty about the Internet's performance, reliability and security are some of the issues which are inhibiting the growth of e-commerce.

Confidence in the constituents of e-commerce needs to be developed so that a legal and secure mechanism of conducting a transaction and making payment is available. To provide this confidence, definite guidelines on various issues as: where does an electronic transaction actually take place in terms of contractual obligations; whom to assign tax responsibilities, where do companies that trade electronically register and to which legal regimes are they subject; how are rights in tangible and intangible forms of property to be protected; what happens when a transaction goes wrong – who has responsibility and liability; what are the audit requirements of companies involved in e-commerce, etc. need to be framed. These issues may be classified as commercial, security and privacy, consumer protection, Intellectual Property Rights (IPR), taxation and socio-economic.

COMMERCIAL ISSUES

Commerce depends on confidence. For electronic commerce to be successful, buyers and sellers must have the same confidence in electronic transactions as they have in traditional kinds of transactions. For a consumer to feel confident about using the Internet, he should be able to verify the identity of the party at the other end of the transaction and should be sure that any agreement made electronically is binding. For example, a buyer might want to ensure that the person they are dealing with is indeed the company's representative, or whether the business is in compliance with certain standards such as a code of commercial practice or a data protection standard. In the same context, a seller might want to know the buyer's identity, something about him or her (for example, whether the consumer is old enough to buy an age-restricted product), or the buyer's ability to pay. Finally, both parties might need some assurance of payment and delivery, an enforceable copy of the agreement, or to know the applicable body of law which governs the transaction.

At present, the identity of the transacting party is verified with password, electronic signatures and Internet Protocol (IP) addresses. However, a more effective system of digital certification and authentication needs to be developed for which efforts are being made around the globe.

SECURITY AND PRIVACY

The main concerns for security in electronic commerce may be defined as the availability of the network when needed, confidentiality and integrity of information systems, minimal unauthorised or malicious access to networks, security of commercial and other messages, assurance that the data and information is only disclosed to authorised persons/entities, protection from unauthorised modification or alteration of information, etc.

At present, Internet purchases are being made mostly by entering credit card and delivery information on a computerised form and transmitting it electronically to the retailer. This is not happening on a very large scale as customers are reluctant to give credit card information online for fear that it will be stolen or misused. In a survey conducted by Price Waterhouse Coopers, 60 per cent of the U.S. respondents said they would like to spend more if they get assurance that their credit card information was more secure and their privacy was better protected.

Insurance coverage should also be extended to this kind of misuse. In India, at present, these kind of credit card transactions are permitted by the credit card organisations in a very limited way.

To ensure security, some other modes of payment are required over the Net, such as debit cards, smart cards and digital cash. In smart cards, personal identification numbers (PIN) in conjunction with cardholder codes are stored on the card on an embedded computer chip. Instead of re-entering name, address and credit card information each time a purchase is made at a different web site, information already stored on the smart card is transmitted to the merchant electronically, saving many steps for the consumer and reducing fraud by automatically validating the consumer's identity. For those consumers who wish to purchase goods or services anonymously, digital cash and stored value cards (cards worth a set amount of money) may be ideal.

Ensuring privacy of personal information, besides security, is also absolutely a must for making e-commerce a success. A survey conducted by Price Waterhouse Coopers in April 1988 on 'Privacy and American Business' regarding online privacy concerns, confirmed the high importance of privacy for Net users. However, the concerns were, anticipatory in nature and 94 per cent interviewees never had experienced any harm. Of the concerns for privacy, the main concerns were collecting personal information from children without parental consent, receiving junk e-mails, unsolicited marketing, tracking of web site visits surreptitiously, capturing of e-mail and their use for marketing without permission, placing personally-identified pubic record information on the Net, etc.

The survey pointed that current web site practices on the issue of privacy are not adequate and privacy notices are rarely seen while surfing. Businesses collect personal information to develop markets and customise services which, at times, is sold or misutilised. Information such as telephone numbers, purchasing habits, age profiles, etc. are sold for marketing purposes. Sale of such information without consent should not be allowed.

Surveyed Net users suggested certain steps that may be adopted as rules and practices. These were posting clear privacy notices on the websites, disclosing information policy, displaying adequate information on the choices available to a user, naming a company official authorised to receive and resolve users complaints on use of information, conducting annual self-audit of compliance and announcing the results publicly, having independent reviews on privacy compliance from firms such as auditing organisations. However, for ensuring security and privacy both technological and legal solutions are required.

Cryptography is one technique, which provides security of data and the reliability of transactions by safeguarding both the confidentiality and the integrity of the data. It uses an algorithm to transform data in order to render it unintelligible to anyone who does not have the cryptographic 'key' necessary for decryption of the data. Cryptography helps in confidential transmission and safeguarding the integrity of data in an open network environment such as the Internet. It also helps in two other problems posed bye-commerce, such as repudiability and lack of security in the payment system.

The technique of cryptography solves these problems by providing mechanisms for establishing the validity of claimed identity of a user/entity (authentication) and from preventing an individual/entity from denying having performed a particular action (non-repudiation). A critical issue presented by cryptography, however, is that it also helps in concealing data related to illegal activities, which limits the ability of the government to protect public safety and national security.

CONSUMER PROTECTION AND INTELLECTUAL PROPERTY RIGHTS

Electronic commerce offers many conveniences to attract consumers, but at the same time, its properties facilitate fraud and make prosecution difficult, leaving consumers vulnerable. The very international nature of e-commerce means that the laws and regulations of one country are not applicable on both consumer and merchant. Electronic commerce, thus, requires novel protection and redressal mechanisms. Though some mechanisms develop automatically through competition, for others a more concentrated effort and international co-operation among industry and governments is required.

Refund policies in digital products, especially, require some innovative thinking as digital products such as software, music, etc. sold *via* electronic commerce may be consumed immediately on downloading by making a perfect digital copy, thus making return of the product for a refund problematic.

Certain measures to protect the consumers, such as mechanisms for verifying information, certifying the goods on international quality standards, notifying consumers of the legal jurisdiction or venue for resolving disputes arising from a transaction, access to education messages describing their rights in the context of electronic transactions are immediately required. A proposal to create an international governmental organisation called the World Consumer Protection Organisation (WCPO) may be a right step in this direction.

Many organisations such as the United Nations, UNESCO, UNDP, UNCITRAL, WTO, WIPO, European Commission, ITU, APEC, have proposed regulations for consumer protection. The World Bank has also proposed policies and programmes protecting consumers. In addition, several national governments have legislated or regulated the emerging online consumer marketplace. An effort should, however, be made to evolve a uniform code applicable on global basis.

Intellectual property issues are also becoming more and more important in an electronic environment. There is a need to protect trademarks and commercial information held in databases. The definition of intellectual property rights itself needs to be redefined in the environment of e-commerce. To provide a better mechanism for protection, various aspects of copyright and related issues of intellectual property rights such as time of publication, use of registered trademarks as domain by unallied parties, etc. and other contentious issues such as legal status of Internet's service providers, right to encrypt, etc. are required to be addressed.

TAX ASPECTS OF E-COMMERCE

The transnational and intangible nature of electronic commerce has direct implications for the ability of governments to raise revenues through established mechanisms. It may open up avenues that legally circumvent national tax structures and facilitating outright tax evasion and fraud.

In view of the new medium of trade, a review of applicability of fundamental principles of taxation on electronic transactions is required. Jurisdictional rules forming the very basis of incidence of taxation are generally based on concepts of physical presence, place of establishment, place of supply or residence of a taxpayer. As electronic commerce is not bound by physical geography, it may become difficult for taxpayers and governments to determine jurisdiction and revenue rights giving rise to a need for action to avoid double or non-taxation.

To achieve this goal, the need is being felt to change the traditional concept of source-based taxation else it may lead to global migration of e-business to low tax or tax haven countries. A proposed alternative to this is residence-based taxation, though that has its own problems. As per Indian tax laws, a company is said to be resident or non-resident on the basis of control and management of its affairs in a place. This will be difficult to establish for a globalised company with management scattered around the globe, communicating by telephone, fax, e-mail or video conferencing. Test of residency and consequent incidence of taxation in the case of an individual is established on the basis of number of days spent in a country. In case of e-commerce transactions (especially for digital products), this test loses its relevance as a person need not stay in a country to earn income from there.

Working Groups on Tax Implications of Electronic Transactions

The Government set-up a working group to examine the tax implications of electronic transactions. The group was set-up by V.M. Muthuramalingam, the then Chief Commissioner of Income Tax, Mumbai. The report submitted by the working group has concluded that the existing tax laws are inadequate to cover e-commerce transactions. It has suggested that the Tax Planning and Legislation (TPL) section of the Central Board of Direct Taxes undertake a study of the issues arising out of taxation of e-commerce transactions.

E-Commerce—Implications of Taxation

1. *Classification of Digitised Products for Taxation Purposes*

The issue to be considered is whether all digitised products are to be treated as one category of goods and taxed on the bases of bits downloaded or to be distinguished between books, music, application software, consultancy services, etc.

Under the existing principles of taxation, these are taxed differently as royalty, service income, etc. Also, in a traditional transaction, the sale of book or music cassette income accrues on sale in the form of profit to the vendor selling the product and accrual of royalty to the creator which are taxed differently under Indian laws. This raises issues of classification of income in e-commerce transactions. In electronic transactions, taxation on the basis of this classification is not feasible.

Use of a different form or medium does not create a different product and should not result in a different basis of taxation, though on grounds of simplicity it may be easier to do so. There may be several kinds of transactions involving digitised information such as data online, use of programmes or database to search and retrieve information, purchasing digitised books, music, consultancy services, downloading programmes or updates to previously purchased programmes, use of interactive products or services such as chat rooms and games, web site hosting and electronic mail and bulletin boards, etc. These transactions need to be classified separately for taxation purposes.

The working group recommended a presumptive tax on a fixed portion of billing or a 'bit' tax. However, there are many problems with the bit tax proposal, such as doing accurate measurement of volumes of traffic, ascribing value to data, difficulty in identifying a taxable transaction. Moreover, the volume of data may easily vary with the technology of compression used.

Taxing such products on the basis of size of information (bit downloaded) thus is not the right criterion. Therefore, both technologies and legal changes are required for appropriate taxation of such products.

2. *Detection of a Transaction on the Internet*

In digitised products, tracing a transaction is not easy without the voluntary disclosure of the same by the constituent. The working group has suggested formation of an international organisation to detect any transaction on the Internet. However, income tax authorities in various countries will have to follow a policy of sharing information.

These transactions may, however, be traced *via* the payment channel. The bank, credit card or similar organisation making payment for such transactions may be held accountable for withholding tax on payment relating to these transactions on the basis of declaration required to be filed by the transacting party. For such withholding of tax, a uniform rate may be worked out.

3. *Concept of Business Connection/Permanent Establishment*

The digitised delivery of products is also giving rise to a need for redefining certain concepts such as business connection or permanent establishment.

Concept of business connection in the Indian Income Tax Act is almost the same as that of permanent establishment used in tax treaties but much wider in meaning. The concept gains importance in the case of taxation of non-resident. Income of a non-resident is taxable only for the portion attributable to business in India, that is, if it can be established that a non-resident has a business connection in India. A business connection involves relationship between a business carried on by a non-resident which yields profits or gains and some activity in India, which contributes directly or indirectly to the earning of those profits or gains. To establish a business connection, there should exist an element of continuity between the business of the non-resident and the activity in India.

The term business connection also has relevance for holding a person as an agent of a non-resident.

The concept of permanent establishment or business connection thus needs to be clarified in e-commerce environment. Certain questions such as whether presence of a server or a web site results in a permanent establishment, whether Internet Service Providers are deemed agents for purposes of determining the existence of a permanent establishment needs to be answered.

(i) *The Status of a Server or a Web Site as a Permanent Establishment*

Under the existing principles in India, a place of management, branch, office, factory, workshop, mine, an oil or gas well, a quarry or any other place of extraction of natural resources including an installation or structure used for the exploration or exploitation, a warehouse or a sales outlet, a farm, plantation or other place where agricultural forestry, plantation or related activities are carried on, a building site or construction installation or assembly project, etc. may be regarded as a permanent establishment.

In view of these principles, the following situations need to be analysed.

Where the server is used for: (i) advertising alone, (ii) advertising and taking orders, (iii) advertising, taking orders and accepting payments, and (iv) advertising, taking orders, accepting payments and for digitised delivery of goods.

The first case is equivalent to a hoarding, which does not fall even in the current definition of a permanent establishment. The other cases may be equated to a warehouse or sales outlet, and thus fall in the current list of permanent establishments.

However, the concept needs to be redefined from the international perspective. In Europe the definition of a fixed place of business presupposes both physical resources as well as personnel who assist the entrepreneur in the use and implementation of the physical resources. This definition is not satisfied by a server.

The concept should also have a certain degree of permanence, which is not only lent by a server. It is very easy to shift the server to a tax haven or to a low tax country without any disruption to any activity. It is also possible to have a number of mirror web sites on different servers located in different countries and a customer could be directed to anyone of these sites. Another difficulty may arise when a web server and parties to a transaction belong to different countries.

Further, a web site can also not be considered as a permanent establishment due to the following reasons. It has no actual physical presence and is highly mobile as it borrows its presence from the server where it resides. The presence of employees is not required in a country to maintain the site. A web site serves the purposes of advertising, order taking and for giving information. To the extent it serves the function of advertising and ordering, it is analogous to a mail order catalogue or a television advertisement. In dispensation of information it is analogous to a location being maintained solely for the purposes of storage or display. None of these quality for being defined as permanent establishment.

The working group in its report, however, states that a computer terminal used to receive and send information across national boundaries and the web site used in e-commerce, should be regarded as a permanent establishment. The report also examines a case where an Indian software vendor obtains software on the Internet from a foreign software vendor and sells the same to Indian buyers. A mutually agreed amount of the sale proceeds is remitted to the foreign vendor. In such a case, since no activity is carried out by the foreign vendor in India, apart from transmitting the software to India from abroad, no portion of the remittance can be brought to tax in India as per the tax laws of India. Such situations emphasise the need for requisite change in existing laws.

(ii) *Assignment of Tax Responsibility*

In Indian tax law, a person employed by a non-resident or who has any business connection with non-residents may be regarded as an agent who is required to fulfil the tax obligation of a non-resident in India. If a person is liable to Indian income tax in an e-commerce transaction, the issue arises whether Internet service provider/web hosts may be regarded as his agent.

In the ordinary course of business, the relationship of an enterprise with its Internet service provider is simply a business contract for services to be provided to the enterprise. An Internet service provider normally does not have any authority to enter into binding contracts on behalf of a business customer and hence cannot be equated to an agent. An Internet service provider is more comparable to a telephone service provider, a postman or a common carrier who does not become deemed agent for delivering mail or facilitating conversation. Similarly, Internet service providers giving space for hosting a web site may also not be considered as agents for similar reasons.

4. *Employee Taxation*

Workforce flexibility in working for a project for a country without having to physically relocate there will also give rise to jurisdictional issues of taxation. For such issues, international consensus on the basis of sharing and taxation of such income needs to be arrived at.

5. *Classification of Income of Internet Service Provider*

Where capacity on the server is leased to others, clarification is needed as to whether existing provisions regarding the rental of storage and display facilities or the leasing of buildings, facilities, equipment or intangible property apply.

Besides, the procedural aspects of taxation will undergo a sea change in view of the availability, reliability and completeness of commercial records generated in an electronic commerce environment to ensure that taxation and tariffs have been appropriately and fairly applied.

However, transactions of tangible goods where only one part of the transaction is concluded on-line and goods are delivered physically, the tax can be easily levied on physical delivery. In digitised products, however, tracing of a transaction for levying taxes is a challenging task.

The business of digitised goods has its own limitations. Items such as a music cassette or a printed book may have more value for collection purposes to a person than its digitised counterpart. Also digitised product has the inconvenience that it can be used only on a computer. Major business on the Internet in the coming years, therefore, may remain to be of tangible items, sending shipment separately for each order from one country to another is not only inconvenient for the company but also expensive and time consuming. As and when, the demand of products from a particular company increases, these difficulties will necessitate establishment of a godown and an agent in that country. Such widespread concern of tax evasion is thus unfounded. The other issues may be sorted out with the help of technological as well as legal developments in this report.

FRAMEWORK FOR GLOBAL E-COMMERCE

In a report *A Framework for Global Electronic Commerce* released by the President of the United States in 1997, five principles have been enunciated to guide governmental action and to give an impetus to the growth of e-commerce. The five principles enunciated are:

1. The private sector should lead. Internet should develop in a market driven arena where government should encourage industry self-regulation.
2. The government should avoid undue restriction on electronic commerce. The government should refrain from imposing new and unnecessary regulations, bureaucratic procedures or new taxes and tariffs on commercial activities taking place *via* the Internet.
3. Where government involvement is needed, its aim should be to support and enforce a predicable minimalist, consistent and simple legal environment for e-commerce. Government intervention should be to ensure competition, protect intellectual property and privacy, prevent fraud, foster transparency and to facilitate dispute resolution.
4. Government should recognise the unique qualities of the Internet and review and revise existing laws and regulations to fit the new electronic age.

5. Electronic commerce on the Internet should be facilitated on a global basis. The legal framework supporting commercial transactions should be consistent and predictable, regardless of the jurisdiction in which particular buyers and sellers reside.

Similarly, some basic principles may be evolved to guide the formulation of rules and regulations governing e-commerce in various countries around the globe. This will facilitate building of a uniform foundation for the development of e-commerce.

IMPACT OF INTERNET ON THE ECONOMY AND SOCIETY

Internet, which is becoming an economical and efficient medium for communication and doing business electronically, is adding conveniences to everyday life. At the same time, it is also changing the society and economy in such a way that it needs proactive action plans by government and other organisations based on proper analysis.

- Today, a lot of things can be done sitting at home through the Internet. A person is not required to go to the market to buy vegetables, day-to-day products, etc., which can be delivered at home by the company. Software programmes, newspapers, airline tickets and music CDs no longer need to be packaged and delivered to stores, offices or homes. They can be delivered electronically over the Internet. Many as yet unthought of changes in distribution strategies and the way business is done are also taking place. Recently, in the U.S.A., even postage stamps can be downloaded from the Internet by using special software.
- Profile of the entertainment industry will change in view of the new medium. Strategies of sales promotion will change. The habits of people in spending their leisure time will change.
- Similarly, the digital economy may bring potential invasion of privacy, easier access by children to pornographic and violent material and hate speech, more sophisticated and far-reaching criminal activities and a host of other as-yet-unknown problems.
- Increased competition, global access and organisational change are affecting labour markets by influencing employment demand, wages and skill requirements. Expanding Internet usage and electronic commerce are not only contributing to

increased demand for 'core' IT workers (computer scientists, engineers, programmers and system analysts) but are also generating new IT occupations, changing skill requirements for some non-IT occupations and raising the minimum skill requirements for many lower skilled jobs.

- Earlier, people were required to advise customers on product features, check availability of merchandise, book orders, collect cash, etc. A retail sale *via* the Internet does not require the presence of a physical store or the same intensity of staff in order to generate the sale. For virtual stores, people with IT skills to develop and programme software, operate and maintain computer servers and networks, design the web site to keep it attractive and user-friendly are required.
- A concept of workforce flexibility is coming which refers to a company's ability to produce products and services with less rigid organisational structures and workers' ability to work without being tied to a desk or an office. Work on the same project can be done in several places or several countries without workers having to physically relocate and enable organisations to deploy resources and operations around the world.

The above changes are taking place at a much faster pace than society can absorb. Educational systems and skill profiles are not changing fast enough to cope with these new developments. A large stratum of a society may find itself not to be in tune with the technological and procedural changes taking place. The importance of experience may get subdued by the necessity of inducting youngsters with new technological exposure. The changing skill requirements pose challenges to the governments to restructure their human resource development programmes to prepare the new generation and to bring in awareness in the older generation. This may necessitate resources to be diverted for anticipated developments.

ORGANISATIONS WORKING ON E-COMMERCE ISSUES

In order to bring compatibility between various countries on the above-mentioned issues, international organisations have started creating the necessary framework. Some of the prominent organisations which have made inroads on such issues include World Trade Organisation (WTO), the Organisation for Economic Co-operation and Development (OECD). United Nations Economic Commission for Africa (UNECA). Asia Pacific Economic Co-operation (APEC), the World Intellectual Property Organisation (WIPO) and the Global Information Infrastructure Commission (GIIC).

Soon with the co-ordinated efforts of these organisations, business communities and governments of various nations, a legal framework suitable for the new medium of doing business will be in place keeping in view the efforts made in this direction.

E-COMMERCE AND DEVELOPMENT IN INDIA

In India, a task force was set-up on Information Technology and Software Development in May 1998. This task force has since submitted its report.

An EDI Council has been established. This is the apex body responsible for laying down the policy framework and direction for promotion and propagation of EDI and electronic commerce, creating awareness and education among the potential EDI functionaries and users, streamlining procedures and practices, attending to legal issues, human resource development and any other issue connected with EDI and electronic commerce.

An EDIFACT Committee (IEC) is also constituted to formulate standards, streamline procedures in line with UN/EDIFACT and maintain Liaison with UN/EDIFACT bodies.

A technical support group is also working under the National Informatics Centre (NIC) which is responsible for helping users in EDI-related software development and for providing technical support.

The Indian government is also evolving a national encryption policy that would facilitate e-commerce and, at the same time, check cyber terrorism and laundering. Soon an Electronic Commerce Bill, Electronic Commerce Support Bill and Information Technology Bill are also expected to be in place. The Cyber Law Bill has already been cleared by the Cabinet.

CONCLUSION

Global electronic commerce can create new opportunities for developing countries like India to take advantage of the benefits of an open world trading system, thus furthering the goals of economic development. However, there is widespread concern on issues arising due to the advent of e-commerce. Some of the issues need to be addressed on an urgent basis, such as development of infrastructure, protection to consumers, development of human resources, enactment of laws governing e-commerce. International co-operation and consensus is required in addressing many of these issues. For the achievement of this goal, widespread support of the business community is an essential requirement in terms of voluntary compliance, greater openness and timely and valuable input.

Many papers and drafts are available over issues pertaining to e-commerce and its possible social and economic impact. Some of the important documents are listed below for further reading:

1. The U. S. Department of Treasury has published a report titled *Selected Tax Policy Implications of Global Electronic Commerce* in November 1996.
2. *Electronic Commerce and Canada's Tax Administration*—A Report to the Minister of National Revenue Commerce was released in April 1998.
3. The United Kingdom Inland Revenue and HM Customs and Excise issued a joint paper on U.K. tax policy on the EC on October 6, 1998.
4. The European Commission has presented an electronic commerce directive.
   The DECO, through its Committee of Fiscal Affairs (CFA) has undertaken a lot of work to develop a co-ordinated international approach to address tax issues in the EC.
5. CFA, which is the main tax body of the DECO, has published a paper titled *Electronic Commerce: The Challenges to Tax Authorities and Taxpayers* for an informal round table discussion between business and Government in Finland, on November 18, 1997.
6. UNCITRAL's Model Law of Electronic Commerce and the Information Technology Bill came in 1998.
7. A framework for Global Electronic Commerce.
8. India's Information Technology Bill and Draft Electronic Commerce Act, 1998.

REFERENCES

A Framework for Global Electronic Commerce. Released by U.S. President William J. Clinton, wwf.iitf.nist.gov/eleccommiecomm.htm

E-Commerce and Privacy—What Net Users Want. A survey conducted by Price Waterhouse Coopers.

E-Commerce Taxation Principles. A GIIC perspective prepared by the Electronic Commerce Committee for the Global Infrastructure Commission.

Electronic Commerce. Report by the Organisation for Economic Co-operation and Development.

The Emerging Digital Economy. A publication of the U.S. Department of Commerce, April 1998.

8

E-Commerce—Perspective and Issues

ARCHANA KAUL

Electronic commerce (e-commerce), the buzzword of the decade, is entirely a phenomenon of the technology revolutions of the late 20th century; in computers and information systems, in telecommunications and also in banking systems and even in postal and delivery services.

What is e-commerce? It is very difficult to give a simple definition of this phrase. Often people talk about e-commerce but very few know what e-commerce is. In simple words, e-commerce is the selling of products and services on the Internet. It is online shopping, bringing a level of convenience. However, in this sense, e-commerce has existed at least for the last 20 years when companies have used the medium of fax and phone to place orders and conduct trade. Privately-run Value-Added Networks (VANs) have been used for EDI (Electronic Data Interchange) and EFT (Electronic Fund Transfer) transactions.

E-commerce is a new term for existing activities being done in new ways. As long as communication networks have been available, they have always been used to their fullest capability by entrepreneurs to create business opportunities. As advanced telecommunications and computer technologies have taken hold in recent years, they have moved to the centre of the international economic infrastructure. The rapid integration of the Internet and other telecommunication-based functions into nearly every sphere of business is what has given rise to the recent international focus on the new world of electronic commerce.

While e-commerce is already sweeping developed economies like the U.S.A., developing countries are also seizing the opportunity to leap from the 'industrial age' into the age of borderless markets. Today, 15 per cent of the over 130 million Web users are buyers; in the year 2002, 50 per cent of the 300 million-plus Web users were estimated to have bought goods worth $ 425 billion. In fact, experts warn that if a company is not on the Net, it may not exist after five years. Of the $ 425 billion, 79 per cent were from the business to business segment and the rest from the business to home segment. Customised interaction *via* the Internet will be possible. Increased revenues, decreased costs and the fostering of community feeling will be the hallmark of the Net economy.

CATEGORIES OF E-COMMERCE

Most transactions in e-commerce may broadly be classified into two main categories:

1. Business to consumer; and
2. Business to business.

The vast majority of the activity to date has been taking place in countries with advanced economies and infrastructure. For developing countries, electronic commerce presents important new opportunities to achieve a more level playing field *vis-a-vis* larger, more developed economies, as it diminishes in-place advantages of cost communication and information and creates huge new markets for indigenous products and services. While many developing countries are beginning to take advantage of e-commerce critical challenges remain to be overcome before the vision of a truly integrated and equitable world economy can be realised.

Business to Consumer Transactions

These are the transactions that most of us are familiar with today, with individual customers buying books and music CDs over the Web, or surfing the Web to find the best deal for some particular item. Here, the merchants setting up shop on the Web deal directly with the end-customer. This category is characterised by a large number of transactions, where each transaction is typically small in volume. The end-customer could be totally unknown to the merchant or might be visiting the shop for a few occasional purchases.

Business to Business Transactions

These are transactions between two businesses or corporations where the product traded is for business use. This category is characterised by a limited number of transactions, where each transaction is typically of larger volume. The end-customer is typically a previously approved or registered customer or at least known to the merchant.

ACTIVITIES OF E-COMMERCE

The different activities that could be carried on electronically include:

Electronic Presentation of Goods and Services

This would include making available e-catalogues on the site, through which the customer could browse to select his/her purchase. It could also include search facilities, where the user could search for items based on its attributes.

Online Order Taking and Bill Presentation

This would include provision for the user to specify the items he wishes to order, defining the terms of payment and delivery and an automated billing system for the users.

Automated Customer Account Inquiries

This could function independent of how the other activities were finalised, online or offline. This would be an integral part of customer support.

Online Payment and Transaction Handling

The merchant may provide or tie up with some third party for the payment verification and special payment methods must be defined and the back end connectivity for these established.

AUTOMATED SUPPLY-CHAIN MANAGEMENT SOLUTIONS

An automated supply chain management solution is a collaboration between a company, its business partners and its customers where various applications talk to each other. One of the benefits of e-commerce is that it is much simpler to integrate supply chain solutions fully to the system.

Customer-relationship management is a field that is receiving a great deal of attention with the spread of e-commerce. Many activities like pre-sale inquiries and post-sales support stand to benefit from the accessibility and speed of the Internet. Once a merchant has set-up his e-shop he is ready with a 7-day, 24-hour storefront reaching a global audience. For the merchant, e-commerce provides reduced transaction costs, more streamlined business processes, less paper-work, reduced costs associated with these transactions and reduced float through the use of EFT. It better enables the merchant to respond faster to customers by providing improved order management, order fulfilment, payment and ongoing customer support. The 'start small, grow fast' advantage helps small enterprises compete on a close footing with larger established firms.

ISSUES

1. The fundamental issue concerning e-commerce is cyber fraud. With exceedingly high potential for growth in e-commerce, estimated by the OECD, to grow from about $ 500 million to as much as $ 5 billion, the potential for increased cyber fraud becomes a concern for all.

   It should be noted that where there is commerce, there will always be those who seek shortcuts, illegal methods to defraud the unsuspecting, or otherwise even misuse the technology of the market for unwarranted illegal gain. In the case of electronic commerce, these technologies can be used in quite sophisticated ways and there have already been many examples of very damaging and disturbing scams and abuse on the Internet. These can include false investment promises, so called 'spam' e-mail advertising that jams mailboxes and servers, various pyramid and get rich-quick schemes or merely the problem of goods and services not being delivered as agreed.

   One of the major areas of Internet fraud relates to software piracy. The Chief Executive of the Washington-based Business Software Alliance (BSA) has estimated that the loss to the software developers on account of software piracy may be up to $ 1 billion a year. BSA represents many large business software developers like Microsoft, Adobe, etc. Through monitoring, BSA has detected as many as 95,000 web sites that offer pirated software called 'Warez' by hackers. Ease of duplication on the electronic medium makes it extremely easy to copy software and distribute it on the Internet.

2. Individuals right to privacy in the electronic age is a large area of concern which many in developed countries consider to be the main barrier for e-commerce. As technology increasingly facilitates obtaining deleted personal information without the knowledge or consent of the consumer, there are strong sentiments in favour of establishing new clear rights and laws to protect unauthorised use and dissemination of such data and otherwise to assure some degree of control over access to private information and invasions of privacy generally.
   The Internet has raised new issues concerning confidentiality of records in terms of restricting access to personal details; into what jurisdictions data are stored and used, as well as protection of financial information disclosed in electronic transactions. The degree of mandatory *versus* voluntary regulation of personal data is one issue of contention as well as the practical enforceability of privacy standards. These concerns apply not only to transmission media but also to computer software which, recent experience has shown, can incorporate revealing information about users without their knowledge.
3. Money laundering by criminals and drug traffickers has always posed a problem for the enforcement agencies. With the growth of e-commerce, the use of electronic money and digital cash is bound to grow. If an individual or a company can purchase and sell goods and services from the comfort of their homes and offices, they would also like to ensure payments and receipts of money electronically. Necessarily, e-money transactions have to be through secure electronic transactions using encryption technology. During the past years, various enforcement agencies in different countries have made co-ordinated efforts to prevent and detect money laundering. However, e-commerce opens new avenues for conducting dirty money transactions, leaving no paper trail and making detection extremely impossible by the enforcement agencies.

4. E-money transfers can now be made without the collusion of a willing bank employee through automated online banking channels. Banks can also be located outside national jurisdictions, beyond the reach of enforcement authorities, but providing banking services to customers located anywhere in the world through the Internet. A criminal can easily open and operate accounts in such a bank sitting in the comfort of his hideout. Multiple transactions using smart card systems can also block tracing back laundered money.
5. Jurisdiction questions cut across nearly all issues in electronic commerce because electronic commerce is inherently indifferent to national boundaries. Differences between laws and policies of different countries can greatly affect the viability and credibility of e-commerce globally.
6. Questions are being raised about the protection of intellectual property rights. Intellectual property having assumed considerable importance in recent years, the future development of electronic commerce rests heavily on two major issues of intellectual property rights. These include: (1) the protection of copyrights and related rights, and (2) the protection of equitable allocation of trademarks and domain names. These concerns have been a primary focus of international deliberations in recent years; for instance, through the World Trade Organisation which has negotiated an Agreement of Trade Related Aspects of Intellectual Property Rights (TRIPs) making intellectual property an integral part of the multilateral trading system.

Because so much of the consumer and business trade that occurs over the Internet involves selling or licensing information, cultural products and technology protected by intellectual property rightholders, this medium is especially susceptible to risks of theft or misuse of protected works.

Both the TRIPs Agreement and Copyright Treaties of the World Intellectual Property Organisation (WIPO) recognise that copyright protection covers compilations of data or other material the contents of which constitute intellectual creations. It has been informally agreed that the impact of digital technology on copyright and related rights has to a large extent, been to enable production and distribution of pirated sound recordings, films, software, CD-ROMs, etc. Despite the legal protection offered by these international agreements, the use of trademarks on the Internet continues to raise important questions, as for example, with regard to jurisdictional authority.

The relationship between trademarks and Internet domain names is also receiving considerable attention. Some of the problems stem from the fact that under each top-level domain (.com, .org, .net, etc.) there can be only one of each particular second-level domain name (per country) and these have been typically allocated on a first-come-first-served basis within each top-level domain. However, some trademarks may co-exist in different categories of products and services, and in different territories.

Another controversial issue is under which jurisdiction(s) the use of a domain name that is identical or similar to a trademark may constitute a trademark infringement, and what remedies should be available to the trademark holder. How best to develop the governance of the domain name system remains undecided, and there is a pressing need for a widely acceptable resolution.

LEGISLATIVE DEVELOPMENTS

Realising the potential of e-commerce, the Government of India is proposing to being a new Information Technology (IT) Bill that would allow enactment of Cyber Laws to regulate Internet-related activities, including electronic communication, e-commerce and information highway based commercial transactions. The Government proposes to set-up elaborate machinery for licensing, monitoring and certifying authorities for this. These authorities would monitor and oversee issues like jurisdiction, origin, authentication, privacy protection, intellectual property, computer crimes being committed *via* the information highway or cyberspace.

Accordingly, through the new IT Bill, the Government seeks to monitor and regulate activities like creating Web pages, advertisements, bulletin boards and, most importantly, e-commerce originating from the country.

The Government has also prepared a draft of Electronic Commerce. The Draft Electronic Commerce Bill of 1998 aims to facilitate the development of a secure regulatory environment for electronic commerce by providing a legal infrastructure governing electronic contracting, security and integrity of electronic transactions, the use of digital signatures and other issues related to electronic commerce. The Draft Act can be summarised as follows:

Part I of the Draft Act outlines the general purpose of the Act, provides definitions for terminology used within the Act and defines the scope of the application of the Act.

Part II of the Act deals with electronic records and electronic signatures generally. It provides that, with limited exceptions, electronic records and signatures should be accorded the same treatment as paper records and signatures for purposes of complying with statutory writing, signature, evidentiary and record-keeping requirements.

Part III of the Draft Act addresses the integrity and authentication of secure electronic records and secure electronic signatures. Secure electronic records and signatures define specific categories of records and signatures that are afforded greater evidentiary presumptions because of their enhanced reliability and trustworthiness. The concept of a secure electronic record or a secure electronic signature will foster the growth of electronic commerce by providing businesses with assurances that records and signatures which meet the statutory definitions of 'secure' records or signatures will be accorded the heightened evidentiary presumptions necessary to make business transactions effectively non-repudiable.

Part IV of the Draft Act addresses issues of electronic contracting. This part deals with the form in which an offer and an acceptance may be expressed and legal recognition of contracts formed in an electronic medium. This part aims to provide increased legal certainty as to the conclusion of contracts by electronic means.

Parts V, VI, VII, VIII and IX of the Draft Act stipulate the legal issues related to the use of digital signatures. Digital signature technology, which utilises asymmetric cryptography technology, has been developed to facilitate secure transactions over the Internet and other computer networks. Although the electronic contracting sections of the Draft Act have been drafted to be technologically neutral, Parts V-IX have been included to establish the rules for the use of the most prominent current technology. Thus, a digital signature issued in accordance with Part V will be presumed to be a secure electronic signature.

Part X of the Draft Act addresses the acceptance and use of electronic records and electronic signatures by government entities. This section authorises any Department or Ministry to accept electronic filing of documents and to issue permits, licenses or approvals electronically. This section also empowers any Department or Ministry of the Government to specify the conditions and procedures for electronic filing or retention of documents. However, this section does not compel any Department or Ministry of the Government to accept or issue any document in electronic form if it does not wish to do so.

Part XI of the Draft Act deals with issues relating to the liability of network service providers.

Part XII of the Draft Act lays down criminal penalties for intentional damage or destruction of information systems or data, intentional 'trespass' into a system and intentional theft of computer services, tampering with data, interrupting network services and intentionally introducing viruses into computers or computer networks.

Part XIII of the Draft Act contains general provisions relating to the use of electronic records.

CONCLUSION

The rapid development of information and communication technologies over the past decade has revolutionised business practices. The meteoric rise of the Internet and the World Wide Web has accelerated the transformation of global commerce, allowing instantaneous, inexpensive contracts among sellers, buyers, investors, advertisers and financiers throughout the world.

Today, real competition is between business models and not between products – when business models change, new leaders emerge. The Government has to re-engineer itself; for example, the present tender route for procurement is so slow that the product may become obsolete by the time procurement is made. We should take lessons from other progressive governments like those of the U.S.A., Canada and Singapore, which enacted laws speedily to facilitate the assimilation of the latest in IT.

The rise of electronic commerce means that the world is about to undergo a great change. As we enter the new millennium, the members of the international community, including governments, private sectors and international organisations, all have an opportunity to work together to ensure that people everywhere benefit from the economic revolution underlying the rise of e-commerce.

REFERENCES

'Bill on Cyber Laws Coming Soon'. *Hindustan Times,* October 21,1999.

Economic Times, September 23, 1999.

Policy Considerations for Electronic Commerce. Discussion Paper from the International Telecom Union (ITU), Telematics, India, May 1999.

Rama, A., 'Start Small, Grow Fast', *Telematics India,* September 1999.

Satapathy, C., 'E-Commerce and Cyber Frauds'. *Chartered Secretary,* July 1999.

9

Emergence of Global E-Commerce—Strategies and Prospects

SAWALIA BIHARI VERMA

The development of Internet-based E-Commerce offers the most exciting business opportunities in the marketplace, which is pressurising business operations all around the world to change traditional methods of conducting business. Organisations that want to stay in business must re-evaluate every aspect of their strategy and operations and incorporate these technological changes into the way they conduct business. Internet based E-commerce is essential for the survival of companies entering a virtual distribution market place.

The lack of integrated applications and the unavailability of universally accepted methods of communication have been a constant plague in the development of electronic commerce. As the Internet develops there is every possibility that e-mail and applications-based technologies will take over from traditional telephony as the common method of communications. Furthermore, the Internet provides an unprecedented infrastructure for moving information. This will have immense repercussions within the commercial world.

BRIEF HISTORY

The rapid growth in business and consumer use of the Internet and the web-beginning with the introduction of the first graphical web browser. Mosaic, in 1992 and the subsequent elimination of the National Science Foundation's (NSF) acceptable-use policy (which prohibited commercial use of the Internet backbone) created the potential for new forms of e-commerce.

These options now are attracting more attention than EDI, are growing much faster and eventually will be much larger, both in terms of participants and in the value and volume of transactions.

As interest in the Web exploded during the mid-1990s and as the number of consumers with access to the Internet at work or at home grew, companies that originally had established web sites primarily for marketing purposes to promote their corporate or brand identity or to provide information about their products, soon became interested in using those sites for sales purposes as well (that is to take orders). In other cases, the Web was used in support of transactions that already had occurred or were ongoing, for example, in tracking of shipments being handled by the major package delivery services. The compelling advantage of the Web as an infrastructure for e-commerce is that it provides a universal software client, the web browser and a ubiquitous infrastructure, the global TCP/IP network known as the Internet that can serve as a ready-made platform for e-commerce. This situation vastly reduced the costs of setting up as an EC merchant because it eliminates the need for each vendor to develop, distribute and support a software client and maintain a dedicated network and dialling access facilities.

INTERNET COMMERCE CAN BE CLASSIFIED AS FOLLOWS

- Business-to-Business,
- Business-to-Consumer,
- Consumer-to-Consumer, and
- Consumer-to-Business.

Although business-to-consumer Web-based e-commerce has garnered more attention recently, business-to-business e-commerce will continue to account for the bulk of transaction dollar volume in the next few years, in part due to existing infrastructure and to compelling financial benefits. Barriers to business-to-consumer e-commerce have included concerns about security and poor performance often experienced by consumers from Internet congestion, slow modems, the use of large graphic files and other factors.

At the same time, business-to-business e-commerce has been accelerated because businesses already have the necessary technology infrastructure. The growth of corporate extranets (intranets that have been extended to include business partners and key customers) has fuelled the growth in Internet-based business-to-business e-commerce.

The two forms of Web-based e-commerce, business-to-business and business-to-consumer, share many common characteristics and technologies. However, they also differ in important ways, in characteristics and technologies as well as in the business drivers for adopting e-commerce.

Common Technology Characteristics of B2B and B2C

- Use of the Web server as a platform and the Web browser as a client.
- Interaction that is often human using computer programme (Web browser) to program (Web server), not direct programme-to-programme (as in the case of EDI).
- Message formats that are not tightly defined or highly standardised (as in the case of EDI). Instead, each web site has its own structure, content, procedures and so on. The only way to interact with that site is to navigate through it with a browser and populate forms by typing into them.
- Technology issues involved in linking a company's web site and e-commerce server to its back-end systems for functions such as generating the content of an online catalogue from a product database or passing orders taken over the Web to an order entry and fulfilment system.
- The need for authentication and encrypting because the transactions are carried out over non-secure networks.

Common Technology Differences of B2B and B2C

There are also important technology differences between the business-to-business and business-to-consumer e-commerce models. For example, the need to process payments *via* credit card securely has been a major driver for the development of the broad range of security technologies and payment systems. However, this need is felt most acutely on business-to-consumer sites because e-commerce merchants expect payment at the time an order is placed and consumers want to be able to pay online to avoid the delay and inconvenience associated with having to mail a check to the merchant. On business-to-business e-commerce sites, this issue is not as pressing because the merchant typically is willing to invoice the buyer and collect payment later and because business customers are used to ordering *via* a purchase order rather than paying immediately *via* credit card. For business-to-business transactions, additional safeguards are built into the existing processes to protect the companies against possible fraud. In the business to business sector, EDI is getting replaced because of the advantage Internet offers to conduct such transactions. In the business-to-consumer e-commerce market, the anticipated benefits to the vendor vary according to the business model for becoming involved with e-commerce initially.

In some cases, merchants have taken a familiar business model, such as catalogue shopping, and transported it to the web as a new medium, using their web site instead of a paper catalogue to provide product information and using online ordering to replace calling an operator to place an order. Today, these web sites may not generate many incremental orders (orders that would not be placed if the company was not on the Web). Merchants are investing in e-commerce to extend their presence to the Web so they will not become visible by their absence, to give consumers and additional mechanisms through which to do business with them; and to gain experience with web-based e-commerce so that when (or it) it becomes a larger part of their sales, they are ready to take advantage of it. Gaining experience with web-based e-commerce is particularly important so that a company can avoid being outflanked by competitors who take advantage of the web more quickly and use it to gain market share. In the future, as usage of the web becomes more widespread and possibly begins to replace (rather than supplement) existing channels, other business drivers may become important as well. For example, expenses of direct mail merchants (such as printing and postage) could be reduced dramatically if web-based e-commerce replaces traditional catalogue sales.

EFFECT OF INTERNET ON VALUE CHAIN

Primary Activities

- Inbound logistics – fast, inexpensive, reliable connection to suppliers.
- Operations – Intra-firm connectivity – Lotus Notes like connectivity through the Web-customer participation, quicker.

- Outbound logistics – fast, inexpensive, reliable connection to distributors.
- Marketing and sales – greatest value added in this area at present. Cost of advertising a product on the Web is just a fraction of the cost of newspaper advertising. Similar cost comparisons will hold for the cost of advertising the same product over TV / radio *versus* the Internet.
- Service – high impact, similar to that on marketing and sales.

Support Activities

- Corporate structure – flatter organisations, disappearing middle layer, whole organisation becomes externally oriented.
- Human resources – Internet as a vast training and recruiting tool kit.
- Technological Development – faster, richer interaction with the rest of the world, sharing of information, collaborative advantage.
- Purchasing – similar advantages as in marketing.

Other Significant Benefits

- Customisation of information as per user needs.
- Interactivity.
- Helps the seller to understand the consumer's needs fully.
- Product promotion and transaction processing is possible in one step – because of this capability of the Web, it can be considered to perform the entire marketing function by itself.
- Unusual feedback, not only what consumers buy, but also what they don't buy, might buy.
- Timeliness of information put out by a firm.
- Information updated frequently.

Market niche coverage – can be made very specific by targeting product promotion towards very specific target groups.

LEGALITY IN QUESTION

Commerce depends on confidence. For the electronic marketplace to flourish in both its customer and enterprise dimensions, buyers and sellers alike must have at least the level of confidence in the outcome of electronic commerce as they have in more traditional kinds of transactions. It must be possible for each participant in an electronic transaction to determine that both the transaction and the market environment in which it occurs are legitimate in the sense that:

- the seller and buyer are who they claim to be;
- the seller has rights of sale over the item in question;
- the buyer has the resources to purchase the item;
- the transaction and payment mechanisms are available, legal and secure;
- the item sold corresponds to its description and is suitable for purpose;
- The purchased item (be it a product or service) can and will be delivered to the buyer.

All of these expectations give rise to some fundamental questions:

- Where does an electronic transaction actually take place in terms of contractual obligations, assignment of liabilities and tax responsibilities?
- Where are companies that trade electronically registered and regulated, and to which legal regimes are they subject?
- How are rights in tangible and intangible forms of property to be protected?
- What happens when a transaction goes wrong—who has responsibility and liability?

The Internet is harmonising the general environment in which electronic communications of all kinds take place. Thus, the electronic transaction environment is moving closer and closer to the individual. As more and more kinds of consumer transactions migrate to the Internet, a number of issues become magnified that are fundamental to the creation of trust in electronic commerce as a way of doing business. By definition, a product vendor using Internet commerce has no physical presence with respect with the consumer. In this respect, electronic commerce is different from the more established kinds of catalogue sales where the location and status of the trader can normally be determined, and, more importantly, a physical record normally exists of the product description and the transaction details. All of this can be missing from an electronic transaction, and, correspondingly, the possibilities for deception and fraud can increase.

The non-territorial and intangible nature of Internet commerce calls into question the adequacy of existing law enforcement mechanisms that are still geared to tangible products and national legislation. On the other hand, Internet commerce can also be used to document the transaction trail in great detail, and to process this information for product development and marketing purposes.

This leads to questions about how to preserve the privacy of the consumer in an electronic environment (including the problem of aggressive direct solicitation). Vendors must also protect the confidentiality of information provided by the customer as part of a transaction. There are many legitimate purchases – medicines and professional services, for example – that consumers may prefer to keep confidential. Preserving consumer confidentiality involves the provision of mechanisms to prevent the use of transaction-generated information in ways that were not intended. It also involves ensuring that safeguards on the use of this information cannot be circumvented by the transportation of consumer databases between legal jurisdictions. At the moment, considerable discrepancies exist between the levels of data protection available in different countries. A primary inhibitor to consumer use of Internet commerce facilities is the difficulty in locating the sources of products, and establishing liabilities, should these products be found not be of the advertised quality, or not fit for the intended use. This situation is exacerbated where intangible products are involved.

To overcome these problems, legal, administrative and technological mechanisms are needed to certify the identity of traders and the validity of guarantees and product descriptions, and to document electronically each stage in the transaction. This could become an especially critical issue for new market entrants who have not already established a commercial reputation in the non-electronic marketplace. One method, at least in the short to medium-term, might be the use of endorsements. New product brands and vendors could enter the electronic marketplace under the 'umbrella' of a firm or brand name that has already established consumer trust in the marketplace.

Credit card firms and platform companies could also perform risk assessment, third party vetting, and rating of new companies. Endorsements could be certified electronically by means of an encrypted accreditation code. Current litigation practices, however, could inhibit development of the endorsement system. Even when the purchasing part of the transaction is complete, consumers still have to be assured that they will receive the products they have purchased electronically in good order.

At present, one of the weakest links in any consumer-oriented Electronic commerce system involving tangible goods is the physical delivery infrastructure. Delivery can also be a problem for intangible products entertainment and information services, for example—where the network backbone fails to provide access, or to delivery adequate bandwidth. In general, most types of on-demand delivery are expensive in most national markets, and these costs tend to increase over time. Business efficiencies realised at the supplier end through Internet commerce should result in more competitive prices to the consumer. These efficiencies can easily be wiped out by delivery costs, especially in countries where regulation keeps these charges artificially high. To overcome these problems, legal, administrative and technological mechanisms are needed to certify the identity of traders and the validity of guarantees and product descriptions, and to document electronically each stage in the transaction.

The prospect's final buying decision can be conveyed online and the affirmation of the sale can also be done on-line, thus closing the deal.

The following are the various issues involved in closing on-line.

Authentication

It means, verifying that the parties to the transaction are who they claim to be. Generally, it involves checking:

- Something a person has, such as a key, a credit card or some other physical device.
- Something a person knows, such as user name and/or password.
- Something unique to a person that can be compared to a known and trusted record of this information, such as a fingerprint, a signature, or a picture ID.

Cryptography using public key technology and digital signatures offers a potential solution to the problems of authentication and non-repudiability. But currently, public key technology does not provide for verification that a public key really is the key of the party in question.

A public key system requires that there be a third party, commonly called a 'Certification Authority, or CA (a new intermediary) trusted by both sender and recipient, to vouch for the validity of the sender's public key.

Privacy

The Internet is public network, and it is quite simple to 'listen in' to the message as it travels over the network from the sender's system to the recipient system, as the listener need only break into one of the systems. As more companies do business on the Internet the potential for break-ins will increase. An ordinary customer may not care much about privacy, but no large corporation would risk paying its bills over the Internet without some assurance that the transactions are safe from prying eyes. In response to the concern about break-ins, Secure Hypertech Transfer Protocol (S-HTTP) and Secure Sockets Layer (SSL) have been developed. In addition, a number of companies including Cybercash Inc., and Visa International in partnership with MasterCard and Microsoft, are working separately to develop payment specific protocols.

Integrity

It is assurance for both buyer and seller that transaction data sent from one party to the other cannot be directed to or altered by an unauthorised third party. In a cash and carry purchase, it is possible to guarantee the integrity of the transaction by simply watching the merchant, checking the change, and verifying the amount on the receipt. In the case of a transaction over the Internet, it is not possible to guarantee integrity with the infrastructure available today.

Guaranteed Delivery

Another requirement of commercial transactions over the Internet is the assurance that the order or message sent is received by the intended party. Without this guarantee, the Internet cannot be used for business-to-business transactions. A company must be able to demonstrate that a critical transaction was indeed received by the intended receipt through some form of signed digital receipt.

Non-repudiability

It means the sender cannot deny having sent the message. It involves attestation of the identity of the sender and the receiver by a trusted third party who holds the identity certificates.

FEW PRINCIPLES TO BE FOLLOWED BY GOVERNMENT WHILE DESIGNING THE CYBER LAWS TO ENHANCE THRUST TO E-COMMERCE

The private sector should lead.

Though government played a role in financing the initial development of the Internet, its expansion has been driven primarily by the private sector. For electronic commerce to flourish, the private sector must continue to lead. Innovation, expanded services, broader participation and lower prices will arise in a market-driven arena, not in an environment that operates as a regulated industry.

Accordingly, governments should encourage industry self-regulation wherever appropriate and support the efforts of private sector organisations to develop mechanisms to facilitate the successful operation of the Internet. Even where collective agreements or standards are necessary, private entities should, where possible, take the lead in organising them. Where government action or inter-governmental agreements are necessary, on taxation for example, private sector participation should be a formal part of the policy-making process.

Government should Avoid undue Restrictions on Electronic Commerce

Parties should be able to enter into legitimate agreements to buy and sell products and services across the Internet with minimal government involvement or intervention. Unnecessary regulation of commercial activities will distort development of the electronic marketplace by decreasing the supply and raising the cost of products and services for consumers the world over. Business models must evolve rapidly to keep pace with the breakneck speed of change in the technology; government attempts to regulate are likely to be outmoded by the time they are finally enacted, especially to the extent such regulations are technology-specific.

Accordingly, governments should refrain from imposing new and commercial regulations, bureaucratic procedures or taxes and tariffs on commercial activities that take place *via* the Internet.

Where Governmental Involvement is needed, its Aim should be to Support and Enforce a Predictable, Minimalist, Consistent and Simple Legal Environment for Commerce

In some areas, government agreements may prove necessary to facilitate electronic commerce and protect consumers. In these cases, governments should establish a predictable and simple legal environment based on a decentralised, contractual model of law rather than one based on top-down regulation. This may involve states as well as national governments. Where government intervention is necessary to facilitate electronic commerce, its goal should be to ensure competition, protect intellectual property and privacy, prevent fraud, foster transparency, support commercial transactions and facilitate dispute resolution.

Governments should Recognise the Unique Qualities of the Internet

The genius and explosive success of the Internet can be attributed in part to its decentralised nature and to its tradition of bottom-up governance. These same characteristics pose significant logistical and technological challenges to existing regulatory models, and governments should tailor their policies accordingly. Electronic commerce faces significant challenges where it intersects with existing regulatory schemes. We should not assume, for example, that the regulatory frameworks established over the past 60 years for telecommunications, radio and television fit the Internet. Regulation should be imposed only as a necessary means to achieve an important goal on which there is a broad consensus. Existing laws and regulations that may hinder electronic commerce should be reviewed and revised or eliminated to reflect the needs of the new electronic age.

Electronic Commerce over the Internet should be Facilitated on a Global Basis

The Internet is emerging as a global marketplace. The legal framework supporting commercial transactions on the Internet should be governed by consistent principles across state, national and international borders that lead to predictable results regardless of the jurisdiction in which a particular buyer or seller resides.

To make Indian Websites Globally Competent the following Issues should be Covered by Cyber Laws

Issues

1. Financial Issues
   Customs and taxation electronic payments.
2. Legal Issues
   Uniform commercial code for electronic commerce.
   Intellectual property protection.
   Privacy.
   Security.
3. Market Access Issues
   Telecommunications infrastructure and information technology.
   Content.
   Technical standards.

1. *Financial Issues*

Customs and Taxation

For over 50 years, nations have negotiated tariff reductions because they have recognised that the economies and citizens of all nations benefit from freer trade. Given this recognition, and because the Internet is truly a global medium, it makes little sense to introduce tariffs on goods and services delivered over the Internet.

Further, the Internet lacks the clear and fixed geographic lines of transit. The taxation of commerce conducted over the Internet should be consistent with the established principles of international taxation, should avoid inconsistent national tax jurisdictions and double taxation, and should be simple to administer and easy to understand.

Any taxation of Internet sales should follow these principles.

It should neither distort nor hinder commerce. No tax system should discriminate among types of commerce, nor should it create incentives that will change the nature or location of transactions. The system should be simple and transparent. It should be capable of capturing the overwhelming majority of appropriate revenues, be easy to implement, and minimise burdensome record keeping and costs for all parties.

Any such taxation system will have to accomplish these goals in the context of the Internet's special characteristics—the potential anonymity of buyer and seller, the capacity for multiple small transactions, and the difficulty of associating on-line activities with physically defined locations.

Electronic Payment Systems

New technology has made it possible to pay for goods and services over the Internet. Some of the methods would link existing electronic banking and payment systems, including credit and debit card networks, with new retail interfaces *via* the Internet and electronic money, based on stored-value, smart card, or other technologies, is also under-development. Substantial private sector investment and competition is spurring an intense period of innovation that should benefit consumers and businesses wishing to engage in global electronic commerce. At this early stage in the development of electronic payment systems, the commercial and technological environment is changing rapidly. It would be hard to develop policy that is both timely and appropriate. For these reasons, inflexible and highly prescriptive regulations and rules are inappropriate and potentially harmful. Rather, in the near term, case-by-case monitoring of electronic payment experiments is preferred.

From a longer term perspective, however, the marketplace and industry self-regulation alone may not fully address all issues. For example, government action may be necessary to ensure the safety and soundness of electronic payment systems, to protect consumers, or to respond to important law enforcement.

2. *Legal Issues*

'Uniform Commercial Code' for Electronic Commerce

In general, parties should be able to do business with each other on the Internet under whatever terms and conditions they agree upon. Private enterprise and free markets have typically flourished, however, where there are predictable and widely accepted legal environments supporting commercial transactions. To encourage electronic commerce, the U.S. government is providing support to the development of both a domestic and global uniform commercial legal framework that recognises, facilitates and enforces electronic transactions world-wide.

Fully informed buyers and sellers could voluntarily agree to form a contract subject to this uniform legal framework, just as parties currently choose the body of law that will be used to interpret their contract. Participants in the marketplace should define and articulate most of the rules that will govern electronic commerce. To enable private entities to perform this task and to fulfil their roles adequately, governments should encourage the development of simple and predictable domestic and international rules and norms that will serve as the legal foundation for commercial activities in cyberspace.

In the United States of America, every state government has adopted the Uniform Commercial Code (UCC), a codification of substantial portions of commercial law.

Internationally, the United Nations Commission on International Trade Law (UNCITRAL) has completed work on a model law that supports the commercial use of international contracts in electronic commerce.

The following Principles should, to the Extent Possible, Guide the Drafting of Rules Governing Electronic Commerce

Parties should be free to order the contractual relationship between themselves as they see fit; rules should be technology-neutral (that is, the rules should neither require nor assume a particular technology) and forward looking (that is, the rules should not hinder the use or development of technologies in the future); existing rules should be modified and new rules should be adopted only as necessary or substantially desirable to support the use of electronic technologies; and the process should involve the high-tech commercial sector as well as businesses that have not yet moved online.

Government should develop additional model provisions and uniform fundamental principles designed to eliminate administrative and regulatory barriers and to facilitate electronic commerce by:

Encouraging governmental recognition, acceptance and facilitation of electronic communications (that is, contracts, not arised documents, etc.); encouraging consistent international rules to support the acceptance of electronic signatures and other authentication procedures; promoting the development of adequate, efficient and effective alternate dispute resolution mechanisms for global commercial transactions.

Intellectual Property Protection

Commerce on the Internet often will involve the sales and licensing of intellectual property. To promote this commerce, sellers must know that their intellectual property will not be stolen and buyers must know that they are obtaining authentic products.

International agreements that establish clear and effective copyright, patent and trademark protection are therefore necessary to prevent piracy and fraud. While technology, such as encryption, can help combat piracy, an adequate and effective legal framework also is necessary to deter fraud and the theft of intellectual property, and to provide effective legal recourse when these crimes occur.

Copyrights

In December 1996, the World Intellectual Property Organisation (WIPO) updated the Berne Convention and provided new protection for performers and producers of sound recordings by adopting two new treaties, namely, the WIPO Copyright Treaty and the WIPO Performances and Phonograms Treaty.

Both treaties include provisions relating to technological protection, copyright management information and the right of communication to the public, all of which are indispensable for an efficient exercise of rights in the digital environment.

Both treaties also contain provisions that permit nations to provide for exceptions to rights in certain cases that do not conflict with a normal exploitation of the work and do not unreasonably prejudice the legitimate interests of the author (for example, 'fair use'). These provisions permit members to carry forward and appropriately extend into the digital environment limitations and exceptions in their national laws, which have been considered acceptable under the Berne Convention. These provisions permit members to devise new exceptions and limitations that are appropriate in the digital network environment, but neither reduce nor extend the scope of applicability of the limitations and exceptions permitted by the Berne Convention.

Government should work for appropriate copyright protection for works disseminated electronically. The two new WIPO treaties do not address issues of online service provider liability, leaving them to be determined by domestic legislation.

Patents

Development of e-commerce will both depend upon the stimulate innovation in many fields of technology, including computer software, computer hardware and telecommunications. An effectively functioning patent system that encourages and protects patentable innovations in these fields is important for the overall success of commerce over the Internet.

Trademark and Domain Names

Trademark rights are national in scope and conflicts may arise where the same or similar trademarks for similar goods or services are owned by different parties in different countries. Countries may also apply different standards for determining infringement.

An Internet domain name functions as a source identifier on the Internet. Ordinarily, source identifiers, like address, are not protected by intellectual property (that is, a trademark).

The use of domain names as source identifiers has burgeoned, however, and the courts have begun to attribute intellectual property rights to them, while recognising that misuse of a domain name could significantly infringe, dilute and weaken valuable trademark rights.

To date, conflicts between trademark rights and domain names have been resolved through negotiations and/or litigation. It may be possible to create a contractually based self-regulatory regime that deals with potential conflicts between domain name usage and trademark laws on a global basis without the need to litigate. This could create a more stable business environment on the Internet.

Privacy

Collection, re-use and instantaneous transmission of information can, if not managed carefully, diminish personal privacy. It is essential, therefore, to assure personal privacy in the networked environment if people are to feel comfortable doing business.

The Information Infrastructure Task Force (IITF) issued a report entitled "**PRIVACY AND THE NATIONAL INFORMATION INFRASTRUCTURE**".

Principles for Providing and Using Personal Information

The report recommends a set of principles to govern the collection, processing, storage and re-use of personal data in the information age.

Data-gatherers should inform consumers what information they are collecting and how they intend to use such data; data-gatherers should provide consumers with a meaningful way to limit the use and re-use of personal information.

Disclosure by data-gatherers is designed to stimulate market resolution of privacy concerns by empowering individuals to obtain relevant knowledge about why information is being collected, what the information will be used for, what steps will be taken to protect that information, the consequences of providing or withholding that information and any rights or redress they may have. Such disclosure will enable consumers to make better judgements about the levels of privacy available and their willingness to participate.

In addition, the Privacy Principles identify three values to govern the way in which personal information is acquired, disclosed and used online information privacy, information integrity and information quality. First, an individual's reasonable expectation of privacy regarding access to and use of his or her personal information should be assured. Second, personal information should not be improperly altered or destroyed. And, third, personal information should be accurate, timely, complete and relevant for the purpose for which it is provided and used. Under these principles, consumers are entitled to redress if they are harmed by improper use or disclosure of personal information or if decisions are based on inaccurate, outdated, incomplete or irrelevant personal information.

The administration supports private sector efforts now underway to implement meaningful, consumer-friendly, self-regulatory privacy regimes. These include mechanisms for facilitating awareness and the exercise of choice online, evaluating private sector adoption of and adherence to fair information practices and dispute resolution.

The administration also anticipates that technology will offer solutions to many privacy concerns in the online environment, including the appropriate use of anonymity. If privacy concerns are not addressed by industry through self-regulation and technology, the administration will face increasing pressure to play a more direct role in safeguarding consumer choice regarding privacy online. There is particular concern about the use of information gathered from children, who may lack the cognitive ability to recognise and appreciate privacy concerns. Parents should be able to choose whether or not personally identifiable information is collected from or about their children.

We urge industry, consumers and child-advocacy groups working together, to use a mix of technology, self-regulation and education to provide solutions to the particular dangers arising in this area and to facilitate parental choice. This problem warrants prompt attention. Otherwise, government action may be required.

Security

If Internet users do not have confidence that their communications and data are safe from unauthorised access or modification, they will be unlikely to use the Internet on a routine basis for commerce. A secure G II requires

1. secure and reliable telecommunication networks;
2. effective means for protecting the information systems attached to those networks;
3. effective means for authenticating and ensuring confidentiality of electronic information to protect data from unauthorised use; and
4. well trained G II users who understand how to protect their systems and their data.

There is no single 'magic' technology or technique that can ensure that the G II will be secure and reliable. Accomplishing that goal requires a range of technologies (encryption, authentication, password controls, firewalls, etc.) and effective consistent use of those technologies, all supported globally by trustworthy key and security management infrastructures. Of particular importance is the development of trusted certification services that support the digital signatures that will permit users to know whom they are communicating with on the

Internet. Both signatures and confidentiality rely on the use of cryptographic keys.

To promote the growth of a trusted electronic commerce environment, the administration should encourage the development of a voluntary, market-driven key management infrastructure that will support authentication, integrity and confidentiality. Encryption products protect the confidentiality of stored data and electronic communications by making them unreadable without a decryption key. But strong encryption is a double-edged sword. Law abiding citizens can use strong encryption to protect their trade secrets and personal records. But those trade secrets and personal records could be lost forever if the decrypt key is lost.

Depending upon the value of information, the loss could be quite substantial. Encryption can also be used by criminals and terrorists to reduce law enforcement capabilities to read their communications.

The administration, in partnership with industry, should take steps to promote the development of market driven standards, public key management infrastructure services and key recoverable encryption products.

3. *Market Access Issues*

Telecommunications Infrastructure and Information Technology

Global electronic commerce depends upon a modern, seamless, global telecommunications network and upon the computers and information appliances that connect to it. Unfortunately, telecommunications policies are hindering the development of advanced digital networks. Customers find that telecommunications services often are too expensive, bandwidth is too limited and services are unavailable or unreliable. Likewise, many countries maintain trade barriers to imported information technology, making it hard for both merchants and customers to purchase the computers and information systems they need to participate in electronic commerce.

Areas of concern include

Leased Lines

Data networks of most on-line service providers are constructed with leased lines that must be obtained from national telephone companies, monopoly or governmental entities. In the absence of effective competition, telephone companies may impose artificially inflated leased line prices and usage restrictions that impede the provision of service by online service providers.

Local Loops Pricing

To reach their subscribers, on-line service providers often have no choice but to purchase local exchange services from monopoly or government-owned telephone companies. These services also are often priced at excessive rates, inflating the cost of data services to customers.

Interconnection and Unbundling

Online service providers must be able to interconnect with the networks of incumbent telecommunication companies so that information can pass seamlessly between all users of the network. Monopolies or dominant telephone companies often price interconnection well above cost, and refuse to interconnect because of alleged concerns about network compatibility or absence of need for other providers.

Attaching Equipment to the Network

Over the years, some telecommunication providers have used their monopoly power to restrict the connection of communication or technology devices to the network. Even when the monopoly has been broken, a host of unnecessary burdensome 'type acceptance' practices have been used to retard competition and make it difficult for consumers to connect.

Internet Voice and Multimedia

Officials of some nations claim that 'real time' services provided over the Internet are 'like services' to traditionally regulated voice telephony and broadcasting, and therefore should be subject to the same regulatory restrictions that apply to those traditional services. In some countries, these providers must be licensed, as a way to control both the carriage and the content offered.

Such an approach could hinder the development of new technologies and new services. In addition, countries have different levels of telecommunications infrastructure development, which may hinder the global provision and use of some Internet-based services. The administration should believe that the introduction of policies promoting foreign investment, competition, regulatory flexibility and open access will support infrastructure development and the creation of more data-friendly networks.

Content

Informational material now accessible and transmitted through the Internet including through World Wide Web pages, news and other information services, virtual shopping malls and entertainment features, such as audio and video products and the arts.

This principle extends to information created by commercial enterprises as well as by schools, libraries, government and other non-profit entities. In contrast to traditional broadcast media, the Internet promises users greater opportunity to shield themselves and their children both from content they deem offensive or inappropriate. New technology for example, may enable parents to block their children's access to sensitive information or confine their children to pre-approved web sites.

To the extent then that effective filtering technology becomes available, content regulations traditionally imposed on radio and television need not be applied to the Internet. In fact, unnecessary regulation could cripple the growth and diversity of the Internet.

The administration should support industry self-regulation, adoption of competing ratings systems, and development of easy-to-use technical solutions (for example, filtering technologies and age verification systems) to assist in screening information on line.

Regulation of Content

Companies wishing to do business over the Internet, and to provide access to the Internet (including U.S. on-line service providers with foreign affiliates or joint ventures) are concerned about liability based on the different policies of every country through which their information may travel.

Countries that are considering or have adopted laws to restrict access to certain types of content through the Internet emphasise different concerns as a result of cultural, social and political differences. These different laws can impede electronic commerce in the global environment.

The administration should be concerned about Internet regulation of this sort, and should develop an informal dialogue with key trading partners on public policy issues such as hate speech, violence, sedition, pornography and other content to ensure that differences in national regulation, especially those undertaken to foster cultural identity, do not serve as disguised trade barriers.

Foreign Content Quotas

Some countries currently require that a specific proportion of traditional broadcast transmission time be devoted to 'domestically produced' content. Problems could arise on the Internet if the definition of 'broadcasting' is changed to extend these current regulations to 'new services'. Countries also might decide to regulate Internet content and establish restrictions under administrative authority, rather than under broadcast regulatory structures.

Regulation of Advertising

Advertising will allow the new interactive media to offer more affordable products and services to a wider, global audience. Some countries stringently restrict the language, amount, frequency, duration and type of tele-shopping and advertising spots used by advertisers. In principle, the cyber laws should not favour such regulations. While recognising legitimate cultural and social concerns, these concerns should not be invoked to justify unnecessarily burdensome regulation of the Internet.

There are laws in many countries around the world that require support for advertising claims. Advertising industry self-regulation also exists in many countries around the globe. Truthful and accurate advertising should be the cornerstone of advertising on all media, including the Internet.

A strong body of cognitive and behavioural research demonstrates that children are particularly vulnerable to advertising. As a result, the U.S. has well-established rules (self-regulatory and otherwise) for protecting children from certain harmful advertising practices. The administration will work with industry and children's advocates to ensure that these protections are translated to and implemented appropriately in the on-line media environment.

The rules of the 'country-of-origin' should be allowed to serve as the basis for controlling Internet advertising to alleviate national legislative roadblocks and trade barriers.

Technical Standards

Standards are critical to the long-term commercial success of the Internet as they can allow products and services from different vendors to work together. They also encourage competition and reduce uncertainty in the global marketplace. Premature standardisation, however, can 'lock in' outdated technology. Standards also can be employed as *de facto* non-tariff trade barriers, to 'lock out' non-indigenous businesses from a particular national market. The United States believes that the marketplace, not governments, should determine technical standards and other mechanisms for inter-operability. Technology is moving rapidly and government attempts to establish technical standards to govern the Internet would only risk inhibiting technological innovation. The United States considers it unwise and unnecessary for governments to mandate standards for electronic commerce. Rather, we urge industry driven multilateral fora to consider technical standards in this area. To ensure the growth of global electronic commerce over the Internet, standards will be needed to assure reliability, inter-operability, ease of use and scalability in areas such as:

- Electronics payments.
- Security (confidentiality, authentication, data integrity, access control, non-repudiation).
- Security services infrastructure (for example, public key certificate authorities).
- Electronic copyright management systems.
- Video and data-conferencing.
- High-speed network technologies (for example, Asynchronous Transfer Mode, Synchronous Digital Hierarchy) and digital object and data interchange).

In some cases, multiple standards should compete for marketplace acceptance. In other cases, different standards should be used in different circumstances. The prevalence of voluntary standards on the Internet and the medium's consensus-based process of standards development and acceptance are stimulating its rapid growth. These standards flourish because of a non-bureaucratic system of development managed by technical practitioners working through various organisations. These organisations require demonstrated deployment of systems incorporating a given standard prior to formal acceptance, but the process facilitates rapid deployment of standards and can accommodate evolving standards as well.

Only a handful of countries allow private sector standards development; most rely on government-mandated solutions, causing these nations to fall behind the technological cutting edge and creating non-tariff trade barriers. Numerous private sector bodies have contributed to the process of developing voluntary standards that promote inter-operability. The United States has encouraged the development of voluntary standards through private standards organisations, consortia, test beds and R&D activities.

A COORDINATED STRATEGY

The success of electronic commerce will require an effective partnership between the private and public sectors, with the private sector in the lead. Government participation must be coherent and cautious, avoiding the contradictions and confusions that can sometimes arise when different governmental agencies individually assert authority too vigorously and operate without coordination.

The variety of issues being raised, the interaction among them and the disparate foray in which they are being addressed will necessitate a coordinated, targeted governmental approach to avoid inefficiencies and duplication in developing and reviewing policy.

Private sector leadership accounts for the explosive growth of the Internet today, and the success of electronic commerce will depend on continued private sector leadership. Accordingly, the administration shall encourage the creation of private foray to take the lead in areas requiring self-regulation, such as privacy, content ratings and consumer protection and in areas such as standards development, commercial code and fostering inter-operability. There is a great opportunity for commercial activity on the Internet. If the private sector and government act appropriately, this opportunity can be realised for the benefit of all people.

DOE TO RELEASE FIRST REPORT ON CYBER LAWS

The Standing Committee to Formulate Cyber Laws of the Department of Electronics (DoE). The report is seen as a significant step that will eventually pave the way for such Internet-related activities as e-commerce and transactions on the Net.

The DoE report lays down the need for new policies in some areas, as well as the need to substantially change and rewrite some existing laws if cyber laws are to become a reality. The report was supposed to be debated on the floor of Parliament.

The committee has already published a study on three aspects to be covered under the new laws. These include Digital Signature Law, New Directions in Intellectual Property Rights and Cryptography Technology and Policy Directions.

According to the report, the cyber laws must encompass all the cases, statutes and constitutional provisions that impact persons and institutions who control the entry to cyber space, provide access to cyber space, create the hardware and software which enables people to access cyber space, or use their own computers to go on-line and enter cyber space.

Some of the key players in cyber law disputes may include phone companies, regulatory agencies, PC companies, software companies, Internet Service Providers, schools, colleges, universities and all persons and companies that have established a presence on the Internet.

The business community has been demanding the opening up of e-commerce transactions on the Net for quite some time now. But the lack of a proper authentication procedure and more importantly laws that recognise Net documents as genuine have been a stumbling block in their implementation.

Explaining the urgency for such laws, the report says "our law is tuned to establish authenticity of a transaction through signature. In the absence of paper, signature needs to be replaced. Legal rules are required to define under what circumstances a person can be bound in respect of an electronic instruction purported to have been issued by him. Electronic devices like identification numbers, call-back procedures and encryption are evolved to establish authenticity of an instruction. But from a legal perspective, the security procedure requires to be recognised by law as a substitute for signature."

The new law will layout the guidelines for the following issues: authentication of instruments; countermanding or reversal of instructions, operational security of the system; fraud, technical failure and errors; allocation of loss; evidence, data protection and record preservation.

10

M-Commerce

RAHUL GANGULI

Internet is the world's largest computer network, the network of networks, scattered all over the world. It was created nearly 25 years ago as a project for the US department of defense. It was a goal to create a method for widely separated computers to transfer data efficiently even in the event of a nuclear war. From a handful of computers and users in the 1960s, today the internet has grown to thousands of regional networks that can connect millions of users. Any single user, company or a country does not over this network.

A network of networks or "Internet", is a group of two or more networks that are:

- interconnected physically,
- capable of communicating and sharing of data with each other, and
- able to act together as a single network.

Machines on one network can communicate with machines on other networks, and send data, files, and other information back and forth. The Internet covers the globe and includes large, international networks as well as many smaller local area networks. The Internet offers access to data graphics, sound software text and people though a variety of services and tools for communication and data exchange.

There are two most important reasons for the popularity of internet: (a) Getting information from the internet, and (b) Providing information on the Internet.

The amount of information available through the internet is

staggering. One can find information on just about anything on the internet. Similarly, providing information on the internet in a commercial manner is called advertisement. The internet has more than 600 million users and therefore we are open to an audience that large our reach is more than 600 million users with minimum cost as compared to traditional means of advertisement.

For most people who are new to the Internet, the first experience is quite overwhelming. Faced with a wide variety and range of features and options, the scope, magnitude and amount of information and other resources is amazing.

Once you know the information that you want to find, how to find it, where to find it and how to access it, the internet becomes the most powerful resource is respective of whether you are using it for: work, education, e-mail, communications, entertainment or is any other walk of life.

INTRANET AND BUSINESS

Internet is a communication network which bridges all the small computer networks worldwide as a whole. Intranet is based upon internet technology in particular to www, to build information systems within organization to accomplish standardization and automation. Fundamentally, it means computing environments which let the users share the information through the internet and web browsers, ultimately it allows a certain organization to build a Group ware within web environment at low cost on top of existing network infrastructure. By doing this, closed organization networks would be interconnected with existing worldwide which results in diverse information that strengthens competitive advantages of the organization. Where the Internet connects people and organizations and information sources by using common protocols to link computers on a public and open-to-all basis, an intranet uses the same common protocols for internal company or group purposes. An intranet can be defined as a network connecting an affiliated set of clients using standard IP like TCP/IP and HTTP or as on IP-based network of nodes behind a firewall, or behind several firewalls connected by secure, possibly virtual, networks.

In general, a web is an unstructured client/server network that uses HTTP as its transmission protocol. The www comprises all HTTP nodes on the Public Internet. An internal web comprises all HTTP nodes on a private network such as an organizations LAN or WAN. If the organization is a corporation the internal web is also a corporate web. When a corporate web connects to tixio or more trading partners, it is often referred to as a business to business web or an extranet.

Business Benefits of Intranets

1. The company and its people have access to the very wide and rapidly increasing range of applications, products and services flowing from the worldwide acceptance of internet methods and the very attractive prices that result from intense competition among suppliers – as well as a lot of free or very low cost applications and information.
2. The skills needed to develop, maintain and enhance applications are converging and companies will be able to obtain technical skills from a wider pad.
3. Internet approach makes employees and jobs more flexible and mobile, since applications and information are readily shared regardless of geography and time zones, and people share a common platform of learning.
4. A common approach to internal information and published information enables significant savings for example print of publication, the information can be accessed by all staff and employees of the company at the same time from different locations.
5. Transfer of files on computers like spread sheets and used documents through a secure connection over the internet.

Why does an Organisation Need Intranet?

Whether the largest market of an organisation is corporate conglomerates or the home computer users, the goal is to reach the customers more effectively and efficiently and provide them with better services. Daily more consumers look to the web for new sources and more businesses look to their internal web, or intranet to process their clients needs in a more cost effective and efficient manner. To remain competitive, all organisations need to keep pace with technological advances.

Large organisations, which use intranets to electronically transmit documents internally, pay back their investment in the technology within six to twelve weeks.

There are various benefits of intranet to the employees and organisations. Some of the benefits are:

(i) Employees can access information they need, when they need it.
(ii) One determines as to who can have access information/ data and to what extent.
(iii) Transactions can be followed electronically.
(iv) Databases can be updated dynamically—as the transaction occurs.
(v) Communications can take place instantly—anywhere in the world.
(vi) Employees can work remotely and remote employees can be hired for their expertise.
(vii) One can access other businesses for ordering, sourcing and contracting.

Relationship of Intranets/Internets with Business

The question arises what is the relationship of internet/ intranets with business? The answer has three parts:

(a) Intranets and business have in common the use of the internet protocols to connects to business users.
(b) Intranets are more localized and can therefore move data faster than more distributed extranets.
(c) The amount of control that network managers can exert over users is different for the three technologies.

On a B2B extranet, system architects at each of the participating companies must collaborate to ensure a common interface and consistence semantics. Since one company cannot reasonably enforce standards on its trading partners, extranet application developers must take it into account a wider range of technologies than is the case for intranets. For example, one company participating in an extranet might be using MS 1E, another netscape and other opera. In order to collaborate *via* extranets, the applications have to perform adequately on all represented platforms.

E-Commerce—Unleashed

Dot com businesses may be falling by the wayside, but the percentage of commerce happening *via* the web continues to grow. Meanwhile, hundreds of millions of cellular subscribers world-wide are gaining access to new wireless data choices, including web enabled cell phones, hand-held computers, PDAS and netebooks. Combine these two facts, and you get an industry with an unbelievable potential called mobile commerce or m-commerce.

Not convinced? How about this: Woman looking for a sub-player in a store and is ready to buy, but she isn't sure if the store is offering the best price using the micro-browser on her cell phone, she quickly determines that your on-line enterprise is selling the player at 10% discount, she purchases it from you right away.

Or you send your subscribers an alert on his palm lap to let him know tickets have just gone on sale for one of his favourite performers, before the subscriber even knows the singer is coming to town within minutes, the customer selects the best seats in his price range and purchases tickets from you.

Whether this conuineces you or not, international data corporation forecasts that $ 21 billion worth of mobile commerce will take place in 2004, while Gartner group predicts that 40% of B2C (business to consumers) e-commerce in the same year will occur over wireless connections. Already, the big e-commerce players like Amazon.com and Yahoo are offering mobile options.

Content and applications must still be developed in multiple mobile formats, security questions continue to dog the industry. And evolving payments systems and networks are barely up to the task.

Wireless Commerce

No longer must a customer be tied to a land line to buy stocks or change airlines reservations. Cell phones, PDAS and devices we haven't yet imagined are getting unwired for commerce. Obstacles include multiple platforms, lack of payment systems, sketchy security and the need for specialised infrastructure.

Because mobile commerce is still fraught with technical problems, most companies would be wire to seek a service provider. A big issue here is security.

This year, companies will extend their e-commerce applications to mobile devices but will rely on existing settlement systems, such as charging a users credit card account. Examples of such applications are financial trading, buying tickets, ordering from restaurants, updating financial portfolios, conducting banking transactions—such as transferring funds between accounts. Financial trading are leading the way, as customers can derive clear and immediate benefits.

Electronic Wallet

Now available in limited form, electronic wallets will facilitate transactions by providing a centralized way for users to maintain accounts and shipping information. Electronic wallets will play an increasingly important role in mobile commerce. Major sites like Yahoo already support wallet mechanisms. Credit card companies are also actively involved this area. Expect dozens of such systems to crop up by the end of this year.

Personalised Technology

This year, new location technology will enable mobile commerce applications that take a user's location into account. Based on user's preferences these applications will give user's access to localised and personal information. For example, after dinner at a restaurant, someone could use his PSA or a cell phone to get a list of movies playing at the closest theatre, obtain show times and purchase tickets.

E-Cash Technologies

Beginning around 2002 new financial settlements systems will allow secure transmission of electronic cash on WAN or LAN. E-cash technologies is one of the pioneers in this area. To buy a coke from a vending machine, for instance, a user will be able to press a couple of keys on a mobile device to transfer electronic tokens—the equivalent of virtuals coins to a machine over a local wireless connection such as Bluetooth. In effect mobile devices could begin to replace cash cheques and credit cards. The implications for every one merchants, consumers and banks alike—are huge. What devices will people be using? Initially they'll use smart phones with micro-browsers—typically based on HDML (Handheld Device Mark-up Language and WAP (Wireless Application Protocol) and handheld computers with wireless modems.

Mobile Commerce—Architecture and Protocols

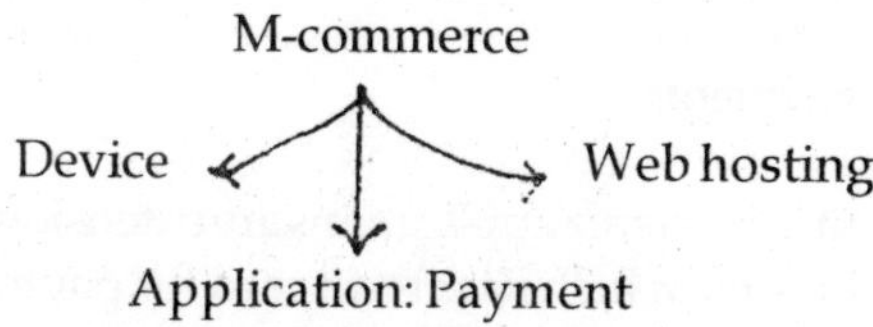

A mobile-commerce application can be broken down into three parts. The user's device, the website hosting the application and the payment mechanism. In addition to this, various gateways come into play. In the simplest model a website would deliver HTML directly to a mobile device, and a protocol such as secure Layer (SSL) would secure communications. To settle transactions, the website would communicate with a financial network either directly or *via* a third party. This structure merely replaces a standard desktop browser with one operating on a mobile device and a wired link with a wireless link, in fact HTML browsers are available for Palm and Pocket PC devices. Most mobile-commerce application developers want to support as many mobile devices as possible. One approach might be to format the content to WML (Wireless Markup Language) which would make the application available to mobile devices with WAP browsers.

Security: A Pair in the ASP

The wireless model we've described raises a serious security concern, since the ASP might decrypt messages received from the mobile unit. As for the security protocols used between mobile units and the wireless ASP or middleware platform, typical protocols include SSL with 3DES encryption.

However, many companies like certicom corp. are developing security solutions based on new methods that are better suited to small devices. The wireless ASP or middleware platform can then translate from these mobile specific security protocols and conventional internet security protocols.

You'll also need to think about user's authentication. Certainly users can enter passwords when prompted SIM (subscribers identity module) cards, now used in GSM (Global system for mobile communications) cellular networks are new methods. These cards uniquely map subscribers to physical cards which the user can insert into various devices.

Settlement and Payments

Most of today's m-commerce applications are extensions of web-based e-commerce solutions, which use credit card for payment. However, as these applications mature and a wide variety of m-commerce transactions broadens, settlement systems will change. Simply put, we need generally available secure electronic wallet and electronic cash mechanisms. No doubt this will take time, but many approaches have already been introduced.

The E-Wallet would hold user's financial information such as credit card accounts, thipping information and various such information. Some wireless ASPs such as Snaz commerce solutions, host such a wallet mechanism and provide a mobile shopping portals for merchants to plug into.

Wireless Application Protocol (WAP)

WAP is built on a layered protocol, making transmission of WAP content possible over almost any available wireless network. These networks include those based on CDPD (Cellular Digital Packet Data) CDMA (Code-Division Multiple Access) GSM (Global System for Mobile Communications).

WAP was designed and is maintained by WAP forum, which was created in 1998, through the joint efforts of Ericsson, Motorola and Nokia. Today the WAP forum includes more than 100 members ranging from handset manufacturers and to consultants.

WAP consists of two components. First is the all important WAP browser, which is responsible for processing hytecode sent to it by the WAP gateway. The WAP gateway creates the interface between the internet and the WAP browser.

In a typical WAP transaction, the browser sends a request to the gateway, which then sends a request to the respective web server on the Internet, the web server responds to the gateway with the requested wireless markup language file. The getway encodes the file into hytecode, which is then transmitted to the WAP browser. Next, the browser decodes the hytecodes and displays the requested website.

Is WAP, Washout?

Mobile Internet is poised for growth in India. The low penetration of home PCS as compared to the exploding numbers in the mobile telephony market implies that for a large number of people, the mobile phone could be the first device to the internet. This is especially true when you look at the projected increase in the number of internet users in the country more than 10 folds in the next three years, at a conservative estimate.

The next group of consumers to enter cyber space will be less tech-savvy, for such a persons, the simple one click away interface of the mobile phone will be far less indimidazing than any PC experience.

In urban India, the average professional spends a high proportion of his/ her time in away – from PC situations with commuting times, traffic jams and fight delays.

Everybody will be WAP enabled!
Banking, Financial Share Trading Services

In an increasingly fast paced, customer-oriented industry wireless access to information is a must have for both customers as well as employees. From banking information and transactions, to corporate money market news, and research data to real time stock quotes and transactions, the world is moving to a WAP enabled wireless 24 × 7 world.

Telecom

Mobile phone began as a voice service. Then came SMS (short message system). Now a wireless internet is revolutionising the face of the mobile industry. Customers are being deluged with everything from basic access to e-mail to local entertainment and leisure directories complete with online booking and directions. A whole new industry of wireless content providers and application developers are stretching the parameters of the rather more conventional telecom services.

The Mobile Internet

Obviously, services that you require whilst you are on the move are generally better suited for 'mobile' internet services rather than the classic web. Some great applications are beginning to emerge for instance . . .

A wireless access to Internet content: Consumers benefit from immediate interactive access to the information they need at that moment, location specific shops, theatre, map, taxi and GPS driver locator.

Wireless access to corporate IT systems and Extranets: Corporates can offer new channels for their services and also create to tally new services for their mobile customers in addition to directory services and intranets.

Wireless access to personal information: Wireless device users can access their e-mails, calendars, to do lists, and even screen text headers for their voice mail messages immediate interest areas like information on sports and news and even horoscopes.

Intelligent Telephony services: Carriers can offer their customers secure access to their personal and other customer related information, billing and other databases in the intelligent Network.

M-Commerce: Access to corporate B2B mission critical legacy applications including inventory, sales automation and SCM applications day-to-day transactions such as buying and selling, goods and services at real time across geography and demographics.

A Wireless Future: The Internet until now, was only available to the few million with access to a PC. With WAP, the fact of internet anywhere, and everywhere has become a reality.

WAP is a *de facto* world standard. Every industry and function will be imported by the access to instant information and data from banking and financial services to the Telecom and software industries.

Thanks to WAP, a business traveller will be able to change his flight bookings or scan the latest stock quotations whilst seated in a coffee shop. He could receive e-mail or send e-mails while miles away from his office or likewise check inventory levels or account receivables from his WAP enabled websited.

WAP in India: It is been less, than a year since mobile operators and internet companies discovered that cell phone was a great way of expanding the scope of the internet and less than a few months. Since mobile subscribers around the world have actually surfed the internet *via* a WAP phone.

India has already ventured into this exclusive market. At a speed, which has been quite phenomenal, thanks to Intense market pitches by both multinational cellular giants like NOKIA and Ericsson who have kicked off this new ball game, and amongst system integrators, e-capital, planetasia.com, IBM and CMS stood out as being active on the WAP front.

In short, the way we work and live is set to undergo a revolution....

- The world is going wireless.
- By 2003, a third of all Internet users will be accessing the internet *via* mobile devices.
- There will be over one billion wireless net users by 2004.
- The WAP industry will be worth more than $ 1 trillion, over the next five years.
- By 2003, every third European, or 219 million users, will be accessing the wireless internet.
- Handset manufacturers representing 90% of the world mobile phone market have committed to shipping WAP enabled devices.
- Telecom carries representing more than 100 million subscribers worldwide have joined the WAP forum.

Source: Fortune, Strategis Group, Forrester, Nokia.com, wapforum.org and wap-intelligence.com.

Bluetooth—The Invasion Begins

Bluetooth, a new wireless interconnected technology standard, is designed to replace many cables we need to connect devices to our PCS or networks. Called a PAN (Personal Area Network), this technology will let you walk into a room and communicate with your PC or other Bluetooth-compliant devices. The Bluetooth specification was created in February 98 by a consortium comprising inventive minds from Ericsson, IBM, Intel, Nokia and Toshiba.

Support for Bluetooth is solid, with more than 1880 adopter/associate member companies signed up to the Bluetooth Special Interest Group.

Bluetooth is a good, low-power data/voice transmission standard that will be a real boon for certain applications. Imagine a cell phone or pager that automatically transfers to vibrate mode when you enter a restaurant or theatre. Or a laptop and GPS (Global Positioning System) that automatically feed a display in your car for directions. One of Bluetooth's design strengths is its low cost. The Bluetooth SIG says integrating this technology should add only $ 5 to the cost of a unit.

Significant steps have been made in overcoming technology hurdles and in encouraging the industry to work together to solve issues of compatibility. Thousands of companies have been driving developments and, as a consequence of this effort, Bluetooth has radically evolved. From the initial concept for a cable-replacement technology a whole new vision of invisible connectivity has emerged. Much more than offering a simple connection between a user's PC and a printer, Bluetooth will provide wireless connectivity to the internet at the office, at home or in other public places.

By simply walking down a road you can easily join or quit dozens of *ad hoc* actworks in streets and buildings, checking for information of personal interest to you imagine being able to receive information on a hotel's facilities while wandering the grounds or to search for information on specific goods while passing through a shopping centre. In fact, Bluetooth projects are already underway in many such public locations in addition to golf courses and airports.

E-Cash

When shopping in Singapore, you pay in Singapore dollars and in Hong Kong you of course pay in HK $. Right? Well get ready for a time when you pay only in e-money.

E-cash is a relatively recent entrant in the complex world of e-commerce very convenient and secure it can be at alternative to traditional methods of on-line payments such as a credit card and even for offline transactions.

E-cash or digital cash or E$, as it is known, was developed as replacement for the traditional concept of money. Basically speaking e-cash is nothing but blocks of data that represent money. It is a payment message bearing a digital signature, which functions as a medium of exchange or value. This data can be transferred from one point to another *via* networks and can be traded as tokens to be exchanged as real money.

These entities intend to promote e-cash as a medium for obtaining products and services, just like real cash. The digital nature of e-cash presents great possibilities for the future of commerce and business, E-cash is stored on computers and mobile devices.

All transactions are secured using complex encryption techniques. The transaction is completed after user verification. The value of e-cash required is taken from the buyer's account and deposited into the account of the seller.

There are three types of e-cash available anonymous and identified type, offline and online e-cash and smart cards.

E-cash *vs.* Paper Money

Similar to paper money, e-cash also works in a two way stream in the real world. You can send or receive e-cash from others. Unlike credit card transactions, it is not possible for others to know or market your personal details on the web from your e-cash transactions.

The Internet is not a very safe place as such security levels are of the highest level standards in e-cash systems. This is made possible using encryption and digital signatures. E-cash providers ensure that it is not possible to have digital cash in more than one location. This means that you cannot have the same unit of e-cash in your hard disk and you PDA at the same time.

We have heard and spoken about global communities, however, currency still varies from country to country. E-cash has an edge in this regard since it is Intended to be truly universal. For example – the e-cash can be used in India and USA. Simply put, it gets things done for you anywhere in the world without having to convert your rupee into the local currency.

It can be split into smaller units more easily than real money. This means that you would no longer have to hear tiresome lines such as "no change". It also does away with dirty and torn notes.

Will it ever make it big?

Now for the big question; when is e-cash going to replace the paper more use? Well not any time in the near future. It will take at least six to seven years before e-cash car replace the money standard in online transactions. There are several factors inhabiting the growth of e-cash at present.

In addition to e-cash sites like flooz.com and benz.com major players such as Microsoft.com have stepped into the Orena. Microsofts latest operating system, Windows XP, comes with a passport, a kind of e-wallet that stares user's credit card information on his PC, which he can later on use for secure and easy on-line transactions, American Express, Mastercard and Visa have also come out with a range of smart cards for on-line transactions.

To first block to e-cash is acceptance. Why is paper money so popular? Simple – everyone accepts it. Anywhere in the world paper money is the standard means of trade credit cards have been around for more than 30 years but still haven't been able to replace cash, completely.

Next comes the case of use. Come on how many of us would like to go through the tiresome process of registering and logging on to sites when we need something as simple as a shirt or a book.

Biggest blow is yet to come, Governments and banks do not like e-cash. They object to the anonymous nature of e-cash transactions. It would be difficult to prevent tax evasions and money laundering if transactions were to become common. This in a way explains why e-cash is taking so much time to develop. Well, nothing did ever come easy and these roadblocks could be seen as part of the evolutionary process for e-cash. E-cash providers are sure to find out a way out of these thorny issues.

CONCLUSION

The need to make the Internet a better environment to work and play in. The need to cut down on the development time for solutions and ensure faster time to market networking today is no longer just about products – its about services that you deliver over the wire.

Necessity is the mother of all inventions. However, not all changes are driven by necessity at least not in India. So has their time come? look closely and you'll realise that it has.

See how enterprises have spent years and years on ERP implementations, on applications that not only streamline processes, but also offer business data. Data that can now be mined for profits. Looks good, but will the companies implement them.

We find that scores of companies setting up huge data centres. Facilities that will eventually house hundreds of dot.com servers generating terabytes of data.

The face of net working is changing and so is business too. E-commerce is now sporting a new look to m-commerce on a large scale, but the question remains, are we ready for it?

11

E-Commerce and the Indian Business: Emerging Challenges and Initiatives

NAVIN PRAKASH

A world of change is sweeping across the business world in the way the companies all across the globe are conducting their business. Indian companies are no exception. The single major factor for such change is IT – The Information Technology.[1] The IT as we know of is not of recent origin. Computers in their earlier *avtars* have been there since the 50s. However, it was only during 80s after the introduction of Personal Computers for the SOHO (Small Office and Home) segment that led to the e-revolution. There has also been a sea change in the processing capability of the computers to deliver the increasing demands of the business.[2]

There is an interesting story about the evolution of the PCs. IBM was the creator of the PCs. According to Stephen H. Wildstrom[3] the first business PC was the IBM 5150. It is interesting to note that IBM was initially rather reluctant to commercially introduce PCs and had grossly underestimated it's market and application potential. However, after the introduction of the first PC, the rest as they say is history. It is significant to note that the essential PC architecture still remains quite like it was during 80s. The following table gives an idea of how power of computers has exponentially increased while the costs have come down making the PCs a mass product in the process.

The mass availability, lower prices and ease of use of the PCs specially after the introduction of GUI (Graphic user interface) and WYSIWYG (What you see is what you get) in the computers,[4] we have

Year	*1981*	*1991*	*2001*
Model	IBM PC	Compaq 486	Dell Dimension
Processor	Intel 8088	Intel 80486	Intel Pentium 4
Speed	4.77 MHz	33 MHz	1.3 GHz
Storage Capacity	160 KB	120 MB (HDD)	20 GB
Cost in $	3,300	2,300	2,300

come to the stage where computers in one way or the other affect our daily lives. Related to this has been the development of the INTERNET – The Network of the Networks – The technology which is changing the way we conduct business. It may be surprising to note that the Internal has been there since the 1970s albeit in a rudimentary form. The first network to evolve was the APRANET (Advance Research Project Agency Network) of the Department of Defense of the Government of the United States in 1969 connecting four host computers to each other. In the 1970s, the network was extended to academic institutions in the U.S. and Europe. Another major development was the introduction of e-mail by Larry Roberts in 1972 as an application of the APRANET network. These were simple applications developed to share and collaborate in the research and academic work. However, they were undoubtedly the starting points for today's e-revolution. During 1980s, TCP/IP (Transfer Control Protocol and Internal Protocol) were developed for the flow of information across APRANET. Another significant development was the releasing of the APRANET to the public domain in 1983 and by 1990, thirty countries had joined NSFNET (National Science Foundation Network), the successor of APRANET. By March 1991, first commercial applications started as newer networking technologies and protocols evolved continuously leading to the present day Internet and World Wide Web. Gradually companies started building their websites firstly for disseminating information and then for e-commerce[5] purposes as well as for B2B and B2C transactions.

> "General Electric is a hundred year old company and seeks every tool and technique it can squeeze out waste. Some say that is the secret of GE's sustained performance over decades. GE

expects to save $ 1 billion from it's internet initiatives this year. Principal amongst these is it's private online Market place in which it will buy and sell $ 20 billion of products and services this year."

"It is estimated that e-commerce related spending will constitute 69% of overall IT products and services spending in year 2005, up from 32% in 2000. The Global market for such products and services are likely to be $ 600 billion in 2005."

"The total e-commerce transaction volume in India is expected to touch Rs. 1,95,000 crores by year 2005 with B2B transaction alone amounting to 1,92,000 crores (98.5%) and the balance made up by B2C transactions."

(Excerpts from the proceedings of the 2-day Seminar – E-Biz India – 2001, organized by NASSCOM (National Association of Software and Services Companies) and the Boston Consulting Group (BCG), Bangalore, Aug. 2-3rd, 2001, as reported in the www.bizpapertoday.com.)

NASSCOM is a professional body engaged in the lobbying and promoting of the Indian software industry. Their estimates even though slightly off the mark, may not be totally unrealistic. With the rapid growth in the Internet application technology and the ease with which transactions can be carried out across the Internet, security and related issues notwithstandings, businesses across the board will find it increasingly attractive to conduct transactions over the net.

Of late there has been a lot of hoopla over the Dot Com companies going bust and several start ups going down the hill with fears regarding the long-term feasibility and sustain ability of the Internet being expressed. This has been more so after the events of 9/11. However, these fears seem quite unfounded as far as existing established businesses are concerned. The brick and mortar companies can substantially increase efficiency and cut down on transaction costs by going on-line through the use of Intranet (Within the company) and Extranet (Networking with their associates, suppliers and vendors on the one hand and wholesalers and retailers on the other) and linking the whole with the Internet for on-line, real time transactions.

It's like the "200 million Indian middle class" syndrome which enticed droves of consumer good manufacturers to the country – and then left them tottering, IT-enabled services, once heralded as the next biggest opportunity for employment in India, don't seem to be living up to their promise.

The now famous 1999 NASSCOM-McKinsey report had generated considerable excitement on the job potential of India's IT-enabled services market, but the ground reality is rather more mundane. The report had famously estimated that the IT-enabled services industry will earn 417 billion $ in revenues and provide jobs to one million in the next seven years. But the actual number of people employed so far is about 70,000 including 18,000 in the much-hyped call center business.

The IT-enabled services industry comprises call centers, medical transcriptions, geographical information systems (GIS) and back office processing. The worldwide information technology-enabled services market is estimated at 600-800 million $. There are around 200 MT (Medical Transcription) units in the country employing between 5,000 to 8,000 people and generating revenues of $ 25-$ 50 million annually. ("After the big infotech hype, it is the time to do a reality check." *The Economic Times*, Sep. 8th, 2001.)

While too much hype was generated over the potential B2C transactions, the fact remains that most of the revenue is generated from B2B transactions over the net. News, Views, Entertainment and Lifestyle Portals which were set-up during the initial euphoria of the dot com wave, were set-up with unclear objectives and poor revenue models depending too heavily on on-line advertising. However, big players like Amazon.Com and Yahoo are still adding on services in spite of mounting losses in the hope that the things will start looking up sooner than later. Predominantly e-mail portals like USA.net are now charging for their e-mail services—others including pioneer Hotmail are likely to follow suit soon. Back home, many portals have vanished but long-term players like Sify and Indiatimes are not only holding forth but also adding up new services.[6] New portals are coming up in spite of the poor revenues in the hope of good times. An indication for things to come up could be recent acquisition of Indya.com by Star Network group.

However, there are several issues associated with the e-commerce aspects, of the internet that need consideration:

- As a technology tool, the Internet can greatly facilitate the conduct of business with supporting IT applications available for integration of a company's suppliers, retail chain members and the customers. This requires upgradation of existing IT-infrastructure (EDI) in order to avail full benefit of the internet. This costs money, but this is money well spent as in the long-run costs are cut, savings made and time saved through decision-making processes getting automated.

- In the long-run it is the commercial aspect of B2B transactions over the net that will sustain the IT business and Internet products than individual users.
- The present Internet connections in India are estimated to be 25 lakh while the Internet users are estimated to be 60 lakh. These numbers are steadily growing. Uppermost in the minds of these users is the issue of confidentiality and security and privacy while buying products over the net, specially while using credit card for payment. Most of the Indian B2C sites accept payment on delivery manually also due to these reasons.
- Then there are issues like validity of contract over the net, tax issues, warranty and currency issues specially while making transactions with a foreign website.
- Another aspect is regarding the IPR (Intellectual Property Rights) and Copyright, Trademark and Patents particularly in case of works of Art, music and literature on display on the net.
- Another worry is regarding increasing Cyber Crimes and Hacking which have the potential of hampering a fully internet adopted company's business.

With the increasing use of IT in the Government sector in India, the Indian Business can also take advantage of the same. Firstly, private sector can help in empowering and enriching consumer awareness levels specially in the rural sector and secondly, there is going to be a large demand for IT related products and services gradually as there is mass implementation of e-governance projects in the Government sector. Similarly, there is large potential in G2B (Government to Business) transactions in future in form of on-line tax payments, on-line clearances, on-line filling up of forms, etc.

These are however, early days for internet in India with a subscriber base of 2.5 million and user base of 6 million. But the potential is huge and gradually the businesses—big or small will have to embrace the new technology. Probably, never in the history has a new technology affected the way organizations conduct their business as the IT and Internet have.

Notes and References

1. Economist Joseph Schumpeter's Fifty-year model refers to technology waves in the modern history, 1780s-1840s—Steam power, 1840s-1890s—Rail, 1890s-1930s—electric power and 1930s-1980s—oil and automobiles. Now the IT represents the Fifth wave. (Quoted in Fred Luthans—Organisational Behaviour, p. 29, Irwin McGraw Hill, 1998).
2. It is estimated that the processing power of computers doubles up every 18 months at present.
3. Technology and you, *The Economic Times*, September 2nd, 2001.
4. It was not the Windows of Microsoft but the Apple Macintosh which introduced GUI for the first time in the PCs.
5. E-commerce is defined as a shift in business paradigm that seamlessly integrates the various business processes through dissemination of real time information.
6. The Indiatimes, an e-portal of the *Times of India* group was recently adjudged to be the best portal overall in a survey conducted by *Digit Magazine*. For e-mail, the largest service used in India is Hotmail followed by Yahoo, Indiatimes, Sify and Rediff.

12

E-Commerce and Corporate Governance

B.B. MANSURI

In the prevailing era of Infotech revolution, business has become a new reality in the form of E-commerce. E-commerce is taking the front seat in all businesses worldwide, as globalization is what organizations are aiming at. This is E-commerce, where the business is done electronically throughout the globe. Most of the traditional business practices are getting obsolete due to the onslaught of an E-environment, E-banking, E-shopping, E-searching are becoming inseparable from our daily routines. The E-revolution is all set to take the countries by a storm and the day is not far when virtually the entire trading universe would be in cyberspace.

Indian organizations are ready for this E-storm and are adopting the E-commerce technologies. Figures suggest that there are about 8 to 10 lakh internet users in India. Some of the larger Indian companies have been using E-commerce for Supply Management, Customer Relationship Management, Business Intelligence through Data Warehousing and even Virtual Enterprises, E-commerce-based business too are leaving their mark in terms of technology competitiveness, business model viability and entrepreneurship. This ensures greater transparency and timely financial reporting which is a pre-requisite.

CORPORATE GOVERNANCE AND REGULATORY INITIATIVES

E-commerce is being adopted as a cost effective solution to various timebound problems facing the Indian corporate. It also offers the best opportunities to break into the fiercely competitive global market and make its presence felt. But the emergence of E-commerce is posing a new challenge to the world to redefine the rules of business and commerce. So, corporate governance is the need of the hour to Indian Businesses to give correct picture. Keeping in view the changing international business scenario, SEBI had set-up a committee under the chairmanship of Kumar Mangalam Birla to formulate the code of governance. Based on this report, SEBI directed the Stock Exchanges to amend the listing agreement between them (Stock exchange). Entities whose securities are listed on the stock exchange are required to comply with the code of governance as stipulated in clause 49.

The SEBI code of corporate governance by virtue of clause 49 of the listing agreement, broadly incorporates the areas of corporate governance. Mandatory requirements relate to board of directors, audit committee, remuneration of directors, board procedure, management, disclosure to shareholders, shareholders report on corporate governance and auditors certificate. The non-mandatory requirements are regarding non-executive chairman, remuneration committee. Shareholders rights to a copy of half-yearly declaration of financial performance and postal ballot.

Schedule of implementation is also provided. In view of the suggestion of Kumar Mangalam Birla Committee Report, the Institute of Chartered Accountants of India has formulated the Accounting Standards on Segment Reporting (AS-17), Related Party Disclosures (AS-18), Consolidated Financial Statements (AS-21) and Accounting for Taxes on Income (AS-22).

Corporate governance extends beyond corporate laws. Its fundamental objective is not mere fulfilment of the requirements of law, but in ensuring commitment of the board in managing the company in a transparent manner for maximizing long-term shareholder value.

Effectiveness for corporate governance system cannot merely be legislated by law neither can any system of corporate governance be static. As competition increases, technology pronounces the death of distance and speeds up communication, the environment in which firms operate in India also changes. In this dynamic environment, the systems of corporate governance also need to evolve.

The committee on corporate governance believes that its recommendations will go a long way in raising the standards of corporate governance in Indian firms and make them attractive destinations for local and global capital.

Thus, the recommendations will also form the base for further evolution of the structure of corporate governance in consonance with the rapidly changing economic and industrial environment of the country in the new millennium – E-commerce.

Experts have argued that the low cost of personal computers, a growing installed base for Internet use, and an increasingly competitive Internet Service Provider (ISP) market will help fuel e-commerce growth in Asia's second most populous nation. *Dataquest*, an Indian computer magazine, has found that the rise of Indian Internet subscribers will ultimately depend on the proliferation of network computers and Internet cable. Cyber cafes will also continue to provide low cost access.

As per a Nasscom-McKinsey study 1999, India has the potential to earn revenues worth US $ 10 billion by 2008 from e-business solutions. (Both the domestic and export markets put together.)

And the Indian players can achieve this goal by increasing their reach, establishing deep relationships, and expanding the scope of businesses covered. As part of its survey on e-commerce. Nasscom also conducted a study on the plans and capabilities of software companies in India. Some of the preliminary findings on e-commerce/ e-business software exports potential are as follows:

- The study revealed that Supply Chain Management optimisation and Customer Relation Management are going to be one of the strongest drivers of the global e-commerce solution market. And more than 72 percent of Indian software houses were found to possess strong expertise in Supply Chain Management and CRM.
- Some of the areas of e-commerce services available are:
  1. Legacy application integration.
  2. Internet application integration.
  3. EDI.
  4. Migration to Web-based models.
  5. New IT frameworks.
  6. Integration with business strategies.
  7. E-commerce training services.

There are still enormous challenges facing e-commerce sites in India. The relatively small credit card population and lack of uniform credit agencies creates a variety of payment challenges unknown in the United States. Increased distribution of online purchases could be complicated by India's complex postal system and an uncertain regulatory environment. Nonetheless, everyone from Yahoo, Microsoft, and IBM to local carpet vendors, hotels, and some Indian ISP's are trying to claim a slice of the rapidly emerging Indian e-commerce market.

The past two years have seen a rise in the number of companies' embracing e-commerce technologies and the Internet in India. Major Indian portal sites have also shifted towards e-commerce instead of depending on advertising revenue. The major in this services being Rediff on the net (www.rediff.com) and India plaza which started a shopping section after their highly successful content site generated WEB visitors. In spite of RBI regulation, low Internet usage e-commerce sites have popped up everywhere hawking things like groceries, bakery items, gifts, books, audio and videocassettes, computer, etc. None of the major players have been deterred by the low PC penetration and credit card usage in India and have tried to close the success world-wide of online commerce. BPB publication went online selling its complete range of computer books about 2 years ago, it might not have the success like Amazon.com, but they definitely have promised the cause of e-commerce in India with at least 1 to 5 web sites like Indiabookshop coming online.

This is not to say that the e-commerce scenario has been bad in India as highly successful e-business like baba bazaar and India mart have proved Indian Banks too have been very successful in adapting EDI Technologies to provide customers with real time account status, transfer of funds between current and checking accounts, stop payment facilities. ICICI Bank, Global Trust Bank and UTI Bank also have put their electronic banking over the Internet facilities in place for the upcoming e-commerce market. The future does look very bright for e-commerce in India with even the stock exchanges coming online providing an online stock portfolio and status with a fifteen minute delay in prices. The day cannot be far when with RBI regulations we will be able to see stock transfer and sale over the Net.

13

Electronic Commerce, Jobs and Skills

ARUN KUMAR

Electronic Commerce is the process of buying and selling goods and services electronically with computerised business transactions using the Internet, networks and other digital technologies. By replacing manual and paper-based procedures with electronic alternatives, and by suing information flows in new and dynamic ways, electronic commerce can accelerate ordering, delivery, and payment for goods and 'services while reducing companies' operating and inventory costs.

It also encompasses activities supporting those market transactions, such as advertising, marketing, customer support, delivery and payment.

— Laudon and Laudon

Example: Odense Steel Shipyards

Odense Steel Shipyards in Denmark is not one of the world's larger shipyards, but it specialises in building the world's biggest ships.

Today, only 15 people run its main steel-construction facility, a gigantic shed the size of 12 football fields. A less automated facility would require 300 people to do the same job.

Odense can generate various different designs that meet the speed and size requirements of the customer.

When the model for a ship is complete, the system generates a complete list of the 4,00,000 parts needed, ranging from steel plates to butterfly valves. The system breaks down the list according to supplier and required delivery date and monitors shipment schedule. Only the smallest and largest-quantity items, such as rivets, are kept in inventory.

Example: Inventory Replenishment System

The "continuous replenishment system" of Wal-Mart sends orders for new merchandise directly to suppliers as soon as consumers pay for their purchases at the cash register.

Point-of-sale terminals record the bar code of each item passing the checkout counter and send a purchase transaction directly to a central computer at Wal-Mart headquarters.

The central computer collects the orders from all of the Wal-Mart stores and transmits them to suppliers. Wal-Mart does not need to spend much money on maintaining large inventories of goods in its own warehouses.

Competitors such as Sears spend nearly 30 percent of each dollar in sales to pay for overhead (that is, expenses for salaries, advertising, warehousing and building upkeep). Kmart spends 21 percent of sales on overhead, but by using systems to keep operating costs low. Wal-Mart pays only 15 percent of sales revenue for overhead.

Today the impact of electronic commerce on employment may be very small and insignificant, but, in the long-run, it is going to cover all of us and effect may be felt more strongly. It is going to effect trade balances of countries. Drastic changes may take place in process of skill matching process between employment opportunities and available work force. It may allow economies to reap the benefits of Increased productivity at the micro level and sectoral level.

The overall effect of electronic commerce on employment will be the net balance, positive or negative, of new jobs, direct and indirect created by increased demand and job losses, due to workers, e.g. retailers or other intermediaries, being replaced by it. Gains and losses may differ by industry, by geographic area, by skill group, etc.

To assess the impact of electronic commerce, it is essential to understand for which industries it is generating or will generate new demand and growth, which types of jobs will be destroyed and which created, and what the overall needs are in terms of skills. These skill requirements place new demands on schools and vocational training facilities.

These changes in the labour force caused by e-commerce under score the need for flexible labour markets and active labour policies that help workers to adjust to changes in these markets.

The Future of Existing Products

1. Telephony, fax, video conferencing and the Internet.
2. Entertainment.
3. Education.
4. Health services.
5. Other professional services.
6. Publishing.
7. Financial services.
8. Letter delivery.

Disintermediation: The process of cutting out the middleman.

Re-Intermediation

1. Advertising/branding.
2. Directories.
3. Search services.
4. Malls.
5. Publishers.
6. Virtual resellers.
7. Web site evaluators.
8. Financial Intermediaries.
9. Spot market makers and barter networks.
10. Intelligent agents.

Job Gains and Losses in E-commerce-Related Industries

1. The "copyright" industry.
2. The Internet industry.
3. Travel agencies.
4. Post offices.
5. Retail.
6. Finance and banking.

Ten New E-commerce Jobs

1. Entrepreneurial consultant.

2. Application developer.
3. Fulfilment specialist.
4. Consumer behaviour consultant.
5. Broker.
6. Network security specialist.
7. E-commerce business analyst.
8. Internet architect.
9. Product manager.
10. Core programmers.

Career in a System of No Careers

The biggest unknown for the individual in a knowledge-based economy is how to have a career in a system where there are no careers.

How do you Manage to have a Career?

Individuals need to manage their own skill portfolio. The question is "Do I manage my skills in such a way that I always have marketable skill?" or do I sit back and say, "My company will make some investment in me and ensure that I have relevant skills and rising wages over the course of my career". Beyond having the portfolio of skills, you need to ask how you can make a greater contribution and help create wealth to sustain your employment by using your skills and creativity. And at some point, you need to take the risk and try something entrepreneurial.

Management of Portfolio of Skills
Boston Consulting Group Growth/Share Matrix

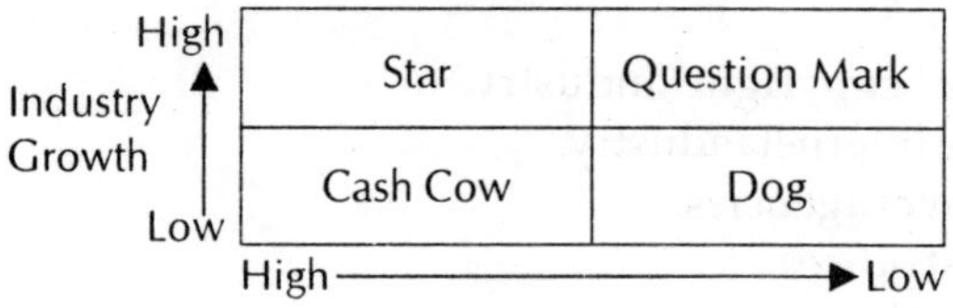

Industry Growth	High → Low	
High	Star	Question Mark
Low	Cash Cow	Dog

Your economic security does not lie in your job; it lie in your own power to produce to think to learn, to create, to adapt. That is true financial independence. It is not having wealth; it is having the power to produce wealth.

— *Stephen R. Covey*

14

E-Commerce—Security Issues

SUNNYKUTTY THOMAS

E-commerce is concerned with buying and selling information, products and services through computer communication networks. In e-commerce, netizens give high priority to the security of information exchanged through Internet. Security, privacy, confidentiality and integrity of the transactions are essential for the success of e-business.

Cryptography is the art of performing secure transactions on the Web. It has become one of the central tools for maintaining privacy and confidentiality and to protect information of real value against hackers and organised criminals.

Cryptography is the art of keeping information private and which is unreadable to another person without the right key. Cryptanalysis is the art of compromising algorithms developed in cryptography. Cryptology is the branch of mathematics that studies the mathematical foundations of cryptographic methods.

Cryptography has become one of the main tools among others, for privacy, confidentiality, integrity, authenticity, non-repudiability, access control, electronic payments, and corporate security. Cryptography, in electronic businesses, helps to ensure that no-one else, other than the intended person, reads the message.

BASIC TERMINOLOGY

Plain text: In cryptographic terminology, the message transmitted through electronic medium is called plain text or clear text. It is the readable form of the document.

Encryption: In order to keep the secrecy of an e-commerce transaction, the message should be made unreadable to others. The process of making the contents of the message unintelligible to the unauthorised reader is called encryption. It is the process of translating the readable form of the document into an unreadable form.

Cipher text: The encrypted message is called cryptograms or cipher text. Cryptographic transformation is done in such a way that each bit, character or word of the plain text is replaced by a bit, character or word of the cipher text.

Decryption: The process of retrieving the plain text from the cipher text is called decryption.

Cryptographers: Persons who do cryptography are cryptographers.

Cryptanalysts: Practitioners of cryptanalysis are cryptanalysts.

Key: The knowledge about cryptographic transformation is technically known as key. In secret key cryptography, a single key is used for both encryption and decryption. In public key cryptography, the encryption key is the public key and decryption key is the private or secret key.

Basic Cryptographic Algorithms

There are two types of encryption algorithms, symmetric (or secret-key) and asymmetric (or public-key). In symmetric algorithms same key or password is used for both encryption and decryption, whereas asymmetric algorithms use different keys or passwords for encryption and decryption.

Symmetric algorithm or secret key cryptography is based on a secret key which is shared by the parties engaged in secure communication. The message sent is encrypted, i.e. transformed using a secret key. The receiver applies the inverse transformation using the same secret key and recovers the message.

(Sender) Plain text	Encryption	CIPHER TEXT	SENT TO	CIPHER TEXT	Decryption	(Receiver) Plain text
	Secret Key		RECEIVER		Secret key	

FIG. 14.1
Secret Key Cryptography

The idea of encryption through transposition and substitution can be clearly understood from the following example. Suppose the plain text is 'sunnykuttythomas'. It is first transformed using transposition usually applied on blocks of characters. For this a transposition key is required. Suppose the transposition key determined is '34521'. The key implies that, as the first step the message should be grouped into 5 character blocks since there are five characters in the transposition key, and then the characters should be permuted using the rule '34521'. That is, replace 1st character by the 3rd character, 2nd character by the 4th character, 3rd character by the 5th character, 4th character by the 2nd character and 5th character by the 1st character. A block at the tail, if any, which has less than 5 characters is left unchanged. By applying the transposition key, the plain text of 'sunnykuttythomas' becomes the permuted plain text of 'nnyusttyukomahts'. The next transformation is substitution. For instance, a substitution rule with key 3 would replace every letter by a letter that is 3 letters away from it in the collating sequence, i.e. A becomes D, B becomes E, C becomes F . . . X becomes A, Y becomes B and Z becomes C. After applying this transformation, we get the cipher text of 'qqbxvwwbxnrpdkwv'. In this example a person who has no knowledge about the transposition and substitution keys cannot decode the message.

The most common secret key techniques are steam ciphers and block ciphers. Stream ciphers can encrypt a single bit of plain text at a time, whereas block ciphers can take a number of bits (typically 64 bits in modem ciphers), and encrypt them a single unit. The most widely used symmetric cipher is DES (Digital Encryption Standard), which is introduced by IBM in 1975 and standardized by the U.S. Government in 1977. DES applies transformation on blocks of 64 bits corresponding to the binary encoding of the message text. A new standard called AES (Advanced Encryption Standard) is being developed which uses 128 bit blocks and 128 bit keys. AES is not yet standardized and DES is still used widely.

Asymmetric algorithm or public-key cryptography is based on two distinct but related keys. Asymmetric ciphers permit the encryption key to be public, allowing anyone to encrypt with the key, whereas only the proper recipient, who knows the decryption key, can decrypt the message. RSA is the most widely used asymmetric encryption algorithm that was developed in 1975 by the researchers – Ron Rivest, Adi Shamir and Leonard Adleman. RSA system works as follows:

Take two prime numbers, p and q (i.e. numbers which cannot be divided evenly by an other number), and multiply together to get their product *N*.

SERIES OF NUMBERS

Normally, if we know only *N*, then it is extremely difficult to determine what the factors *p* and *q* are if *N* is sufficiently large. In cryptography, *N* assumes a value that is greater than 500 bits (150' digits). The message is written as a series of numbers, each of which is smaller than *N* but has approximately the same length as *N*. Each of these message numbers *M* is then multiplied by itself *e* times. Then, the result of this set of multiplication is divided by *N*, and only the remainder of that division is kept and is the encrypted message. To decrypt the message, the recipient uses another specially chosen number *d*, which is typically a very large number (of the order of half the length of *N*). This number is chosen so that if we now multiply the encrypted message with itself *d* times, divide by *N*, and keep only the remainder, then we get the original message back. The only way known to find *d* is to know *p* and *q*.*e* and *N* is the public key, which is published, while *d* is the private key, which must be kept secret, *e* and *d* are symmetric in that using either as the encryption key, the other can be used as the decryption key. Through this method, electronic documents can be signed.

Digital Signatures

In e-commerce, authentication is one of the most important factors to build a trustworthy relationship among the parties. Authentication is done by signing documents. In order to make electronic documents legally usable, it is necessary to have a mechanism that provides a means to authenticate the author of a document. Digital signatures are used for authentication.

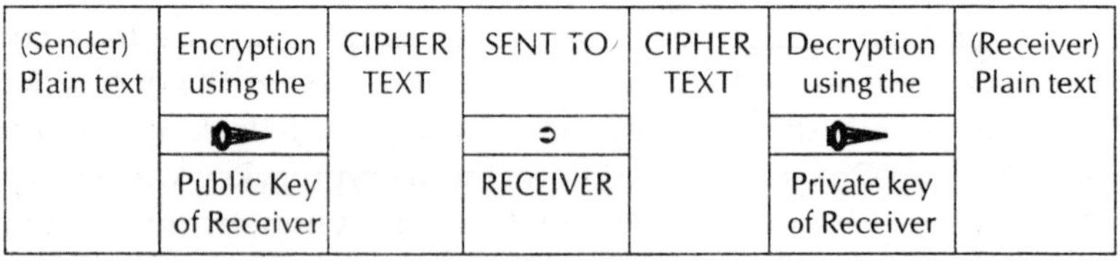

(Sender) Plain text	Encryption using the	CIPHER TEXT	SENT TO	CIPHER TEXT	Decryption using the	(Receiver) Plain text
	Public Key of Receiver		RECEIVER		Private key of Receiver	

FIG. 14.2
Public Key Cryptography

A digital signature is a small data created using some secret key, and there is a public key that can be used to verify that the signature was really generated using the corresponding private key. It is used to verify whether the message really comes from the claimed sender or not.

A digital signature is not scanned image of a hand written or typed signature. The digital signature is an electronic substitute for manual signature. It is an identifier composed of a certain sequence of bits, that is created from the message through a hash code. Hash code is a function that reduces every possible message to a fixed number of bits. Hash functions generate message digests or hash value. No matter how big the file is, the hash will always be the same length, and therefore hash value will be different for every message. The hash function is a one-way function. It is possible to generate a message digest or hash value from the message. But it is not possible to find a message that would fit exactly the hash value. The hash code can be seen as a seal on the envelope.

A digital signature of an electronic document is typically created by computing a message digest from the document. The resulting string is then encrypted using the private key of the signer using a suitable algorithm. The resulting encrypted block of bits is the signature. To verify a digital signature, the recipient decrypts the signature using the public key of the sender. If the signature decrypts properly and the result matches that of the message digest, the signature is accepted as valid. The most widely used method of making and verifying digital signature is RSA algorithm.

The technique of signing an electronic document can be well understood from the following:

Suppose a sender wants to send an electronic message to the receiver and authenticate the document by putting digital signature, the following are the steps:

1. Sender chooses a random key. He encrypts the plain text using the random key and sends the cipher text so arrived at to the receiver.
2. Now the receiver is unaware of the random key used for encryption. Receiver needs key used for encryption in order to decrypt the message. Therefore sender encrypts the random key using the public key of the receiver and sends it to the receiver.

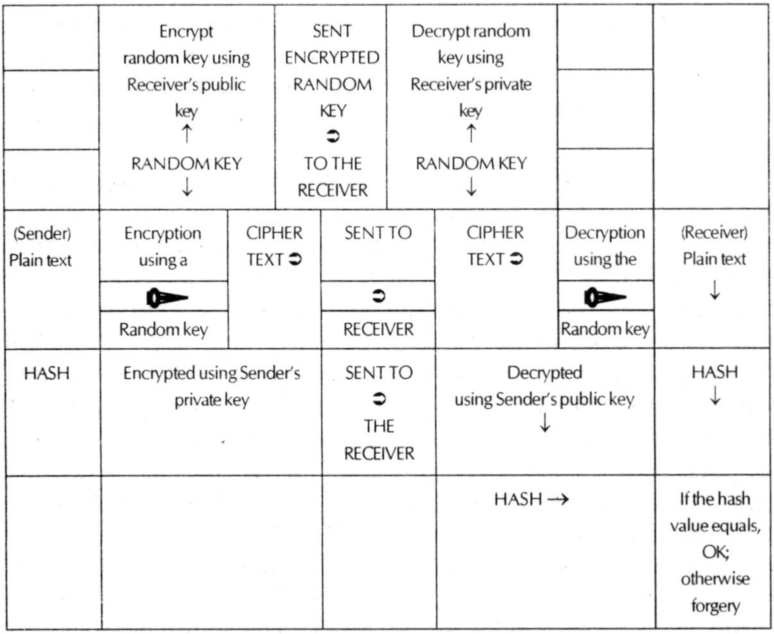

	Encrypt random key using Receiver's public key ↑ RANDOM KEY ↓		SENT ENCRYPTED RANDOM KEY ➲ TO THE RECEIVER	Decrypt random key using Receiver's private key ↑ RANDOM KEY ↓		
(Sender) Plain text	Encryption using a Random key	CIPHER TEXT ➲	SENT TO ➲ RECEIVER	CIPHER TEXT ➲	Decryption using the Random key	(Receiver) Plain text ↓
HASH	Encrypted using Sender's private key		SENT TO ➲ THE RECEIVER	Decrypted using Sender's public key ↓		HASH ↓
				HASH →		If the hash value equals, OK; otherwise forgery

3. Receiver decrypts the random key which is encrypted by using the private key and obtains the original random key.
4. Receiver can decrypt the cipher text by using the random key and gets the original message or plain text.
5. Now the receiver has to be convinced as to the identity of the sender. Signature of the sender reveals his identity.
6. In order to sign the message, the plain text is hashed using a hash function. The hash value, being the digital signature, is tied to the document being sent.
7. Hash value is encrypted by the Sender using his private key and sent to the Receiver.
8. Receiver decrypts the hash value using the public key of the sender. Since we are able to decrypt the hash with the public key of a certain person, it proves that the message comes from that person. Only the person who owns the private key is able to create a message that can be decrypted using the public key.
9. Similarly, Receiver can calculate the hash value of the plain text using the known hash function.

10. If the hash value calculated under step 8 and 9 equals, it can be concluded that the transaction is cent percent OK; otherwise a fake message.

Cryptanalysis is the art of deciphering encrypted communications without knowing the proper keys. Even though techniques are emerging for attacking cryptosystems, cryptography stands accepted as a reliable art for ensuring secrecy and authentication to electronic documents.

15

E-Commerce at Work—Trends and Projections

K. RAJESHWAR RAO AND D. RAVI

The objective of this paper is to analyse the evolutionary process of e-commerce, the way it is working, its distinction from traditional business, its limitations and precautions, the Indian scenario and finally the trends and projections thereof.

EVOLUTIONARY PROCESS

With the advent of information technology, every aspect of human life is transforming at a rapid pace. Geographical boundaries, which were pervasive for the earlier generation, are losing their identity. We can see and talk to people across the globe without any prejudice. New products are entering the market at a faster rate, communication is no longer a barrier even for people living at remote places. Information is available 24 hours a day—a feat, which was unpredictable and unthinkable in the past. The Internet[1] has shrunk the world into a global village. Globalization of economy is resulting in intense business competition in products and services. It is therefore, important that corporate sector worldover, has to reach out beyond their traditional market places. In doing so, it is equally imperative to ensure that cost is kept to the minimum so that the entry cost of doing business in the global market place, and maintaining competitive edge, do not become deterrent to a global business model. Electronic commerce (E-commerce) offers solutions that address both.

E-commerce is the catchword today and the whole world is

looking forward to the day when all work can be done at the desktop defying the laws of motion. E-commerce can change the life styles of people significantly. Banking, finance and shopping are some areas that will undergo a radical change. Everything will move on the click of mouse. E-commerce uses web[2] to bring together customers; vendors and supplier. It presents abundant opportunities for businesses. E-commerce helps us to purchase products or services without having to deal with middlemen.

E-COMMERCE AT WORK

Commercial transaction over an electronic medium is known as e-commerce. In simple terms, electronic commerce is a process of two or more parties making business transactions *via* computer and some type of network. This includes business-to-business transactions, online retail and digitalization of financing industry. Some experts argue that e-commerce includes all steps that occur in any business cycle such as placing ads, completing invoices and providing customer support. This term 'e-commerce' is often used interchangeably with IBM's coined term e-business. Zwass defines e-commerce as "the sharing of business information, maintaining business relationships and conducting business transactions by means of telecommunication networks." He points out that e-commerce includes not only buying and selling of goods but also various processes within individual organizations, which support that goal. Applegate L.M. view that e-commerce is more than simply buying and selling goods electronically. It involves using network communications technology to engage range of activities up and down the value-added chain, both within and outside the organization.

According to Kalakota and Whinston, four different types of information technology are converging to create the discipline of e-commerce. These include electronic messaging such as fax and e-mail, sharing a corporate digital library to promote collaborative work, electronic document interchange utilizing Electronic Data Interchange (EDI) and electronic funds transfer, electronic publishing to promote marketing, advertising, sales, and customer support. Applegate L.M. has identified three classes of e-commerce applications viz. customer-to-business, business-to-business and intra-organizational. Currently, most commercial Internet applications focus on using web to direct company's marketing message to end customers. On the other hand, the Intranet is an internally focused application used to disseminate information throughout the company. While EDI has been dominant in business-to-business applications, companies are just beginning to implement Internet technology that could dramatically alter their trading partner relationships. These business-to-business applications of Internet technology are called "extranets". The development of extranets provides a link between the firm's Internet and Intranet strategies that will broaden the definition of e-commerce.

The operation of e-commerce involves five steps as per details given below:

1. When a customer enters the merchant's web site, selects the products to be purchased and enters the shipping instructions, the merchant's server then returns a summary of the selected product, its price and transaction identity (ID) code.
2. After the selection of the product from the merchant's web site, the customer has to click the pay button. Then Cyber Cash[3] wallet appears. The next step is to indicate the credit card number and click 'ok' to forward the order and the encrypted payment information to the merchant.
3. On receiving the order from the customer, the merchant forwards the encrypted payment information digitally signed and encrypted with his private key to the Cyber Cash server. In the process, the merchant cannot see the consumer's credit card information.
4. The Cyber Cash server receives the information, takes the transaction behind it's firewall and off the Internet, unwraps the data within a hardware based crypto box, reformats the transaction, and forwards it to the merchant's bank over dedicated lines. The merchant's bank forwards an authorization request to the issuing bank *via* card associations or directly. The approval or denial code is sent back to Cyber Cash.
5. Cyber Cash returns the approval or denial code to the merchant who passes it on to customer. All these steps (from 1 to 5) will take roughly 15 to 20 seconds on a computer.

UNDERLYING TECHNOLOGIES

The underlying technologies in e-commerce have to be taken note of, before proceeding further. The important among them are Internet and EDI.

(a) Internet

When two or more computers or other devices are connected together so as to enable them to communicate with one another, they form a network. The largest network used for computers in the world is 'Internet'. Internet protocols are incorporated in client-server architecture. The client-server[4] architecture is implemented for delivery of applications on Internet. The Internet is so vast that it is like an electronic cloud encircling the earth. The power of Internet as the global access tool, was realised with the arrival of world wide web. World wide web is a recent addition to the Internet. Its popularity has increased automatically because it is easy to use, colourful and rich in content. Today all, that a person needs is a computer, a telephone connection, a modem and an Internet account with an Internet service provider. He can buy flowers, airline tickets and even a car.

(b) Electronic Data Interchange

Electronic data interchange may be defined as application-to-application transfer of documents through computers in a standard format. These formats look like standard forms and highly structured. It is a fast and safe method of sending purchase orders, invoices, shipping notices and other frequently used business documents common to various business processes. EDI can be applied at various layers of business process such as ordering, acceptance, manufacturing, delivery, shipment and custom clearance.

EDI is very effective in reducing costs and improving efficiency. It is estimated that 95 percent of fortune 1000 companies are using it. It is considered as foundation of e-commerce. EDI saves businesses and consumer's money by lowering the cost of handling or processing the business documents such as invoice or purchase order. It increases the accuracy of transactions. Retyping of important business information is eliminated thereby reducing the chance of errors. EDI ensures a smooth flow of information. Orders can be processed, goods shipped and invoices sent, all in one day. Greater volume of business can be performed without adding personnel and other costs.

LIMITATIONS AND PRECAUTIONS

The existing legal framework in several countries is not properly placed to encounter the challenges of digital age. They need to adopt a global approach to ensure uniformity in statutory and administrative instruments. Several modifications in the existing statutes may have to be introduced in several countries across the globe, to enable them to participate effectively in e-commerce.

In e-business, security plays a very important role, especially in the context of dealing in finance, banking and insurance. Security of transactions depends upon certification by a trusted third party, preferably a government body. Global electronic commerce requires the establishment of global certification system. The common apprehensions on the Net are.... Is money securely travelling on the Net? Are the bank accounts safe? Consumers must be able to select a mode of payment and the software must verify their ability to pay. This involves credit cards, electronic cash or purchase orders. Since transactions on Internet go through so many computers between buyer and seller, no transaction is secure. Credit card numbers and other sensitive information could be easily stolen. Therefore, the system should enable e-commerce by providing safe, convenient and quick payment system between consumers, merchants, banks and individuals and by processing them in real time and passing the authorization codes back to the merchants concerned, safe and secure.[5]

The tampering of network information could be prevented through a process of encryption.[6] Encryption scrambles the data sent to web site, in an unintelligible string of seemingly random characters. Authentication is required between the client and server to ensure that they know each other in no uncertain terms.

Credit card companies are structured to use certificates of identity (software codes) to authenticate web sites and web surfers. These certificates are 'digitally signed'[7] with a unique code and issued by a trusted third party, known as Certification Authority (CA). CA is a third party to a transaction between a customer and a merchant and is used to build 'trust' relationships. Once a web site has registered with a CA, the 'browser can ask the CA – 'is this the correct code for the company?' The reply will confirm the accuracy. Today, the card companies are employing two methods for ensuring security of information viz. Secure Socket Layer (SSL)[8] and Secure Electronic Transaction (SET).[9] If one of these to methods has to become industry standard, it must be accepted and implemented by all the vendors, financial institutions, banks, transaction processors, credit card companies and customers.

TRADITIONAL *VS.* ELECTRONIC BUSINESS

Although e-business is a new concept it supersedes traditional business in several respects. A few significant among them are analysed below:

1. E-commerce as a medium or marketing, is less expensive than traditional marketing. In traditional marketing, a product goes from a producer to a distributor, to a retailer and then to a customer. These changing hands result in a increase in the price of the product. But in e-business, a producer can directly get in touch with the customer. This enables producer to sell the product, at a lesser price than it is available in the market.
2. E-business offers businesses to be open 24 hours a day, 7 days a week, giving customers access, at any time, day and night. It enhances buying process by providing an interactive environment in which each buyer can customise the purchase.
3. When more and more customers get in touch with the marketer, the chances of selling the products will increase. Customers of 21st century are moving towards learning more technical education, particularly in the field of information technology. As more and more people become aware of e-business, directly or indirectly, it will increase the customers and business.
4. Modern organizations have realised that e-commerce can give them a competitive edge. A company with minimal investment can tap the entire world market. E-commerce enables businesses to reach new customers and partners with extended marketing and selling techniques.
5. Internet is an attractive medium of sharing knowledge. Customers can acquire information about latest and innovative products. Moreover, a web merchant can provide information about various new uses of the existing products.

INDIAN SCENARIO

India is uniquely positioned and it has to start from the scratch. There is need to develop high speed, long distance backbone network that will interconnect the entire world. The existing business rules need to undergo radical changes and new business strategies have to be evolved. The Indian Evidence Act, 1897 does not take cognizance of the electronic transactions. Reserve Bank of India does not allow credit card information to be supplied over the Internet without a legally binding signature. The Government of India has formulated certain guidelines to make e-commerce a reality.[10]

Some Indian banks are already successful in adopting electronic commerce and EDI technologies to provide customers with real time access status, transfer of funds between current accounts and stop payment facilities. Customers will be able to inquire into their accounts and transactions, and take printout statement of accounts request for transfer of funds between their accounts. It will provide customers access to their depository accounts also. Some Indian banks are already offering Net banking facilities. Many other banks are planning to offer e-banking services in future. The Industrial Credit and Investment Corporation of India (ICICI), Citibank, IndusInd Bank, Global Trust Bank are the 'Net' banking premiers offering a range of online services. The ICICI launched its online banking services in October 1997. Its infinity Internet banking service provides remote banking facilities information. It offers account details and statements, financial modelling tools that allow simulation of various deposit options to arrive at an optimum combination and transfer of funds between accounts. About 6000 customers are using ICICI's online banking services. Citibank's Citidirect Internet banking gives freedom to customer to bank any time anywhere. The bank customers can view or take printouts of their accounts, order cheque books, transfer funds, even pay utility bills, etc. IndusInd Bank offers a range of cyber banking options. About 5000 IndusInd Bank customers are availing the online facilities.

If true e-commerce (particularly business-to-consumer) has to take off in India, there is a need to bring out 'cyber laws' that recognize the validity of electronic transactions. Electronic purchase orders need to have legal validity. There is a need for recognition of digital signatures. Issues relating to export and import of goods and services (across the border) and sales tax (points of origin and destination) need to be clarified. To have better exposure to these issues, let us consider an example. Suppose a company in India wants to look into the electronic catalogue of an American company and places an order for products for which payment will be made electronically. This scenario raises certain fundamental problems such as what is the legal status of the contract? Which company has legal jurisdiction over the contract? Currencies of these nations are different and exchange rates are likely to vary. Given the differences in financial regulations and practices, how is payment made and confirmed? What taxes and custom charges apply to these products and services? How are the charges 'policed' and 'collected' and who has to pay?

The situation gets even worse in dealings relating to knowledge business, for example software development, which is done purely on Internet. Further to take advantage of global e-commerce, there is a need for full convertibility of rupee. In India at present, rupee is fully convertible on current account only but not on capital account. While those few who possess dollar cards can transact globally, the rest can look forward to some brisk rupee shopping for now.

It is time for India to restructure its legal, business and communication infrastructure. If it fails to do so, it will cost heavily. A recent relevant example is Ludhiana in Punjab, which suffered heavy loss in business. Ludhiana is known for its export of hosiery and sports goods. Recently, exporters noticed an inexplicable drop in sales. Further enquiries revealed that business is being lost to Pakistani exporters across the border. The reason for this was neither quality nor price, but the exporters in Pakistan have put their products on the web. Increased convenience and communication has led to the loss of business to India.

India has to evolve a legal framework for the recognition of its global intellectual property rights, patents, copyrights, in order to enable global organizations to offer their products and services to the masses. In the words of N. Vittal, Chief Vigilance Commissioner of India, "e-business is a goose that can lay down eggs. Allow the goose to egg laying stage. Don't kill it". He listed six C's that are required for e-business to grow in India, they are computer density, connectivity, content, cyber law, cost control and common sense.

TRENDS AND PROJECTIONS

There is a great deal of business already in the pipeline on the Net. Market projections by leading analysts (e.g. Forrester Research) indicate that the value of e-commerce would be around $ 300 billion by 2001 and $ 660 billion by 2003. Contrary to initial estimates, the biggest chunk, (approximately 80%) of e-commerce is likely to be 'business-to-business', rather than 'business-to-consumers', although the latter would be more visible. In 1999 alone, 100 million shoppers are expected to spend an estimated $ 15 billion in the cyber marketspace. The US Department of Commerce in a report (April 1998) titled "The Emergence of Digital Economy" predicted that e-commerce may account for more then $ 300 million annually by 2002. According to Frank Gens, Senior Vice-president of Interent Research at International Data Corporation, e-commerce will generate as much as $ 900 millions sales between 1999 and 2002. According to a report by e-Marketer, an Internet reporting and research firm, a new user is joining on the Net for every 1.67 seconds.

In India in the past 2 years most of the e-commerce transactions are targeted at NRIs with gift delivery services, books, audio and videocassettes, etc. The most popular among these include REDIFF on the Net, INDIAPLAZA which started a shopping section, and BPB Publications which went online selling its complete range computer books since 2 years.

At present, the Internet in India is growing at the rate of 10 percent per month. The info-communication penetration in INDIA is 1.3 per 100 persons as against the world average of 10. Out of 6,04,374 villages only 2,67,832 villages have telephone lines in India. Telephone services are very expensive. It may affect India's participation in e-commerce. However, the Government of India have realized the importance of informational power. Recently, one of the recommendations of Task Force on Informational Technology has recommended for conversion of all STD/PCO booths into info-kiosks. The Internet subscribers in our country have risen to 1 million in four years, compared to 8-10 million subscribers in China. The present Net advertisement revenue is only Rs. 10 crores from a market that is more than Rs. 700 crores. Experts predict that Net users in India would increase to 25 million in the next 5 years. Many Indian exporters are finding new ways to penetrate the West with e-business for selling the Indian Mystique: Yoga, astrology, silk, ayurveda, etc. A departmental store in India has announced plans to sell groceries on the Net. New companies are delivering and planning to deliver customized newspapers over the web. Nirula's went on the web selling pizzas. Many people in India have been routinely buying cinema tickets over the Net!

E-business phenomenon is globally acceptable and India is no exception. E-business alters traditional concept of time and space. An Indian company with minimal investment can tap the entire world market. Although penetration of PCs in India is relatively low compared to developed economies, the growth rate is high. Even in the current slow pace of economy which India is passing through, PCs have registered a growth of 43 percent in the first 6 months of this fiscal year. We, may see soon, more than 1 million PCs for the first time in Indian market. This increase in awareness of computers promises prospects for a significant growth of e-business in India.

NOTES AND REFERENCES

1. Internet is a large set of networks that communicate with each other, often over telephone lines. It enables individuals, organisations and the government to share information across the world.
2. Web is a series of interconnected documents stored on computer sites commonly called as web sites.
3. Cyber Cash is a realtime, secure, digital signature-based credit card authentication service developed by Cyber Cash Inc. It acts as an intermediary between consumer, merchant and credit card clearing house.
4. Client is an application programme that provides the front-end entrance for the use and resides on the use's computer and responsible for interfacing with the user by accepting input and displaying data. The server is an application programme that provides services requested by the client and generally resides on a computer. The server is responsible for performing tasks directed by the client.
5. The system could become unsafe and insecure in the following way . . . once a client's system is connected to the target destination through the Internet, all the resources of destination system are available to the client. It is easy for the server system to get compromised when illegal or unauthorized users enter the system through mis-configured software. Illegal users can enter the system through security breaches in the operating system software. The generic Internet Protocol (IP) network is inherently open, susceptible or vulnerable to illegal listeners and attack from external invaders.
6. Encryption normally works in the following way—a message in its original form (plain text) is encrypted into an unintelligible form (cipher text) by set of procedures know as encryption algorithm used as a variable called keys and the cipher text is transformed back (decrypted) into plain text using the encryption algorithm and the key.
7. Digital signature means any letters, characters, numbers or other symbols in digital form attached to or logically associated with an electronic record, and executed or adopted with the intention of authenticating or approving the electronic record.

8. SSL is a method for hiding the information sent by a web browser and web server to each other. When a web site is scanned it is possible for other people to see the information. Credit card numbers personal data and other information is open to the technologically sophisticated professionals (eavesdropper). SSL is designed to defeat that purpose.
9. SET is a protocol developed by VISA, Matter Card and other technology leaders is a collection of encryption and security specifications for ensuring secure payment transactions over the Internet.
10. On 4th November 1999, the union cabinet has approved the proposal to introduce the 'Information Technology Bill, 1999' in the coming session of the parliament to enact cyber laws to regulate electronic communications, trade and commerce and prevent computer crimes in the country. The Bill envisages legalisation of electronic signature on the Net, which would give sanctity to credit card transactions and boost e-commerce business. The Bill seeks to amend the Banking Act, the Indian Evidence Act, the Telegraph Act and the Companies Act to bring them in line with the new law. It proposes to set-up elaborate machinery for licensing, monitoring certifying authorities for enactment of cyber laws. The authorities would monitor and oversee issues like jurisdiction, origin, authentication, privacy protection, intellectual property and computer crimes being committed *via* the information highways in cyber-space. Cyber laws are laws that govern electronic transaction on the Net. According to Department of Electronics (DOE) Government of India, 'cyber law' typically encompasses all the cases, statutes and constitutional provisions that impact persons and institutions who control the entry to cyberspace, provides access to cyberspace, create hardware and software which enable people to access cyberspace or use their own computers to go online or enter cyberspace. In terms of issues, cyber laws can be broken down into many parts like digital signatures, cryptography law, privacy law, liability of service provider, digital IPR, cyber laundering and e-cash to name a few.

REFERENCES

Anurag Sharma, "Policy Issues in E-commerce", *Software Review*, January, 1999.

Atul Dingra, "Marketing on the Internet—Strategies for Success", JIMS 8 M, April-June, 1999.

Dennis P. Curtin, Kim Foley, Kennalsen, Eathleen Morin, *Information Technology*, Tata McGraw Hill.

D. Krishna Sunder, "Electronic Commerce—The Future Challenges", JIMS 8 M, July-September, 1998.

D.V. Jagadish, "The Tidal Wave of E-commerce will hit us sooner that we may Believe"—An INTERVIEW, *Data Quest*, 15th January, 1999.

Frederick J. Riggins and Hyeun-suk (sue) Rhee, "Toward a Unified View of Electronic Commerce", Communications of ACM, October, 1998.

Kavita Kaur, "Online Banking—Cheques and Balances", *Computer Today*, August, 1999.

P.D. Kaushik, "Opportunity Online", *Global*, 31st May, 1999.

Ravi, "The First Thing to do is to be Aware", *Economic Times*, 9th September, 1999.

Srinivas, Vijay, "The State of E-commerce", *Computers Today*, 16th April, 1999.

16

Impact of E-Commerce on Accounting

S.K. SINGH

Internet growth has led to a host of new developments, such as decreased margins for companies as consumers turn more and more to the Internet to buy goods and demand the best prices, University of Michigan Business School professor, C.K. Prahalad said.

The Internet means that traditional businesses will change because "incumbents (in markets) and large firms do not have the advantage" just by virtue of being there first or by being big, he said.

In the last two decade, Information Technology has played a key role in transforming the way business is conducted. With each new wave of technology, it has brought about fundamental changes. In all these, the one technology that has truly been an effective agent in changing the fundamental ways to doing business is none other than ubiquitous thing that everyone knows as Internet.[1]

More and more of commerce is becoming electronic. It signifies many opportunities and challenges for accounting profession as well.

WHAT IS INTERNET COMMERCE?

The US-based Aberdeen Group describes it thus: "Internet Commerce is a term used to describe the automation the full range of interactions across corporate borders between companies and people from marketing to sales, order placement to invoicing and payment, product distribution and customer service — by establishing computer-to-computer service — by establishing computer-to-computer communication utilising the infrastructure and standards of the Internet."[2]

In other words, Internet Commerce – the fusion of electronic commerce based on Electronic Data Interchange (EDI) with Internet standards – is a new frontier transforming how business work. After realising tremendous return on investment with corporate Intranets, businesses are using E-commerce on the Internet to reach outside the company boundaries to change the way business is conducted with their customers, suppliers, and partners – wringing out expense, improving customer service and vastly reducing cycle-time.

By 2002, it is estimated that $ 500 billion of business will be transacted on the Net – is that each time this forecast is updated, the figure tends to increase by 30 percent. IBM transacts business worth approximately $ 5 billion over the NET.[3]

IMPACT ON ACCOUNTING SERVICES

Supply Chain Management[4]

Internet Commerce involves several applications. Among the more important ones is Supply Chain Integration. A supply chain is an interlinked set of partners and operations – from design through delivery – that enable an enterprise to provide products or services. The electronic integration of this chain can increase reliability of transactions; streamline interactions, real-time data and information sharing; and allow for benefits take many forms, such as lower administrative and transaction costs, shorter time-to-market cycles, better targeting, higher market acceptance, and increased short control of the flow of materials, supplies, and services.

Traditional approaches to supply chain integration (such as EDI) have linked only the largest and most established partners, and have generally done this through proprietary systems. Building on the ubiquity and standards of the Internet enabled EDI tools to enterprise electronically and integrate all members of its supply chain – large and small, with either established or intermittent relationships – to form full extranets.

There are four principal aspects of supply chain integration. They are: **electronic transmission, information sharing, workflow automation, and real-time interactive buying and selling.**

Electronic transmission eliminates the need for re-keying, provides automatically generated audit trails, and triggers operations such as automatic order confirmation.

Information sharing opportunities enlarge the exchange of ideas all along the supply chain.

Workflow automation automatically routes work-through routine processes, reducing the time it takes to complete projects.

Real-time interactive buying and selling becomes a reality when an entire supply chain is electronically linked through Internet standards.

Clearly, if companies have to survive the coming millennium and live to see another day, they will have to quickly adopt this new medium just to be in the race. Already companies have come to realise the old rules and models no longer apply. In fact, nearly 68 per cent of US companies believe that adopting E-Commerce demands a re-evaluation of traditional business models. Additionally, accordingly to the Web Tech. Survey, of those currently conducting E-Commerce and those intending to go on-line, 64% expect pay back within a year.[5]

Data Mining[6]

The more you go for E-Commerce, the more you accumulate data in your computer warehouses. The data available at storehouses can help in various ways to accounting and financial functions in a more scientific and logical way.

The technique employed is data mining. Data mining offers intelligent retrieval of information. And, unlike analytical tools, it can be automated to run continuously in the background, saving direct managerial time. All data mining tools are driven by cutting-edge applications in Artificial Intelligence, that stream of computer science which seeks to make machines behave intelligently, not just blindly fast, e.g.:

Neural Networks

Software that mimics the structure and functioning of the human brain, it can identify patterns, arithmetically, combining the numerous variables associated with a given data-point. It can be used to build non-linear predictive models that learn by studying combinations of variables, and how such combinations affect datasets.

Decision-Trees

A mathematical method of following the effect of an event, or decision, on successive events, the process continuously breaks datasets into smaller, separate groups, and traces causes common to seemingly-unrelated data.

Genetic Algorithms

Such software, aimed at identifying patterns and connections between disparate data, is built using the lesson learnt from how micro-organisms evolved *via* natural selection and genetic combinations.

Fuzzy Logic

Instead of using binary choice — hot or cold, good or bad — the software describes every condition as a combination of the 2 extreme stages in varying proportions. This helps identify linkages that binary choices do not allow.

How are associations made by data-mining tools? Their magic lies in the algorithmic approach they adopt in sorting the data, primarily in three different ways:

Association

Data is divided into sets, each representing a single bundle of transactions; the shopping-list of a single buyer, for instance. The contents of hundreds and thousands of sets are compared to find out how often particular items are associated detergents, also buy soaps. The higher the figure, the stronger, obviously, is the association between them. In a variation, the same data can be analysed over a period of time to understand associations between sequences of events.

Clustering

The objective is to segment a seemingly amorphous mass of data into smaller, distinctive groups. For instance, the data pertaining to credit-card spending, covering a huge range of sums, products, locations, and dates, can be plotted in a four-dimensional space. Each dimension is partitioned, each compartment being defined by specific ranges for each of the dimensions. The data is then automatically divided into these segments, and the contents of each are explored for linkages.

Classification

The most commonly-applied data-mining technique, it uses a preclassified set of examples to teach the software which parameters are important for a particular form of classification. For instance, in a fraud detection transactions identify the parameters that the tool uses as pointers to predict recurrences in other cases. In a variation, the classification is made not in a binary—Yes/No—form but in one involving scores, which must then be interpreted for conclusions.

CONCLUSION

It is amply clear that the rise of E-Commerce has changed the business practices in every sphere ranging from marketing to finance and accounting. Instant orders, delivery, payment, recording of transactions have become the call of the day. On the other hand, E-Commerce has opened up new dimensions for accounting. Now it by virtue of E-Commerce only that it has ensured its better participation in information decimation for better management decision as well as strengthening key concepts like supply-side management. E-Commerce has enabled to tie-up all the participant of the trade in one line. Their efficient and effective approach could E-Commerce has enabled the business to record host of the data relating to all aspects of business in their machines. This spells another opportunity that the same data can help in deriving many cross-breaks and relationships to take better decisions.

NOTES AND REFERENCES

1. *Hindustan Times*, 18 June, 1998, p. 12.
2. "Internet Commerce—Leveraging the Net for Profit", Internet Commerce Supplement, *Data Quest*, September 30, 1998, p. 6.
3. Excepts from Intel's Business Strategy by its CEO Craig Radford Barrette, "Inside New Millennium Computing", *Business Today*, November 22-December 6,1998, p. 102.

4. "Internet Commerce—Leveraging the Net for Profit", Internet Commerce Supplement, *Data Quest*, September 30, 1998, pp. 10-11.
5. "Internet Commerce—Leveraging the Net for Profit", Internet Commerce Supplement, *Data Quest*, September 30, 1998, p. 11.
6. S. Chandrashekhar, "Mining Decisions from Data-Mining", *Business Today*, December 7-21, 1998, pp. 106-7.

17

B2B: Another Blood Bath?

YOGESH UPADHYAY AND SHIV KUMAR SINGH

Clearly, companies and consumers are discovering that global networking and other technological innovations are powerful assets if used as competitive weapons in their day-to-day activities. These activities also permeate organisations where increased demands of the efficient collection, dissemination, and processing of information are evident because of various economic factors – global competition and other market forces – and consumer demands for high service and improved quality. These demands are forcing companies to integrate previously isolated "islands of automation" into coherent weapons.[1]

Today, the emphasis has shifted from this narrow focus to the invention of entirely new business applications for reaching and getting close to the customer. And while earlier efforts resulted in small gains in productivity and efficiency, integrating them into the Information Superhighway will fundamentally change the way businesses done, these new ideas demand radical changes in the design of the entire business process.[2]

E-business is tiny at present, but Forrester Research, an Internet consultancy, estimates that this will increase to more than $1.5 trillion in America by 2003. Internet bulls calculate that this would be equivalent to about 13 per cent of GDP.[3]

As we get ready to enter the next century, yet another fundamental redefinition of time and space called the Internet promises to bring about unprecedented changes in society.[4] It is shaping the very nature of competition by leading it towards perfect competition.[5] It has transformed the very way business is conducted.[6]

Internet growth has led to a host of new developments, such as decreased margins for companies as consumers turn more and more to the Internet to buy goods and demand the best prices, as observed University of Michigan Business School professor, C.K. Prahalad said:

> The Internet means that traditional businesses will change because "incumbents (in markets) and large firms do not have the advantage" just by virtue of being there first or by being big, he said.

The Net economy is fundamentally different from the physical economy in terms of leveraging information, knowledge and speed for coordination and collaboration between trading partners and knowing and fulfilling customer requirements.

THE E-BUSINESS VALUE CHAIN: WINNING STRATEGIES IN SEVEN GLOBAL INDUSTRIES

A global survey of 331 companies and in-depth interviews with 42 senior executives in seven global industries was conducted by The Economist Intelligence Unit and KPMG. The survey examined how major international firms in seven global industries are transforming their supply chains, internal operations, distribution channels and customer relationships to ensure their survival in the digital age. The report is invaluable to anyone involved in developing their company's e-business strategy or evaluating their competitors.

Several cross industry and industry-specific trends highlighted by the survey are:

- 57% of survey respondents believe that e-business is transforming their company's role within their industry.
- Companies have found it difficult to bypass their traditional intermediaries. Instead, customers are looking at new ways of working with the middle man.
- Senior management is only adequately involved in their firm's initiatives are 42% of surveyed firms.
- The greatest barriers to e-business lie within the corporate, with 58% of respondents citing re-engineering business processes as the biggest obstacles they face.

List of Industries and Companies Interviewed

Automotive

Atutobytel, Autonation, BMW, Ford, Renault, Volkswagen.

Chemicals

Celanese, Ciba Speciality Chemicals, ChemConnect, Eastman Chemicals, Imperial Chemical Industries.

Communications

British Telecommunications, Cable & Wireless, Deutsche Telekom, Ericsson, Ignite (BT), Pacific Century Cyberworks, SBC Communications.

Consumer Markets

Dairy Farm (Jardine's), Diageo, Fort James, Harvey Norman, IGA, Office Depot.

Electronics

Hitachi, Infineon (Siemens), NCR, Nortel, Singapore Technologies, Taiwan Semiconductor Manufacturing Company.

Financial Services

Abbey National, Commonwealth Bank of Australia, Credit Suisse, Development Bank of Singapore, ING Group, Wells Fargo.

Pharmaceuticals

AstraZeneca, Aventis, European Medical Network, Glaxo Wellcome, OmniComm Pfizer.

Key Findings

E-business is working its way through every industry. Familiar ways of operating are changing, as companies integrate more tightly with customers and suppliers. The Internet is promoting some companies to specialise in a particular part of their industry's value chain, while others are looking to expand their activities—blurring the lines traditionally separating different industries and changing relationships with customers and partners.

The research led to the following conclusions:

The Internet is transforming industry value chains

Of survey respondents, 57% say that e-business is transforming their company's role within their industry. For example, many electronics manufacturers are moving up the value chain to offer e-business advisory services. At the same time, new web-enabled competitors are appearing at each point on the value chain, threatening companies' accustomed sources of value.

Intermediaries are changing, not disappearing

Companies have found it difficult to bypass their traditional intermediaries—37% of survey respondents say that a reluctance to disintermediate intermediaries poses a very major obstacle to their e-business plans. Instead, companies are searching for new ways of working with intermediaries. For some financial service firms are attempting to turn insurance salesmen into customer-service agents, and many pharmaceutical firms are web-enabling relations with wholesalers rather than selling directly to pharmacies or patients.

For online distribution, companies are developing a "portfolio of options"

Rather than attempting to drive customers to a single sales channel, executives believe it is important to let customers choose among several options. Many chemical companies, for example, are enabling their customers to buy from them through online marketplaces, corporate extranets and system-to-system connections, as well as through in-person channels.

Online B2B exchanges will grow in importance, but they must change to meet user demands

Online marketplaces such as ChemConnect and Global NetXchange are becoming an important tool for sales and procurement—19% say that industry-specific online exchanges are important for their supply chain management today, and 48% say they will be in 18 months. But in interviews, executives expressed dissatisfaction with current offerings, wishing to see more specialised and customised products. Of survey respondents, 55% said that the ability to customise an exchange's products and services is a very important feature.

The main obstacles to e-business are internal

The greatest barriers to the implementation of e-business strategy lie within the corporation: a need to re-engineer business processes (58% cited this as very significant) a lack of e-business skill (50%), and a lack of integration between front- and back-end systems (45%).

Senior Management involvement is too low

Research indicates that successful e-business strategies require highly involved senior managers. Of companies surveyed, 58% say senior management is very involved in implementing e-business strategy. This means, however, that at the remaining 42% of companies, senior management involvement is inadequate.

Companies are using e-business to expand products and services

To meet escalating customer demands and to prevent products and services from becoming commodities, companies are using the Internet to provide value-added products and services. According to 74% of respondents, this is a very important objective for their e-business plans. Examples include the "Virtual ISP" service offered by some telecommunications firms – a service that allows companies to brand their own ISP service – and the efforts of automakers to allow consumers to order customized cars *via* the Internet.

Companies are using e-business to reach new groups of customers

The Internet is turning out to be an effective way of reaching new customers, particularly customers overseas. According to 62%, this is a very important goal for their strategies. In interviews, executives said that they consider online marketplaces as the most efficient way to do this.

Executives hope to improve internal and external collaboration with e-business

The Internet is turning to be more than a sales and purchasing channel. According to 71% of respondents, improved collaboration with business partners is a highly important objective for their e-business strategies and 70% say that improved knowledge management is highly important. Alliances intensive industries, such as pharmaceuticals, are especially concerned with collaboration, with 82% citing improved collaboration as highly important.

No consensus has emerged on where to place e-business operations

Companies are severely split on the question of whether to form a separate e-business unit – 46% believe they need to. Some argue that to compete with dotcoms, e-business operations must be independent and flexible. Others say that for the online and physical operations to truly support each other e-business must be integrated into the lines of business. Our interviews suggest that the answer depends largely on the company's culture and competitive strengths.

E-business investment will continue to shift to B2B

Recognizing that some of the quickest benefits of e-businesses are likely to come from business-to-business initiatives, companies are increasingly devoting their investments to B2B. Currently, companies spend on average 57% of their e-business investments on B2B activities, in 18 months this number will increase to 62%.

E-VALUATING INDIA INC.[7]

On India Inc.'s digital frontiers, there is paucity of pioneers. Even as the world's biggest corporations extend their businesses at warp speed form the bricks-and-mortar marketplace to the binaries-and-bytes market space, and migration across the e-border has only just begun in this country. For corporate India, e-commerce – and its fastest growing component, Net-based business – is still largely uncharted territory.

A survey on the status of E-commerce has been conducted by KPMG, covering a sample of 116 companies operating in the country –

FIG. 17.1

Current Levels of Website Development

Intermediaries only
Limited Transactions
Full transactions
Backend Databases linked to web

Auto/Manufacturing
Chemicals
Communications
Consumer markets
Electronics
Financial Services
Pharmaceuticals

Less than 10% 10-49% More than 50%

Within 18 months, however, companies expect to make dramatic progress. Financial services, electronics and consumer markets will still have the most advanced websites, with more than a third having fully integrated systems. But many companies in other industries will have caught up.

Automotive/manufacturing will still trail, with only 12% offering websites linked to back-end databases, but on average, one quarter of communications, pharmaceuticals and chemicals will have such capabilities.

Source: EIU Survey.

more than two-thirds of which have a turnover of over Rs. 100 crore— the survey evaluates the perceptions, status, and triggers of the use of e-commerce in Indian companies.

Conceptually, India Inc. is plugged into the digital future. At more than half the 116 companies surveyed, e-commerce constitutes a substantial part of, or is crucial to, corporate strategy compared to the microscopic 4 per cent where it is of no importance yet. In fact, all corporates are willing to make the necessary investments in technology so long as they are confident of earning satisfactory return on their investment. The implication: e-commerce is, increasingly, being seen as a strategic tool to gain competitive advantage.

How Important is E-commerce to your Strategy?

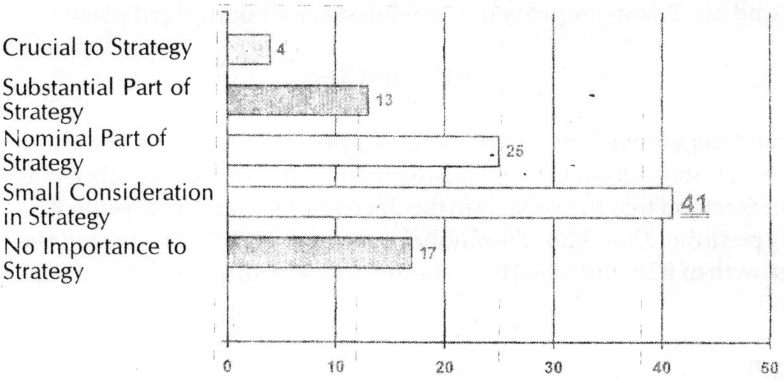

Source: KPMG India Electronic Commerce Survey Report, 1998-99 adapted from *Business Today*, March 22, 1999, pp. 80-83.

In generic terms, the benefits are of 3 kinds:

- Opening up new markets;
- Improving productivity; and
- Automating Supply Chains.

The first, of course, is the primary advantage that e-commerce should be offering companies as they extend their operations into the virtual market space. But, both in terms of expectations and actual gains, the benefits appear to be focused more on operations than on e-commerce. Specifically, the 2 most important pay-offs that corporate India expects e-business to yield are improved customer-service and productivity. The actual benefits that they are reaping are slightly

What Benefits are you Getting from E-commerce?

Improved Productivity
Improved Product Quality
Improved Customer
Reduced Costs
Sortened Supply Chain
New Product Development
Reaching New Customers
Improved Cash-Flows

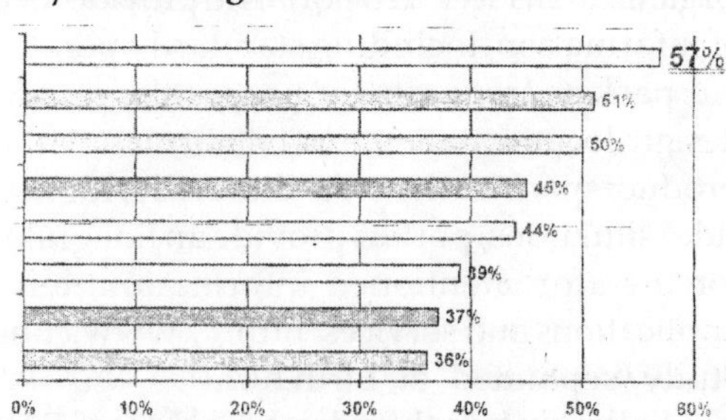

Source: KPMG India Electronic Commerce Survey Report, 1998-99 adapted from *Business Today*, March 22, 1999, pp. 80-83.

different, though improved productivity and product quality are No. 1 and No. 2, with improved customer-service taking third place.

THE DEBACLE

The recent debacle of dot coms have impressed corporates to rethink their strategy of e-commercialising their business. Till recently it was understood that the debacle in the dot coms has much to do with B2C hype rather than B2B. The Global Survey of KPMG also hinted the growth of B2B. But latest trends show a downfall in the value of B2B, too.

B2B

B2B (meaning "business to business") portals are a relatively recent development. Almost always by definition a vortal (vertical portal), B2B portals combine many of the real world functions performed by:[8]

- Trade magazines.
- Professional bodies.
- Contract brokers.
- Purchasing consortia.

The common themes of shared purpose, economies of scale, market focus, are leveraged by the internet strengths of scale and reach, and low cost communications.

B2B portals are rising in demand as more organizations seek to improve relationships with business customers/suppliers. Similar to the position of the enterprise portal's stature as a "next generation intranet", the B2B portal represents an advanced form of extranet. Organizations seek B2B portals to provide focused, controlled delivery of information, including standard operating procedures; policies; bid packets/requests for proposals/requests for quality; product design documentation; and bills of material/inventory/order status/ product specifications. Additionally, for demand chain (or B2B sell-side) situations, portals provide an integrated environment not only for the aforementioned information, but also for access to key applications and services. http://www.consumergoods.com/Tech Study/seperated_at_birth.html[9]

Following pathfinder launches of B2B portals for a few key industries, a number of service providers are now appearing who offer a flexible B2B portal framework that can be adapted to a range of portal needs.

It seems reasonable to expect that B2B portals will follow the route of other portals, and we should expect to see more and more highly specialised portals appearing—and the sub-division of existing B2B portals. In due course, a tier of over-arching meta-portals are likely to appear, consolidating access to specialized B2B portals by sector, geography, or other criteria.[10]

When they first appeared on the scene a year or two ago, the Web's business to business (B2B) companies held out a bold promise to use Internet technology to bring a drastic change in business world. Today, the companies are in big trouble.

First came the news of Ariba, a pioneer of the B2B software market, slashing forecast and people. Followed by a profit warning from Commerce One, its closest rival, leaving both Wall Street and analysts startled. So is it all over for B2B exchanges?[11]

According to the *Wall Street Journal*, some of these B2B companies would be lucky if they themselves can stay open for business.[12]

Gartner Consulting has forecasted a bloodbath in business-to-business e-marketplace during the next one year, with 90% of the dotcom companies unlikely to survive. Things will, however, start looking up from 2002-03.[13]

The Biggest Myths about B2B[14]

Follow the Money

B2B is not about how much revenue can be generated online, according to analysts, but rather about making connections with business partners.

"The idea of pure online sales as something onto itself has a very limited potential," according to Jupiter Media Metrix analyst. Most B2B works toward relationship building.

According to Gartner, "B2B is more about the process than a single transaction." Implementing a B2B strategy is a decision that reaches though the entire organization and will affect every department.

The B2B process could include buyers and sellers collaborating on designs, supply chain management and work flow management. A study released in June by Forrester Research supports this view, saying that firms must master dynamic collaboration—the sharing of information not only across the enterprise but outside the enterprise—to achieve their next big B2B breakthrough.

B2B Follows B2C

Companies hoping to translate business-to-consumer (B2C) e-tail success would do well to realize that B2B and B2C are not even broadly the same. B2C e-tailers sell goods on a first-come, first-serve basis, but most B2B is done through negotiated contracts that allow the seller to anticipate and plan for buyer demands.

The nature of B2B is radically different than B2C. It is a much deeper and longer term process than B2C. One e-tailer preparing to test the B2B waters is Amazon.com. The Internet behemoth recently announced that it will open a new division later this year catering to corporations, libraries and other institutional buyers.

One potential problem Amazon faces is that selling on credit means shipping orders before they are paid for, which could affect the company's cash flow.

"Depending on the size of the order, it could add to Amazon's problems," Gibs said.

B2B is for All

Some companies jump on the B2B bandwagon without analyzing whether buying and selling online is right for their business. Thinking we have to do something 'e' now, just because everyone else is doing it," is a mistake, according to Shu, adding that some companies "jump in without thinking it through".

Although all companies could benefit by using tools that automate business processes, B2B is generally "not for everyone".

B2B is Simple

Early on, the perception was that integrating supply chains was reasonably quick and easy. Covisint, the e-marketplace backed by the major automakers, is a prime example of the difficulties inherent in B2B e-commerce. When Covisint was first announced in February 2000, its founding partners—General Motors, Ford and DaimlerChrysler—expected it to be live within 30 days and predicted that it would eventually handle $ 750 billion in annual purchasing. However, more than a year later, the online auto marketplace is not fully operational.

All Aboard

One of the biggest challenges facing B2B is not technology, but corporate culture. Analysts said that the mental resistance to adopting B2B can be a greater problem than any technological hurdle. The harder task is changing the culture and convincing humans to think in a new way. It is very difficult. For, it's very hard work to get users to commit.

King added that convincing buyers and sellers to use e-marketplaces was cited as the top B2B challenge by the 25 industry-sponsored marketplaces (ISMs) Forrester surveyed for an upcoming report.

B2B is IT

One of the biggest ways companies oversimplify the B2B e-commerce process is by viewing it as simply a project for the information technology (IT) department. The rush to automate, many companies fail to properly evaluate their businesses for inefficiencies.

Moving sloppy, inefficient business processes online usually does not solve a company's problems, the analysts point out. They recommend that companies should fix their internal problems before migrating their business systems online. Like, if a company has a problem with an inefficient system, software is not going to help. Software also cannot totally eliminate the need for human intervention.

B2B is Dead

Despite the obstacles, the missteps, and the misperceptions, B2B is not failing. There's been lots of gloom and doom that the Internet is dying. However, the truth is that "companies have made incredible headway in the past year and a half." Gartner predicts that B2B e-commerce will reach $ 919 billion in 2001 and $ 1.9 trillion in 2002. The research agency is also pretty bullish on what B2B can accomplish.

THE STATE OF AFFAIR

As per a report[15] of the thousands of online exchanges set-up within the last year and a half, hundreds never made it off the pages of the news release, and of those that did, a huge number have either gone bust or are teetering on the brink of bankruptcy.

Last month, Ventro Corp., which owns and operates B2B exchanges, closed two of its key marketplaces, chemical exchange Chemdex and medical industry exchange Promedix, resulting in a loss of $382.5 million. Year-end losses totalled $618.1 million, 11 times greater than the $48.6 million less for 1999.

Dell Computer Corp. quietly closed its exchange, Dellmarketplace.com, which connected its customers with third-party suppliers of office goods and services, in February. Earlier, in Washington, DC, and Delaware electric utility Potomac Electric Power Co. (PEPCO) said it was closing its office supplies and services exchange due a lack of uptake from buyers and suppliers.

Traffic Still Slow in the B2B Lane

As the list of new portals continues to lengthen, it is nevertheless becoming increasingly clear that a portal launch does not necessarily augur immediate B2B success. Customers are not flocking to the portals as quickly as expected and even those who make the trip are often unwilling or unable to make transactions.

Jerry Jasinowski, president of the National Association of Manufacturers (NAM), said that in a recent survey of 2,500 manufacturers, 68 percent of those responding said their companies are not using electronic commerce as a forum for business transactions.

"The prospects for robust B2B Internet-based communication, distribution and service are extremely promising," he observed. "But our survey shows that most manufacturing companies are still at a rather basic level when it comes to integrating the Web into their corporate business activities. While 80 percent claim they have a Web site, the vast majority offer only an information storefront. Furthermore, only 10 percent say that their current business process technology systems are fully automated."[16]

Only the large, public marketplaces—Covisint in the automotive industry, Transora in consumer packaging goods and Exostar in aerospace and defense, for example—are still visible. But try to eke out hard data about transaction volume, or actual savings, and it's like trying to penetrate a heavily guarded fortress.

No Participants

But the biggest factor holding back exchanges is the lack of suppliers, analysts said. "Nobody, not one of the big vendors nor any of the public exchanges has really made a concerted effort to bring in the small and medium suppliers," said Joshua Greenbaum of Daly City, Calif.-based Enterprise Applications Consulting. This apart less than one percent of the world's suppliers are connected to online exchanges. "But if they don't get every supplier involved they won't get critical mass and the exchanges will just remain a bunch of press releases."

WHAT WENT WRONG?

Though the facts are ninety percent of all e-commerce conducted in 1999 involved online business-to-business (B2B) deals, according to the US Department of Commerce. Additionally, a study by Gartner found that B2B e-commerce revenues reached US$433 billion in 2000, a 189 percent increase over the $145 billion in revenues raked in by B2B e-commerce in 1999.[17]

"So what happened?" the Journal said. "For one thing, there has been a slowdown in corporate spending on all kinds of technology. But it also turns out that B2B and B2C had a lot in common after all. Both sectors overstated the extent to which the Internet was changing the world of old line businesses."[18]

B2B models and technologies were viewed as an effective tool to achieve transformation. But companies made a basic mistake. They viewed B2B as a 'quick-win' technology initiative.[19]

Allured by the inexpensive worldwide reach of the Internet, most companies decided to participate in global e-marketplaces.

Some joined existing e-marketplaces while others decided to set-up their own. Unfortunately, majority of these e-markets just focused on automating transactions. The technology was there but business issues were never addressed.

B2B collaboration is a means of using the Internet technologies to enable a set of complex cross-enterprise business processes allowing them to share information, workflow and decision-making.[20]

"There was a general perception that since all applications were Web-based, somehow the software could be designed, debugged and implemented in these 90 day time frames and work, when it had never been proven and tested," said Bruce Richardson, an analyst at industry research firm AMR Research in Boston. International Data Corp's Leo Lipis agreed. "They're certainly not even meeting the expectations that were set for them a year ago," he added.[21]

Thomas Chen, ZDNet Asia observes, "Most portals are very much focused on consumers and catalogues with some transactional capabilities, but the question is whether they can make the leap to provide a marketplace or exchange-type functionality," said Brand. "And even if they can do that technically, is the market there to support it?"[22]

B2B PORTALS IN INDIA

The total portals at present in operation in India,[23] are—

- Auction India — Buy and sell any type of new and second hand machinery and industrial assets.
- Auction Portal — Complete B2B auction portal where you can see surplus inventory, liquidate excess stock and display products.
- B2B Connect — Affiliated to Aptechs — a reputed computer training institute, it is a programming service provider of e-commerce solutions to companies, based on JAVA.
- Bargain Shop — Discounts, sales, offers, exchange schemes, prizes and gifts make this a one-stop site for bargains.
- Bharatiya — An e-commerce and low-cost internet solution provider with online store.
- Biz-Horizon — A common platform for buyers and sellers interested in anything relating for their business.
- Chemicals — Online chemical bazaar acting as a unique electronic marketplace using software for Indian chemical business for all buyers and sellers.
- Commodity India — Get information on all the commodities in the market along with the prices at the domestic and international market.
- Construction — A great help to the buyers and sellers of the construction industry to get all kinds of materials and equipment for construction.

- Consultancy to Multinationals – Delhi-based consultant firm offering B2B portal services, laying emphasis on telecom, datacom, computers, and capital goods sectors.
- Cyber World – One of the fastest growing firms in the field of Internet, portal design, ASP and computer education.
- DBS Internet – Firm offering B2B services and global expansion to rich career opportunities and business enterprising solutions on the Internet.
- Directory of Indian exporters – Directory of Indian exporters and importers. Get free web pages and hosting.
- E-com server – Hyderabad-based firm providing state of the art B2B solutions.
- E-simplest – A complete solution to deliver enterprise, web, customized solution and traditional solutions for e-commerce.
- Electric Mela – Your gateway to the electrical industry.
- I three – India's best B2B solution provider of top technology, with news and articles updated everyday.
- Impact – Provides solutions in e-commerce.
- India Business Club – India Business Club is a complete B2B portal which helps all class of business people to improve their business.
- India chem – Buy and sell chemical and pharmaceutical products.
- India e-commerce – A comprehensive list of B2B portals for different products available in the country.
- India echo – The first auction provider for the trading of agricultural products.
- India engineering – Marketspace for manufacturers and engineers to get relevant and important business information for the engineering industry.
- India for Everything – A B2B portal providing complete web solutions.
- India Invest – News and information on tenders and a facility to make your business website for free.
- India market – Get a glimpse of all the sellers and buyers dealing in auto ancillary, chemicals, computers, construction and others.
- Indiacore homepage – Provides information on India's developments in telecom, IT, roadways, ports and terminals, mining, aviation, railways, law centre.

- India – Get all the information about this B2B and other value-added services in travel, finance, health and shopping.
- Indian Bazaar – A common platform for manufacturers and exporters to facilitate trade.
- Industrial Products – A virtual trade center to get all kind of information on industrial products required by you.
- Info Brick – Get all kinds of web-solutions and software programmes.
- InfodriveIndia – Get a glimpse of the exports and imports of the company with the names of the items to be exported and imported in the country.
- Kaashyap Radiant – India's largest ESP providing B2B, B2C and e-commerce solutions.
- Meclai online – Information on the currency rates, risk hedge calculator and tracker services.
- Meet Venture – Providers of expert consultation, web portal for your business, e-commerce development and design, and business directories.
- Mergers and Acquisitions – Buying and selling of companies to diversify, expand or to start new business and also registers buyer's requirements without paying any fees.
- Office Manager – Get all the requirements that your office needs starting from basic office supplies like staplers, scissors, filing, computer accessories.
- Oil market – Comprehensive information for buying, selling and trading of edible oils, non-edible oils, oil extracts, oil meals and other related products.
- Online Chemicals – Trading online related to chemicals to support the business exchange platform online and to the thousands of focussed buyers and sellers.
- Pack – Comprehensive database of packaging products along with free packaging consultancy. Plus it also allows you to auction and advertise online.
- Paper and pulp industry – Online trading of paper listed in the category section of paper and pulp industry.
- Paper exchange – One of the first B2B paper and pulp portal which gives a list of all the machineries, equipment, which are used in the paper industry.
- Planet India – One of the most powerful portal for B2B, C2C and B2C solutions.

- Polyesters Online – Information on the Indian polyester industry along with news and offers to buy and sell products online.
- Sango Soft – Dedicated to make e-commerce into reality for all kinds of business. Also help for companies to conduct their business online.
- Satyam – A leading company providing information on the distributors and dealers of plastic products.
- Seek and Source – For sellers scouting for new markets and buyers seeking the right suppliers.
- Spun online – Facilitates e-commerce amongst the industry, in order to improve business efficiency.
- Steel – Trade steel in global market along with news and information of all products, services, prices, related to steel.
- Steel Exchange – One of the first companies offering online 626 solutions for the steel industry.
- Steel Udyog – Details about the traders, manufacturers, importers and exporters in the steel industry.
- Suppliers – A buyer and suppliers network which helps search different suppliers who provide all the services and products you need.
- Tenderpoint – Solution providers to different companies needing services and a continuous flow of business opportunities to help them grow.
- Tenders online – Online collection and submission of tenders. Services like representation during tender opening follow-up and reporting on order finalisation.
- Textile products – A common platform for buyers and sellers for facilitating trade in textile products.
- The Cheese Room – UK-based graphic design studio providing a variety of creative design services as well as print and distribution.
- Trade to Gain – An online auction site which sells almost everything in trading requirements.
- Web India – Facilitates Indian businesses to sell products, explore import/export opportunities and explore the possibility of technical collaboration.
- World chemicals – A powerful marketing tool for the chemical and pharmaceuticals community to exchange online.
- Yantri Enterprise Solutions – A packaged application service which facilitates you with B2B, B2C, C2C, software engineering and software project management.

Down but Not Out[24]

Nevertheless, analysts still believe there is a place for online exchanges in business-to-business commerce. "There is no question that expectations outpaced reality," said Morgan Stanley's Digital Transformation Group Peter Pashigian, vice-president of Morgan Stanley's Digital Transformation Group, which invested in e2open, among others.

"If you think of it as a pendulum, it swung too much to one side last year, but now it's swung too much to the other. The answer is it should be somewhere in the middle, because the same business problems still exist," Pashigian said. According to AMR's Joan Harbin, author of a new report on exchanges, due out this week, electronic marketplaces are here to stay.

Harbin's team reviewed data from the top exchanges in 10 industries from a list of more than 1,400 survey recipients. "Though money is changing hands, no one's profitable yet," Harbin said, adding that AMR saw revenues crossing exchanges in retail, chemical, utilities and some in aerospace.

For example, CheMatch.com, an online exchange in the chemical industry, completed more than $ 450 million in transactions in 2000. And since going live in October 2000, $ 9 billion worth of electricity has been traded *via* Tradespark, an exchange in the utilities sector.

All of which supports an important point. Exchanges that automate buying and selling of commodity goods, such as plastic or electricity, are taking off fastest because the transaction is simpler than the more complex collaborative planning and design processes required for other products, such as cars. "But broader-scoped exchanges are floundering in their attempts to deliver capability," Harbin said, pointing to companies like Covisint and Transora.

THE WAY OUT[25]

Some of the success stories in the Collaboration space are Walmart, Dell and Cisco. It is important to note that these companies did not have the sole intention of improving the operational efficiencies but also coming up with radically new business models and innovative ways of providing customer value.

In case of India Global management consultant A.T. Kearney says India is yet to realise the full potential of the business-to-business (B2B) transactions, much like the rest of Asia, but held considerable unexploited potential. As per a study conducted by Kearney, India is in Wave One, which means high-end, almost ready, state of country readiness with advantages of early global penetration, specifically in the European markets.

India, like the rest of Asia, has not done too well in the B2B space but it holds vast potential. This can be judged from the fact that 10 per cent of the $85 billion business revenue generation target from Asia is expected to come from the Indian B2B space by 2003, said the vice-president and managing director south-east Asia of Kearney, John Yoshimura.[26]

To ensure successful B2B collaboration, the key aspects are re-aligning enterprise-wide business strategies, adoption of trading partners, developing multi-enterprise business processes, sound implementation approach and choosing the right consulting and systems integration partner.

Part of the problem is the level of technological complexity that is required to make online B2B business work. Most of the technologies available today, according to Kammerer, are "patchwork" solutions that do not replicate real world conditions nor add enough value to the process to make B2B attractive to businesses.

To really take advantage of B2B, businesses actually need to build a layer of technology around themselves to connect into portal and marketplaces, to have the flexibility to switch from marketplace to marketplace and still have the ability to conduct end to end, seamless transactions. That's a tall order, and it's going to cost a lot.[27]

Enterprise-wide business strategy is the first step. Define the value proposition for collaborative commerce for the enterprise, identify all collaborative opportunities and evaluate the financial and operational aspects.

Adoption of trading partners: A strong value proposition needs to be defined to make it lucrative for the trading partners to come on board. A strong process also needs to be in place.

Cohesive multi-enterprise business processes. Companies who take a methodical and strategic approach would succeed in B2B collaboration initiatives.

Companies in India currently overvalue secrecy and under-estimate the value of sharing information. If this mindset is changed, there is a lot to be gained.

CONCLUSION

It could be fairly concluded on the basis of the facts and opinion discussed above that their lies a vast untapped potential in India as far as B2B is concerned. For a resource constrained country B2B is a boon to effectively utilize scarce resources. A sure way to achieve the same is by effectively utilizing the strengths of B2B. India has one advantage over developed countries. It has a learning curve that can be utilized in implementing B2B effectively. The success and failure stories of B2B shall surely help in devising the future.

REFERENCES

1. Ravi Kalakota and Andrew B. Whinston, *Frontiers of Electronic Commerce*, Addison-Wesley Publishing Co, Inc., 1996, p. iii.
2. Ravi Kalakota and Andrew B. Whinston, *Frontiers of Electronic Commerce*, Addison-Wesley Publishing Co, Inc., 1996, p. 2.
3. The Economist adapted from *Economic Times*, Investor's Guide, 1 November, 1999, p. 5.
4. *The Economic Times*, 28 October, 1999, p. 15.
5. Dr. Yogesh Upadhyay and Dr. S.K. Singh, "Perfect Competition: From Myth to Reality", *Delhi Business Review*, An International Journal of Society for Human Transformation and Research, Vol. I, No. 2, July-December, 2000, pp. 119-24.
6. Yogesh Upadhyay and Dr. S.K. Singh, "E-Commerce: Opportunities for Accounting", *Third Concept*, An International Journal of Ideas, July 1999, pp. 37-39.
7. "E-valuating India Inc.", Based on KPMG India Electronic Commerce Survey Report, 1998-99, *Business Today*, March 22, 1999, pp. 80-83.
8. http://www.practicalportals.com/B2B_portals.html
9. http://www.consumergoods.com
10. http://www.practicalportals.com
11. B2B exchanges: Down, but not out, http://infotech.indiatimes.com
12. B2B sector in trouble: WSJ, http://infotech.indiatimes.com
13. Bloodbath in B2B marketplace: Gartner, http://infotech.indiatimes.com
14. The biggest myths about B2B, http://infotech.indiatimes.com
15. B2B exchanges: Down, but not out, http://infotech.indiatimes.com
16. Mick Brady, E-Commerce Times, March 16, 2000.
17. The biggest myths about B2B, http://infotech.indiatimes.com
18. B2B sector in trouble: WSJ, http://infotech.indiatimes.com
19. So, what went wrong with B2B? http://infotech.indiatimes.com

20. So, what went wrong with B2B? http://infotech.indiatimes.com
21. B2B exchanges: Down, but not out, http://infotech.indiatimes.com
22. B2B taking shape Thomas Chen, ZDNet Asia, http:www.zdnetindia.com
23. http://www.in.lycosasia.com
24. The biggest myths about B2B, http://infotech.indiatimes.com
25. So, what went wrong with B2B? http://infotech.indiatimes.com
26. India yet to realise B2B potential: Kearney, June 06, 2001, http://www.zdnetindia.com
27. B2B taking shape Thomas Chen, ZDNet Asia, http:www.zdnetindia.com

18

E-Commerce: Contracting World and Expanding Markets

SAWALIA BIHARI VERMA

Science and technology have brought about drastic changes in the traditional mode of living. Rapid inventions and advances in science have made man the master of his own destiny. Of the thousands of inventions and discoveries that have marked the twentieth century, computer is the one that will go down in history as one of the remarkable achievements that human made in the present millennium.

Computers find applications in almost all the fields from space research to agricultural research. Owing to the application of computers, rapid speeds and needle-precise accuracy in calculations and error-free decision-making and predictions have become possible in almost all the fields. Computers find usage in almost all the branches of commerce and trade. Of late preparation of the final statements of companies has become the simplest job thanks to the computerised accounting methods that have changed the erstwhile complicated jobs as the easiest ones.

This paper on E-commerce aims at presenting a picture of the general applications of E-commerce in the first part and its impact on and challenges to accounting practices in the second part.

INTERNET AND E-COMMERCE

Internet, as we all know, is a huge global network of hundreds of computer networks which links more than 170 countries in the world. It links computers of different types, sizes and operating systems. It is a global community of over 50,000 inter-connected computer networks. According to one estimate, more than 50 million people are connected together and the number of users has been growing almost 15 per cent per month.

Internet, which is network of networks, helps in the international linking of businesses, universities, libraries and research organisations with millions of users. Commercial transactions and activities carried the electronic medium of Internet is called E-commerce. In E-commerce, commercial activities, are conducted electronically. In the context of the web, an E-commerce site is a website that accurately enables a customer to buy products or services. It is a store that is open 24 hours a day /7 days a week. It is operated at a fraction of the costs involved in staffing a business location throughout the week. According to a report, in 1998 E-commerce had a worldwide sales turnover of about $7 billion.

Wide Use

The use of Internet and E-Commerce offers unrivalled opportunities for business and commerce. A company can reach out to a global market with the help of well-designed web-pages and can display their product-range in the most effective manner. Marketing a commodity through effective advertising and reaching out to millions of customers in a fraction of second, mail transfers, stock market information and travel and tourist information have all been made easier with the judicious application of E-commerce technology now-a-days. Companies are trying to do better service to their customers, sell them more products and services, retrieve strategic information about their likes and dislikes and save money by streamlining their own operations.

Impact of E-Commerce on Business

The role of computers and Internet in business is to change raw structured data available in a set of rolls into meaningful information for decision-making and improve the quality of data by forcing discipline in data collection and consistency in operations. The success of business primarily depends upon the timely availability of information. The difficulties of delay and accuracy illustrate the law of information. "Information we have is not we want; information we want is not all we need and the information we need is not available." So estimations, comparisons, predictions and decision-making were some of the major problems faced by businessmen in the past. To overcome these difficulties E-commerce suggests an effective alternative by its very nature of functioning. With the rapid speed and effective functioning of E-commerce great improvement can be achieved in all the areas.

CHALLENGES BEFORE THE ACCOUNTANTS—AN INTROSPECTION

1. It is a Wide Global Network

E-commerce has a vast marketing potentiality. It serves as a powerful customer service tool. It keeps production up-to-date. Customers are able to have access to the information they need on demand. E-commerce website opens up new markets. Since Web is a global medium, properly executed E-commerce strategies enable businesses to reach out to customers they never knew existed. New customers can crop up in the next town or on the next continent.

Advertising and personal selling were once considered to be effective sales promotional techniques. With the entry of E-commerce there is going to be a vast expansion of the customer base. Personal selling and advertising are slowly losing their prime importance. Now web-sites serve as an effective advertising tool; also they convert probable buyers into actual buyers who place online orders immediately according to their needs.

Challenges before the Accountant

Given the above background, the accountant now has to make an assessment of browsers who seek information about the product to be sold through websites. Based on the number of browsers, he should classify them product-wise, area-wise like national and international customers and try to make an estimation of the actual orders likely to be placed by online customers. Since the estimation made by the accountant forms the basis of actual production, his job becomes much more complicated and challenging. This is an area which needs serious thinking and further probe.

2. Online Payment

With the mode of payment being credit card/debit card nowadays, payments are made electronically without carrying cash to the counters. Also tele-banking has been gaining wide acceptance nowadays.

Challenge before the Accountant

Journals and ledger books are going to be replaced with online cash registers and electronic ledgers. The imminent danger in a debit payment through card is that there is every possibility that one may clandestinely decipher the secret code numbers and pass words of other customers and make payments from their cash balances. How to keep strangers at bay from making fraudulent payment is yet another problem which requires through investigation by accounting professionals. So electronic crime is yet another challenge to be tackled judiciously. In tele-banking too, customers do not visit bank premises for both withdrawals and deposits. Here illegal transfer of funds by fraudulent means has to be checked.

3. Simultaneous Updating

In E-commerce, global access is available at our doorstep. Customer surveys, sales estimations and payments are done electronically.

Challenges before the Accountant

Since E-commerce updates payments and estimations 24 hours a day/7 days a week, estimations or calculations made at one point of time may prove to be fallacious the next day and the next week. Also it is really a problem to make a meaningful bifurcation between serious and non-serious buyers.

THE FUTURE

Instead of resorting to age-old techniques of survey, mailed questionnaire and person-to-person contact, online worksheets and hot-linked lists of clients are becoming the order of the day. Instead of hot currencies, cyber-cash is gaining acceptance slowly. Given the vast potentials, E-commerce is the buzzword for the dynamic merchants of the future generation. The barriers to entry into E-commerce have traditionally been three-fold. First, the tremendous expense of E-commerce sites has kept many businesses at bay. Secondly, the unfamiliar nature and complexity of the Internet have made many business owners feel unqualified for making Internet business decisions. Thirdly, the increasing incidence of electronic crimes prevents potential sellers and buyers from entering this web world. The world indeed has been shrinking and the customer base, the marketing network and cyber-cash have been expanding beyond our imagination.

If accountants could provide solutions to the questions that have been raised in this paper, both global business and the profession of accounting would derive innumerable benefits in the long-run.

REFERENCES

Introduction to the Internet-UCW-End-user Computing under Windows 95—Part 2—First Computers.

Ralph F. Wilson, "Getting Customers to Plunk Down Credit Card", *Web Marketing Today*, pp. 1-3.

Ralph F. Wilson, "Give Something Away, The Classic Web Marketing Strategy", *Web Marketing Today*, Issue 11, April 15, 1990.

Ralph F. Wilson, "How to Sell Products Directly on the Web", *Web Marketing Today*, Issue 18, July 27, 1996.

19

E-Commerce: A Business Revolution

P.V. JAYAKUMAR

E-commerce is the most remarkable facet of the emerging – "digital economy". The advent of the internet in the recent past has paved the way for commercial and financial transactions becoming easier, speedier and cheaper through access to an online global marketplace which has no geographic boundaries.

WHAT IS E-COMMERCE

E-commerce is nothing but electronic commerce. It is the use of IT (Information Technology) systems to carry out the process of buying and selling of goods and services. It includes the use of IT for Electronic Data Interchange (EDI), databases of customers and products, electronic fund transfers, value-added networks, interactive voice response, customer service systems, sales and marketing on the internet, electronic catalogues, and anything which simultaneously involves technology and business/commerce.

E-commerce is mainly divided into two categories: Business to Business (B2B) and Business to Consumer (B2C). Business to business involves electronic business transactions between trading partners. Business to consumer involves electronic business transactions between a business and an individual consumer. B2B transactions account for the major chunk of e-business globally.

B2B IN E-COMMERCE

In normal business you need to have a product or service to offer.

You can have the product directly from a producer, or from a distributor or even produced by yourselves. If it is the latter, you should have a place to sell them from. Then you should take care of the marketing aspects. The process of accepting orders, money, billing, delivery of products or service, etc. require more attention. You may have to think of having customer service section also for the smooth conduct of the business.

In e-commerce you can see all these factors with a little difference. You must have a product or service to offer. But the place of transaction changes: it becomes a web site. Proper marketing tactics are to be applied here also. There should be online facility to accept orders, money and billing, etc. Monetary transactions normally take place through credit cards. Proper delivery of products should be ensured through an external source. For products like software and information the delivery can be through the web itself, i.e. through the file downloading technique. An imperative of designing an e-commerce operational model is the exceptional ability to organize the operations of a company and clearly understand how all these can be coordinated to achieve the corporate objective.

THE ATTRACTIONS OF E-COMMERCE

In e-commerce the transaction cost is very low as the order-taking cost and customer service costs are very less. Cost of staffing and the role of middlemen are negligible since it is managed by the web. This will help to offer the product at a lower rate. With the help of IT tools the customer interaction becomes very easy without any extra cost. Similarly when a customer reads the description of a product he can also see the comparison of similar products of other companies. Hence, if a customer is made happy with these type of facilities and interaction, he is likely to purchase again from your company.

In general, higher revenue, faster external access to internal information, 24 × 7 (24 hours a day, 7 days a week), customer support, reduced communication cost, faster information dissemination, better external information gathering and customer goodwill are the attractions of e-commerce.

The main points to be thought of while venturing into the e-business are: the technology cost involved is higher, higher salary to be paid for the sophisticated staff and the ongoing system upgradation cost, etc. In comparison with the tremendous prospects of e-commerce these factors may not be dampener.

PRESENT SCENARIO OF E-COMMERCE

The total global market for e-commerce in 1999 was estimated at US $ 114 billion. It is expected that by 2003 it will be US $ 3.1 trillion and the users are expected to number more than 200 million. The Indian share during the year 1998-99 was Rs. 131 crore which as per the study of NASSCOM (National Association of Software and Service Companies) is expected to reach Rs. 10,000 crore by the end of 2002. A major portion of this will be from B2B transactions.

GENERAL ISSUES WHICH SEEK A GLOBAL SOLUTION IN E-COM

The main problem faced by the Government in connection with e-commerce is the taxation of e-business. The rules regarding taxation is different from country to country and even State to State. Since there are no geographical boundaries for the e-business it is a matter of serious concern as whom to tax, where to tax and how to tax, etc. Moreover, a stringent and unscrupulous taxation system may turn to be a jolt to this flourishing industry. At the same time changing the mode of business should not help anyone to evade tax. Hence while devising a tax rule, due care is to be taken for not hampering the prospects of e-business as well as to check any undue advantage through e-business. Another problem is the security of the transactions. At present the credit card number of a person can be used by another if he knows it. At present it is very difficult to book such culprits. Experts in the field of e-commerce opine that the introduction of a global currency can make the monetary transactions easy.

PROSPECTS IN INDIA

Emerging trend indicates that our country's future in the IT field is very bright. The shopping experience in India is not a pleasurable one due to reasons like acute parking problem in shopping areas, crowded pavements, poor customer service, difficulty in getting one's choice, etc. Similarly, since more and more people in the cities are getting on to the net a greater part of their business is likely to move into the cyber world. Cyber laws and other related Acts are to be properly enacted in our country to protect and promote the e-business.

Our share in the e-business during the past shows that the e-business has taken a right step in our country also even when there is no legal framework for its adequate protection. So let us hope that our country with all its potential software expertise and resources will play a prominent role in this global revolution of e-commerce.

PART II

INFORMATION TECHNOLOGY AND E-COMMERCE

20

Information Technology and E-Commerce

PEEYUSH KR. PANDEY AND SUNIL KR. PANDEY

"Let all the light come towards me, through all directions."
— *Rig Ved*

The word "Problem" means nothing but the lack of information and it arises only either by no information or by less information. We must try to obtain information as clearly stated by the Rig Veda Shloka, "Let all the light come towards me, through all directions, effectively, clearly and promptly.

For effective problem solving we must have information through various sources, fortunately, the last decade in the global arena has witnessed a drastic and tremendous growth in the field of information technology.

Right from the telegraphic and postal services, the latest communication media, computer and Internet services enable us to get prompt access to required information, i.e. we have turned from postal to portal.

Telephone, Computer and Internet (T.C.I.) which are the main tools of today's information technology will turn from demand top need of tomorrow's human life.

With information technology computers have made a significant impact on all directions of our day-to-day life for e.g. education, reservation, Internet trading, electronic market, net-banking, net entertainment, communication and so on.

Information Technology (IT) has replaced the conventional ways to handle the technical and operational problem by introducing the much faster and more convenient method, which is based on its ability to access large and complex pools of data.

Initially computer could process information contained in the form of text only. A text is written with letters, digits and other characters, which we can read. Later it was also realized that the information contained in the form of image, audio, video can also be processed, the pressing demand for storage and retrieval of data represented in multiple form like text, image, graphic, audio-video has given a new direction to the computer scientist and technologist to process information stored in multiple formats. All this has revolutionized information technology.

The fast growth of IT led to search of new technique for conducting effective business and commercial activities on the Internet. In today's hezille, mobile and versatile life commerce is undergoing a revolutionary phase when the medium of communication between the consumer and trader is electronic. We now cannot imagine commerce without advance technology. Yesterday's P-commerce (paper-commerce) now has changed in today's e-commerce. Let us make ourselves ready for any other type of commerce in future which definitely will be more advanced than e-commerce.

Commerce with wonderful value 'E' has brought revolution in every functional area of business organisation with special mention to service sector. Through e-commerce we need not to visit a shop for buying product, no need to carry hard cash in our pocket and need not to wait for delivery of information, the main vehicles for e-commerce are Internet and www.

E-commerce refer to the electronic media in place of conventional paper, for exchange of business information by using EDI, e-mail, EFT and other network-based technology.

EDI

In the Electronic Data exchange the concept of paper was replaced by the electronic exchange of information, it is actually a way of replacing manual data entry with electronic data entry. The essence of EDI is to estimate processing and data re-entry delays.

For banking and financial transactions business organisation, and such item which may be produced in electronic form such as music, video games, electronic books and information on demand and information-based services, EDI is the powerful information-based technique.

EDI can be used to electrically transmit orders, movies, shopping notes, receiving advice and other standard business correspondence between trading partners.

EFT

Electronic Fund Transferring is the advance system of transaction where fund transfer in the form of paper currency is replaced with the electronic transfer.

Smart cards, credit cards are other alternate of paper currency, payment can be made on the internet using plastic currency.

EDI consists of standardized electric message formates for common business documents and similar documents of these electronic transaction sets enable the computer in one company to communicate with the computer in the other company without producing actual paper document.

To take full advantage of EDI's benefit a company must computerized its basic commerce records and mutual agreement for EDI exchange.

CONCLUSION

The need of Information for either solving problem related with business organisation, commerce, market, opportunity, threat, strength, weakness or to make ourselves as a knowledgeable person is beyond doubt.

In real sense all thoughts are now able to come toward us by the development of information technology through computer, telephone and other media in the form of information.

New phase replaced the old one with the development and innovations that is what happened with the information and commerce activity too.

E-commerce based on EDI, EFT, e-mail and other technology focus on shrinking the world. If the whole world is within the reach, we cannot serve it effectively, efficiently and thoroughly without replacing our conventional ways of commerce practices. Fortunately, e-commerce provide chance to spread us. For this we must keep ourselves within the contact of the latest information technology change and development, so that we can acquire the best possible things available in world.

21

Information Technology in Enterprise Resource Planning

SUBODH KESHARWANI

To survive, thrive and beat the competition in today's brutally competitive world one has to manage the future. And the key to managing the future lies in one's ability to effectively manage the wide influx of information. In order to deliver high quality information to the decision-makers at the right time, in order to automate the process of data collections, collation and refinement, organization have to make Information Technology an ally, harness it's full potential and use it in the best possible way.

ERP (Enterprise Resource Planning) is one such area, which has completely revolutionized the business environment. Many industries and business system have reengineered the process and have gone for adopting ERP. Organization, which are yet to do so are seriously working to prepare themselves for adopting ERP.

Information Technology (IT) is revolutionizing the way in which we live and work. It is changing all aspects of our life and lifestyle. The digital revolution has given mankind the ability to treat information with mathematical precision to transmit it with very high accuracy and to manipulate it at will.

IT has many roles to play in any organization. All organizations have certain objectives and goals to achieve. For any organization to succeed, all business units or departments should work towards this common goal. But each department or business functions in the organization will have it's own goals and procedures. The departmental objectives can sometimes be conflicting.

E.g. The finance department might want to cut down the advertising budget, where as the marketing department might want to reduce the inventory level, but the production people might want to have more stocks.

The success of an organization rests in resolving the conflicts between the various business functions and making them do what is good for the organizations as a whole. For this, Information Technology is critical. Every body should know what is happening in other parts of the organization. *It is not enough that each department manages it's activities efficiently, it should also help other departments manage their functions efficiently*. For this to happen, the organization should cease to function as islands of information, each working in isolation. Each and every employer should know what his/her counterparts are doing, how his/her actions and decisions will affect the other departments. This kind of information sharing was difficult in the early days now with the advancements in Information Technology this is possible.

IT has a crucial role to play, both at the organizational level and at the departmental level, at the organizational level it should assist in specifying objectives and strategies of the organization. IT should assist in developing and supporting systems and procedures to achieve them. At the department level, IT must ensure a seamless flow of information across the different departments and develop and maintain an enterprise wide database. This database will eliminate the need of the isolated data islands that existed in each department and make the organization data accessible across the departmental boundaries. This enterprise-wide data sharing has many benefits like automation of the procedures, availability of high quality information for better decision-making, faster response.

EVOLUTION OF ERP

The evolution of ERP solutions has a long history. Earlier packages used to come in different forms and in a non-integral fashion. But slowly the need was felt to integrate various segments of an enterprise and go beyond back office and front office. With the growth of Business to Business (B2B) requirements and large databases, and the rise of concept like Supply Chain Management, JIT and to order manufacture, ERP has become a compulsory addition.

When companies were small and all the different managerial functions managed by a single person, the decisions were made, keeping in mind the overall company objectives. But as companies grew, managing the entire operation became impossible for a single person. More and more people were brought in and the different business functions were given to different individuals when the organization became larger, each person hired people to assist him/ her and the various departments as we see now, evolved. The size of departments began to increase as more and more people were required to do the job.

As the department became large, they became closed and water-tight, each had their own set of procedures and hierarchy. People, at most levels within a department, would just collect and pass information upward.

Thus information was shared between departments only at the top level. Although IT provided the perfect answer, in the haste, most developer ended up developing need-based, isolated and piecemeal information systems that were non-compatible and it is no wonder than that IT implementation automated only the existing applications and not the business functions.

Most of this happened because it was not integrated into the corporate strategy. To draw real benefits from a technology as powerful as IT. One has to devise a system with a holistic view of the enterprise. Such a system has to work around the core activities of the organization and should facilitate seem less flow of information across departmental barriers. Such system can optimally plan and manage all the resources of the organization and hence, they can be called as ERP (enterprise resource planning) system.

MEANING OF ERP

ENTERPRISE – "An Enterprise is a group of people with a common goal which has certain resources at its disposal to achieve that goal. The group has some key functions to perform in order to achieve its goal."

RESOURCES – "Resources included are Money, Manpower, Materials, and all the other things that are required to run the enterprise."

PLANNING – "Planning is done to ensure that nothing goes wrong. Planning is putting necessary function in place and more importantly, putting them together."

Therefore, Enterprise Resource Planning or ERP is a method of effective planning of all the resources in an organization.

MISCONCEPTION IN ERP

There are many misconceptions about ERP. The first one is that:

ERP is a Computer System?

Solution: Yes computer system and IT are integral part of an ERP system, but ERP is primarily an enterprise-wide system, which encompasses corporate mission objectives, attitudes, beliefs values operating style, and people who make the organization.

ERP is for Manufacturing Organization Alone?

Solution: This assumption is basically due to the way in which ERP was historically developed from the methods of Material Requirement Planning (MRP) and Manufacturing Resource Planning (MRP-II) which are relevant to manufacturing organisation.

But in reality, the concept of enterprise-wide planning of resources is not limited to any particular segment of industry.

IT Role in ERP Implementation

Successful implementation is the obvious goal of any organization that has chosen to go in for enterprise resource planning. Any ERP implementation is a special event since it involves the entire organisation over a period of time. It brings together different functionality, people procedures and ideologies and leads to sweeping changes throughout the organization.

ERP implementation is one of the fastest growing segments in the information technology industry today. To take advantage of emerging technologies and business practices and meet the evolving business requirements of a thriving industry, companies like People Soft, SAPAG, Baan, Qad, IFS, Ramco, etc. had launched their product in this field.

As we know that Information Technology is a mixture of computer Hardware and Software. If one can left the other stops. And as far as movement of ERP is concern it can work when the Information Technology is in its full flow.

Participants in the ERP Buying Process

The buying centre in any parts of the organization that plays any of the following roles in the purchase decision:

- Those who request that some ERP must be purchased. They may be users who initiate the proposal and help define the ERP requirements.
- Those who will use the software or service. In many cases, the users define the specifications and also provide information for evaluating alternatives.
- Technical personnel.
- People who decide on ERP requirements and/or on vendors.
- People who decide the proposed actions of deciders or buyers.
- People who have formal authority to select the vendor and arrange the purchase terms.
- Buyers may help shape product specifications, but they play their major role in selecting vendors and negotiating. In more complex purchases, the buyers might include high-level managers participating in the negotiations.

Within an organization, the buying centre will vary in the number and type for different classes of products. According to a pentagon research survey, the average number of people involved in a buying decision ranges between three and four. There is a trend toward team-base buying. Another pentagon survey found that 87% of purchasing executives at fortune 1000 companies expect teams of people from departments and functions to be making buying decisions in the year to target their efforts properly, business marketers have to figure out.

Who the major decision participants are?
What decisions do they influence?
What is their area of influence?
What evaluation criteria do they use?

REQUIREMENT OF ERP IN ANY ORGANIZATION

Before the start of any ERP selling process, the salesperson should find out the suitability of his or her ERP for a particular organization and should accept the fact that will be certainly required by

- Organizations who have a vision for leadership. To be a leader, it is necessary that the organization make the best use of the available resources.
- Organizations which are customer services driven.
- Organizations that are under tremendous pressure to be competitive because if fierce competition and are expected to perform above their level to sustain their position in the market place.
- Organizations that enter an already crowded market.
- Any organization in which the business processes is too complex and which, therefore, requires the highest level of coordination among its employees. To achieve this, they requires data from all departments that are integrated for correct decision-making and analysis.

THE FUNCTIONAL MODULES WHERE THE ERP HIT

ERP comprises a number of distinct yet seamlessly integrated modules that cover almost all your functional requirements.

ERP Functional Modules

Financials	Sales	Purchase	Receivables and Payables
Retail	Inventory	Funds Management	Budgeting
Multi-Currency and Forex	Asset Management	Production and Costing	Production Planning
Payroll	B2B Transactions	Branches and Profit Centres	Executive Info. System

Financials

ERP takes care of complete Financial Accounting of the enterprise over the web. It maintains all the books and records that are essential for proper book-keeping and accounting. All transactions affect and update the entire system, and all reporting is on the fly, for the most accurate information at all times.

Sales

ERP enables you to manage all aspects of sales-orders, deliveries, invoicing, and your customer databases with comprehensive sales analysis.

Purchase

Empower the Purchase function just like Sales, Indents, orders ERP covers all aspects of Production, including issues quality control, material receipts, purchase invoices and your to and receipts from Production, multiple Bills of Material, supplier database and comprehensive Purchase Analysis.

Receivables and Payables

Complete management of receivables and payables with bill-wise accounting, due dates and overdue bills, interest calculations, ageing analysis, ABC analysis and a lot more Production batches, cost sheets, standard costing, variance reports and the valuation of Work in Progress.

Retail

ERP includes a Point-of-Sale billing system with barcode label reading and printing, quick billing and collections.

Inventory

ERP offers total Inventory Management for all kinds of businesses. With unlimited products, grouped as appropriate, Quality Control, valuation on multiple bases, stock ledgers and list, ABC analysis, fast moving goods, dead stocks ageing analysis and more. ERP offers complete Reorder Management enabling you to achieve efficient management of stocks depending on minimum, maximum and reorder levels specified by you for each item of stock.

Funds Management

ERP enables you manage funds efficiently. For each ERP maintains your complete customer database. And does kind of transaction type, you may specify its effect on funds flow, Extensive Sales Analysis. Sales Analysis reports give you total sales information, sorted and presented by products parties, time periods, ERP offers you a forecast of funds based on or in any combination.

Budgeting

You can implement a complete Budgeting and Performance Analysis ERP enables you to manage all aspects of sales. Raise system, offering all variance reports, and periodically generating Quotations on customers. Book Sales Orders. Make Deliveries critical information and timely alerts. Variances can be configured Raise Invoices. You may also link Quotations to Orders, Orders to lead to locked transactions, or their being sent for authorization.

Multi-currency and Forex

ERP supports accounting for multi-currency operations with exchange rate tables, transactions in any currency, accounting and reporting in all currencies and accounting for forex gains and losses.

Asset Management

The system maintains complete records of fixed assets with all details of the assets and their location, with reminders for insurance expiry, AMC renewals and more . Depreciation can be computed in multiple ways, and assets can be revalued if required.

Production and Costing

ERP covers all aspects of Production, including issues to and receipts from Production batches, cost sheets, standard costing variance reports, and the valuation in work in progress.

Production Planning

ERP enables you to plan for material requirements based on a production planning process. The system reports inventory requirements based on work orders initiated, stocks committed and existing stocks. You can determine the optimum mix of inputs at all times.

Payroll

All your Payroll functions are taken care of. The system maintains the employee database, salary structures, and attendance and leave records. It generates pay slips and salary sheets, and all the statutory records essential for PF, ESI, Professional Tax and other such.

B2B Transactions

ERP is a virtual portal that can be accessed by customers, distributors, suppliers, and auditors. Anyone with a computer and a modem, and the necessary access permissions! They can place orders and monitor deliveries, and view account statements. Improve your servicing efficiency by letting your business associates manage their own interaction with your enterprise. All reporting can be individual, grouped, or instantly consolidated across the enterprise.

Branches and Profit Centres

You can integrate and perform accounting for an unlimited number of branches and Profit Centres. These can be grouped, as required and all reporting can be individual, grouped, or instantly consolidated across the enterprise.

Executive Information System

ERP offers the finest suite of user-friendly, instantaneous and relevant reports — tailored to individual requirements. A powerful Report Writer allows creation of your own reports with user specified contents, layout formatting, formulae, and conditions. Reports can be pre-scheduled, and also e-mailed to specified persons. A powerful Query Writer lets you define and save queries. Query reports can then come to you in a scheduled manner, or on demand.

ERP MARKET OF TODAY

A. Market has changed from internal optimization to external collaboration based on the present business focus on —

- Customer relationship,
- E-commerce, and
- C-commerce.

B. This challenge has been met through the development of web enabled ERP systems.

Web enabled ERP or extended resources planning (XRP) systems add the following functionally to the ERP suite –

- Customer relationship management (CRM),
- Store front/ E-channels,
- Supply chain management, and
- E-procurement.

From the above article it is clear that Enterprise Resource Planning play pivotal role in building and boosting the performance of any organization but one thing which we have to kept in our mind that it is Information Technology without it ERP did not move single steps. So in a gist form we can say that without IT, ERP is like a boat without rudder.

22

IT in Our Lives

A. RANGA REDDY

Information Technology (IT) has revolutionised the *modus operandi* of marketing, business and administration. The business horizon is humming with words like internet, world wide web (WWW), cyberspace, information super-highways, etc. These are changing the way of handling customers; order receiving and processing; and networking and integrating business system. The internet is a world-wide, self-governed network connecting thousands of smaller networks, and millions of computers and people of mega sources of information. This is a technology that shrinks vast distances, blurs political, ethnic and national boundaries. Technology experts are anticipating that the internet and the WWW would become the centre of commercial universe. Electronic markets will eliminate the need for intermediaries and that direct contact between manufacturer and customer will bring down the cost of transaction and the cost of the final product. It is possible for customers and suppliers to transact business at any time in any part of the globe, without having to come together physically, especially with the development of optical fibre technology, videophone and tele-conferencing facilities. The UN believes that in today's world, accessible telecommunications is now a human right as the same footing as health care and literacy. Consider that 62 per cent of North Americans currently have internet access, the number is less than 1 per cent in Africa.

The IT industry both software and hardware is characterised by vast consumer side scale and scope economies which are incomparably larger than the supply side network economies in industries like pipelines or electricity distribution. In East Africa, the internet has been effectively used to make micro-loans to small entrepreneurs. These and many such innovative efforts would help India tide over the emerging problems of a digital divide. Information and communication technologies could enable even the least developing countries to leapfrog traditional problems to modern information age.

IT has significantly transformed the distribution system. Effective use of IT in distribution can help companies reduce inventories, delivery time, and stock-outs, respond faster to market changes, reduce rush orders, cut down over production, reduce unnecessary movement, reduce paper work, and plan production better. IT is drastically changing the distribution systems. IT has also greatly contributed to the retail revolution, which is sweeping the entire world. Retailing has now become a global business. The retailing revolution has shifted as such from fragmented to consolidated, local to global, low technology use to high technology, owner-operated to systems driven, traders to retail brand managers, mass marketing to individualized relationship customisation and market place to market space. Retailing in developed markets is increasingly becoming net-tailing or e-tailing. E-commerce is becoming more prevalent in business to business marketing. In developed countries tele-marketing has been progressing. Tele-marketing blossomed in the U.S. in the late 1960s with the introduction of inbound and outbound Wide Area Telephone Service (WATs).

Global business indeed is increasingly becoming e-business. Extra-net also links dealers, retailers and distributors so that a company can have better controls on the delivery of finished goods.

There has been an explosive growth in the use of internet and e-commerce world-wide. Between 1993 and 1997, the number of internet hosts (computers connected to the internet) grew from one million to 20 million, by 2001 that figure is expected to rise to 120 million. The value of the global internet commerce is huge. Estimates of it range from 1.3 per cent to 3.3 per cent of Gross Domestic Product by 2001 – about $ 0.5 to over 1 trillion.

Indians have made a glorious imprint in the new economy particularly in the software sector. The Silicon Valley provides ample tribute to the entrepreneurial potentials of Indians. Back home, there are number of firms which have achieved spectacular success. Infosys started out with a Rs. 10,000 capital, in February 2000, it was worth Rs. 66,000 crore and more than a hundred of its managers were each work over a million dollars. Another in NIIT, which has franchise (like MacDonald's) 750 computer schools in Indian bazars and in 31 countries. On February 22, 2000, Azim Premji had become the third richest man in the world on Forbes ranking, based on the market capitalization of his software company, which crossed Rs. 2,00,000 crore or 11.3 per cent of India's GDP. With this wealth, Premji could pay for India's fiscal deficit and still have money left over.

Information technology has brought tremendous change in day-to-day activity of common man to entrepreneur. The number of mobile subscribers went up from 10.4 million at the end of 2002 to 28.20 million in December 2003. The average monthly growth in mobile subscriptions are 1.5 million new users in 2003. According to the Telecom Regulatory Authority of India, the primary reason for the unprecedented growth was a 50 per cent decline in tariffs over the previous year. At present, mobile telephony tariffs are just 5 per cent of the rate that prevailed in 1995, making it the lowest in the world. Delhi and Mumbai continue to be the biggest markets. However, the States of Gujarat, Maharashtra, Andhra Pradesh, Karnataka and Tamil Nadu have a combined base of 8 million mobile subscribers, which is more than all the metros combined. During 2003 around 17.5 million mobile subscribers were added, bringing the total to 28.20 million against 42.0 million fixed lines.

Railways have initiated four mission programmes in the field of traction and rolling stock, track and bridges signal and communications and fog vision instrumentation have been jointly identified by RDSO and IIT, Kanpur. Successful trials of the anticollision device (ACD), named as '*Raksha Kavach*' have been completed. Already applied for 3,465 kms. and 10,000 kms. are in progress. Further, the frontiers of the much-acclaimed customer friendly computerized Passenger Reservation System (PRS) have been expanded with the introduction of internet booking and also introduced computerized Unreserved Ticketing System (UTS), which has won the appreciation of the travelling public. Again, e-ticketing will be introduced in the reservation segment, in which passengers will get their reservations booked through internet and occupy their reserved seats on the basis of a computer generated slip. In addition to it, in the event of delayed departure of Rajdhani, Shatabdi and Jan Shatabdi trains by more than 30 minutes, passengers who so desire can get information regarding this on their mobile phones through SMS.

To tackle the inconsistencies a major was launched in Akola

district of Maharashtra as usual, blackmarketing on the beginning of year 2000 to detect bogus ration cards. The data was entered into the computers at the District supply office at various Tehsils. Efficient publicity was given. The data collected during survey is compared with the existing ration card registers and bogus ration cards are thereafter removed. This gives a saving at least Rs. 50-60 million to government each year.

A farmer of Madhya Pradesh logs on the website of the Chicago Board of Trade. He gets the prices for Soyabean commodity futures. A drop in prices on the Chicago Board augur a drop in prices here. If it goes up there, it goes up here also. E-choupals allow farmers to check both future prices before going to market. It gives them access to total weather conditions, soil testing techniques and other expert knowledge that will increase productivity. E-choupals may offer a model for developing nations and is a new form of liberalization.

IT PARKS

Government of Andhra Pradesh gave considerable stress on creation of IT Parks through provision of certain incentives and initiatives. The salient features of this initiative are that IT parks can be built in residential, commercial, institutional and industrial zones without payment of any conversion charges. IT parks with a total space of over 30 lakh sq. ft. are likely to come up during the years 2001 and 2002 taking the advantage of the policy. The Government has catalyzed the creation of Hitech city – a world class IT infrastructure facility. There is also a plan to create the infrastructure required for setting up of a hardware park near the proposed International Airport at Shamshabad. An area of over 5000 acres around the Hitech city is being notified as Cyberabad to give a fillip to the development of IT infrastructure in the area on world class lines. The government is also attempting to disperse the benefit of IT to the other parts of the state by promoting setting up of IT parks at Vizag, Vijayawada, Tirupati and Warangal in a phased manner in conjunction with STPI. The e-seva has become more popular with the urban middle class in Hyderabad. It is planned for extension to 56 other towns with a total of 146 centres. These are basically collection centres for various bills/fees like telephone, electricity, trade license fee, etc., applications from the citizens and are integrated with several departments.

Bharat Sanchar Nigam Limited (BSNL) introduced India Telephone

Card (ITC), which would offer special concessional calling rates to people going to pilgrim centres such as Tirupati and Sabarimalai. Similarly, it is now offering a special package for Haj pilgrims, which offers a 25 per cent concession in ISD tariff for calls to Saudi Arabia. Special facilities offered include setting up of free telephone at airport terminals for handling Haj pilgrims. In Andhra Pradesh, BSNL was working on a special scheme for providing 3,000 cellular connections to Andhra Pradesh police at Rs. 300 a month rental with Virtual Private Network (VPN) free facility, which would enable police personnel to speak within their group, virtually free of cost.

E-SEVA SYSTEM

The TTDs (Tirumala Tirupati Devasthanams) administration had introduced e-seva system for devotees to regulate the timings of darshan, which has been quite successful. Internet booking of Kalyanams and Darshanams has also become popular with pilgrims. By introducing information technology in seva, lot of time, money was saved and also reduced unfair trade practices like corruption, delay, negligence and indifference towards devotees. Further, it would be introducing Sri Venkateswara Information Technology Trust, which would be used to modernise the administration, and after free education and food to orphans under Balamandir Trust.

IT has reduced the distances and blurred the political, ethnic and national boundaries. Electronic markets would eliminate the middlemen bringing in direct contact the producer and consumer. Telemarketing is progressing in developing countries at a fast pace. Infosys, Wipro, NIIT are emerging giants in developing IT both in urban and rural India.

23

IT and Business: A Means of Rapid Development

SAWALIA BIHARI VERMA

INTRODUCTION

Information is the lifeline of any matter related to business. The development of information technology (IT) helps in the development of people, their living standards, day-to-day marketing activities and many more activities. IT is leading towards cost effective solutions, with a small size, higher speed, more flexibility and greater performance. It covers new developing areas in the field of technology, such as telecommunication network, internet, intranet and electronic commerce (E-commerce).

Business firms are, today becoming highly competitive in most parts of the world. They are under great pressure to transform their operating environment in order to effective face the challenge of ever-increasing competition. Most business firms are trying to give information about their products or services and deliver in the shortest period of time and to ensure customer satisfaction with the developing technology. With the development of electronic commerce (e-commerce), we can buy/order goods and services at an electronic speed. Without going anywhere we can order and buy a product. The world has now become a global village where distance is no longer a matter.

Importance of IT

IT has come as a force to cause our cultures, customs and communities move forward and advance human civilization. In the process, it will find new applications and create new jobs and equality. IT changes traditional work habits and work norms, i.e., the work environment, to modern efficient and effective work activities. These work activities are performed in offices, factories, government agencies, business units and universities as IT provides new tools and techniques to deal with the knowledge, with far-reaching implications for the future decision-making process. Using IT, information in exchange at electronic speeds, saves time and information is available in no time. IT is used in insurance companies, banks, travel agencies, medical departments or institutions and many other establishments for dealing or interacting with people to fill forms, consider insurance claims, accept premium payments, make prompt payment arrangements, negotiate over differences, etc.

IT Infrastructure

A suitable IT infrastructure is necessary for meeting the information needs of managers, supervisors and other business-related people. It is necessary to plan the IT infrastructure and develop it in the light of the needs and priorities of an enterprise. A common IT infrastructure helps reduce the costs per user, increasing the likelihood of people making efforts to use it and sustain its use for it being a success at a later stage when the user matures. The elements of an IT infrastructure are as follows:

Information

Information is the most important element of an IT infrastructure. It is a common resource and needs to be developed and shared for better utilization.

Service

Information services are facilities for the generation of information and they are dynamic. An IT infrastructure must have services for the generation of information on a regular basis.

Network

IT is a physical system for linking the users of information with the stock of information as well as the process of generating information.

IT Resources

Information is generated by processing facts which are represented by symbols, such as alphabets, digits, diagrams, graphs, pictures, etc. These are popularly known as data. For the purpose of developing services for the generation of information, one has to have processing resources or IT resources. These resources may be broadly classified into four categories, namely, hardware (computer hardware), software, data and human resources.

Hardware

Hardware/computer hardware refers to computer systems and associated equipment including communication links. With the rapid advancement in computer hardware technology, a large variety of computer systems with varying sizes, speeds and functional features are available.

Software

The sets of inter-related computer programmes are collectively called computer software. Software is the lifeline of an IT infrastructure and it makes a computer hardware function.

Data

Data are collections of facts or events represented in the form of symbols, such as digits, alphabets, pictures, graphs, etc. Computing, processing and storage of data are the essential functions of any IT infrastructure.

Human Resources

Human resources are the important resource of IT. The effectiveness of an IT infrastructure is a function of the type of IT personnel available to it. In fact, the best computer hardware, software and data may be spoiled and may cause havoc if the human resources are not competent, honest and reliable. Qualities like competence, honestly and reliability are critical to any work environment. Thus, human resources having the above qualities are the most important resource of IT.

Business Information System

A business information system is a set of procedures using an IT infrastructure in a business enterprise to generate and disseminate desired information. Such a system is designed to support decision-making by the people associated with the enterprise in the attainment of its objectives.

A business information system is no longer meant to be used only by the employees of an enterprise, namely, the manager and the operating staff. The infrastructure should aim at providing information for all those who are associated with the enterprise in the achievement of its goals. These include shareholders, investors, customers, vendors, statutory bodies, industry promotion bodies, employees, unions, etc. in addition to the prime users, the manager and the operating personnel in the business enterprise.

Business Information Systems in India

The use of modern IT resources for a business information system is yet to gain momentum. Indian business was, till recently, under no pressure to transform itself because of the protection given by the Government in the form of licensing system. With the opening up of the economy, Indian business is feeling the impact of fierce competition, both from domestic and foreign rivals. As a result, the Indian corporate world is waking up to shake up the dead wood and have a fresh look at the changing business scenario.

Information Technology and People

Information is required for day-to-day matters. For knowing about a place, a product and other matters like social incidents, weather forecasts etc., we need information. With the development of IT we have been able to know about them, which has helped to plan for the near future. We can talk on the telephone with friends, relatives, etc. staying at far places for their business or study. Now the whole world has become a small family. Again, with the development of electronic commerce, one can demand a product for purchase on the electronic media in no time and buy it without going to the producer's or supplier's place. It saves time and money and leads towards the rapid advancement of people.

Electronic Commerce (E-Commerce)

Internet based E-commerce is now accepted as one of the most important developments in conducting business. This is how the World Trade Organisation (WTO) defines E-commerce: "The production, distribution, marketing, sales or delivery of goods and services by electronic means is known as E-Commerce. A commercial transaction can be divided into three main stages: the first stage is the advertising and searching stage; ordering and payment is the second stage and the third stage is the delivery stage. Any or all of these may be carried out electronically and may, therefore, be covered by the concept of E-Commerce."

Types of E-Commerce

E-Commerce comprises four broad types of activity. They are: (i) Business to business, (ii) Business to consumer, (iii) Business to government, and (iv) Inter-organisational. Of these, Business to business is the biggest one today. E-Commerce takes two forms: (a) direct e-commerce, and (b) indirect e-commerce. Direct e-commerce takes place where the product or service, viz. music or professional advice, is delivered directly to the buyer electronically. Indirect e-commerce takes place where the product is ordered on the net but is delivered in a normal way. The following diagrams (diagram 1, diagram 2 and diagram 3) show the different types of e-commerce activity, the two important forms of e-commerce and the processes of direct and indirect e-commerce, respectively.

Advantages of E-Commerce

There are various advantages of e-commerce. Some of the advantages which relate to business are given below:

(1) *Minimizing inventory costs*

Inventory cost can be minimized by adopting just-in-time systems and enhancing the firm's ability to forecast demand more accurately.

DIAGRAM 1

Types of E-commerce

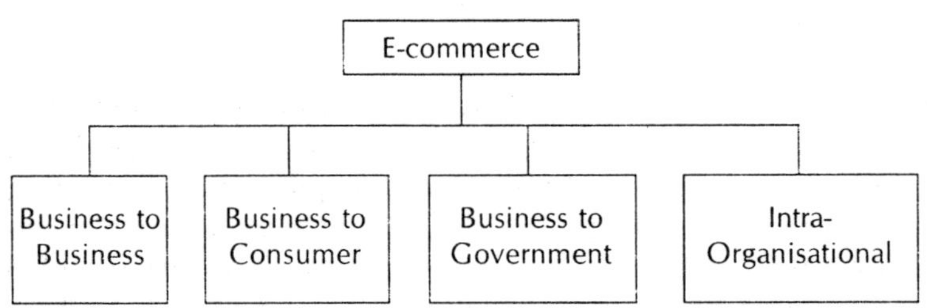

DIAGRAM 2

Terms of E-commerce

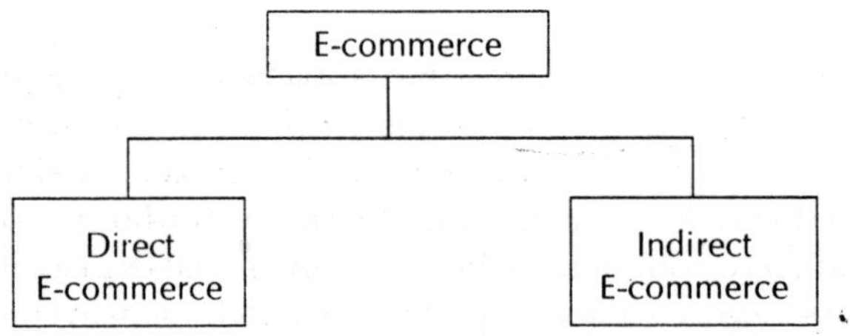

DIAGRAM 3

Processes of Direct and Indirect E-commerce

A. Direct E-commerce

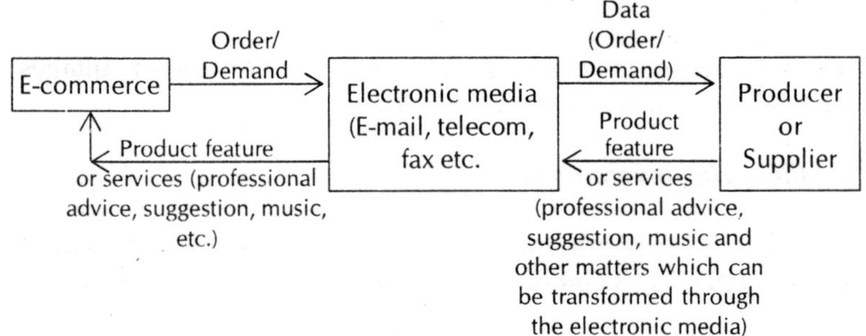

B. Indirect E-commerce

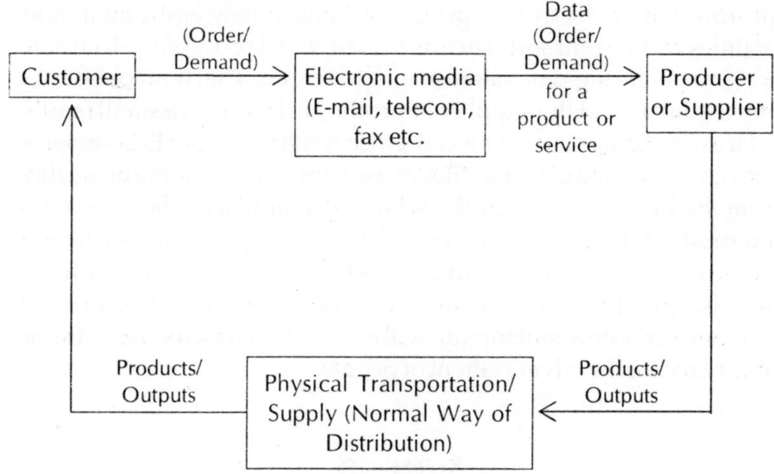

(2) *Improving customer service*

It has been found that, since under e-commerce many services can be put on-line, it can provide both before and after sales services.

(3) *Reduced distribution cost*

Because of the use of electronic machines, the time needed to process orders declines by 50 to 96 per cent. Thus, the distribution cost reduces.

(4) *Global reach*

The internet provides a large or small company with an opportunity to make information on its products and services available to all the potential customers in the world at a minimum cost and in a very short time.

CONCLUSION

Information Technology (IT) is finding applications in business activities, offices, factories and many other areas vital for meeting basic human needs. The office of the future concept, with electronic technology, is aimed at creating paperless offices to document file and transmit information at electronic speed. It relates to new equipment and facilities of different sorts such as E-mail, word processor, electronic filing, conferencing; data-based management, fax. The common people, the customers and the supplier or producers belong to a small family so far as day-to-day business is concerned. With the help of E-Commerce one can buy a product for domestic use from his/her home or locality from the producer or supplier who is at a far place. The internet is required in the trade policies of both the developing and developed nations. Free trade over the internet will be the dream of many trade unions, practitioners world-wide. With the globalisation of commerce, the new millennium will have a special focus on electronic commerce for the advancement of people.

References

Books

1. M.S. Swaminathan, *Information Technology: A Dialogue*, McMillan India Ltd., 1993.
2. Sam Pitroda, *Exploding Freedom*, Allied Publishers Ltd., 1993.
3. Muneesh Kumar, *Business Information System*, Vikas Publishing House Pvt. Ltd., 1998.
4. Dr. Sawalia Bihari Verma, *Rural Development through Electronic Media*, Avishkar Publication, Jaipur, 2004.

Journals

1. "Information Systems Management", *Information Systems Computer World*, July 1-15, 1998, Vol. 3, No. 17.
2. *Computers Today*, 16-30 November, 1999.
3. *Yojana*, August, 1998, Independence Day Special.
4. *Yojana*, Vol. 43, No. 4, April 1998.
5. *Yojana*, Vol. 43, No. 10, October 1999.
6. *Panorama Year Book*, 1998.
7. *Frontline*, December 4, 1998.
8. *Business World*, 25 October, 1999.
9. *Business World*, 8 November, 1999.
10. *Business World*, 22 November, 1999.
11. *Business India*, October 18-31, 1999.

24

Supply Chain Management in E-Business

SITARAM SHARMA, SHIV KUMAR JILOKA AND BUCHESHWAR MANDAL

Supply chain is the network of organizations that are involved through upstream and downstream linkages in the different processes and activities that produce value in the form of products and services in the hands of ultimate customer. Supply Chain Management is an external integration or inter-related functions of the firm with its channel members, vendors, and all third party logistics service providers who contribute in the flow of goods (raw-materials, semi-finished and finished) and related information from the point of inception to the point of consumption with efficiency. In other words, SCM is an integrated management of various functions in the areas or materials, operations, distributions, marketing and after sales services with a customer focus perspective so as to bring synergy in various processes across the organization with a view of optimizing the total cost. It refers to a managerial process of a joint approach of all supply chain participants to design, develop and operate a system, which responds to customer expectations by making available right quantity of right quality products at right time and place in right physical form at a right cost so as to offer best customer service in cost efficient manner. The business world has come to refer to networks of companies, business partners and affiliates as "chains", Michael E. Porter of the Harvard Business School first established the term "value chain" to describe the range of inter-linked activities that a business uses to make and sell its goods and services. According to him, the process or activities by which a firm delivers value to its customers as the firm internal value chain.

A supply chain is the link that moves products between suppliers, manufacturers, wholesalers, distributors, retailers and finally consumers. It is a network of facilities and distribution options that performs the functions of procurement of materials, transformation of these materials into work-in-progress and finished products and finally providing availability of these finished products to customers. The complexity of the supply chain may vary greatly from industry to industry and organization to organization. It is the combination of art, science and management that goes into improving the way the company finds the raw components, manufactures that product and delivers it to customers.

FIVE BASIC COMPONENTS OF SUPPLY CHAIN MANAGEMENT (SCM) ARE AS FOLLOWS

1. Plan

This is the strategic portion of supply chain management, a strategy for managing all the resources that go toward meeting customer demand for the product. A big piece of planning is developing a set of matrices to monitor the supply chain so that it is efficient, cost effective and delivers high quality and value to customers.

2. Source

Choose the suppliers that will deliver the goods required for the product, besides develop a set of pricing, delivery and payment processes with suppliers and create matrices for monitoring the timely delivery and improving the relationships.

3. Make

This is manufacturing and scheduling the activities necessary for production, testing, packaging and preparation for delivery.

4. Deliver

This refer to as "logistics," i.e. to coordinate the receipt of orders from customers, develop a network of warehouses, pick carriers to get products to customers and set-up an invoicing system to receive payments.

5. Return

The problem part is to create a network for receiving defective and excess products back from customers and supporting customers who have problems with delivered products, along with after sales service support.

Therefore, coordination between the various components in the chain is the key in its effective management. Supply chain management can be compared to a well-balanced and well-practiced relay team. Such a team is more competitive when each player knows how to be positioned for the hand-off. The relationships are the strongest between players who directly pass the baton, but the entire team needs to make a coordinated effort to win the race.

An example of a supply chain for a single product is very simple, i.e. raw material is procured from vendors, transformed into finished goods in a single step, and then transported to distribution centres, and ultimately to customers. Realistic supply chains have multiple end products with shared components, facilities and capacities. The flow of materials is not always along an arborescent network, various modes of transportation may be considered, and the bill of materials for the end items may be both deep and large.

Throughout the supply chain, there are *some absolutely critical and predictive questions* the system should accurately and quickly answer:

1. When will specific orders really ship?
2. Which orders will be late?
3. Why will these orders be late?
4. What are the specific problems that are delaying the schedule?
5. What are the future schedule problems and when will they occur?
6. What is the best schedule that can be executed now?

Generally, an effective SCM approach must focus on:

7. Flexible supply and production processes that can very quickly respond to changing customer demand.
8. A short-cycle, demand-driven order-to-delivery process.

9. Accurate relevant information that is available on demand throughout the supply chains.

SUPPLY CHAIN INTEGRATION

The major components: marketing, distribution, planning, manufacturing, and purchasing are organized independently and work the supply chain management cohesively. These components have their own objectives and these are often conflicting. Marketing's objective of high customer service and maximum sales conflict with manufacturing and distribution goals, which are designed to maximize output and lower costs with little consideration for the impact on inventory levels and distribution capabilities. Purchasing contracts are often negotiated with very little information beyond historical buying patterns. The result of these factors is that there is not a single, integrated plan for the organization as there are as many plans as businesses. Clearly, there is a need for a mechanism through which these different functions can be integrated together. Supply chain management is a strategy through which such integration can be achieved.

Over the past decade a combination of economic, technology and market forces has compelled companies to examine and re-invent their supply chain strategies. Some of these forces include the globalization of businesses, the proliferation of product variety, increasing complexity of supply networks, and the shortening of the product life cycles. To stay competitive, enlightened companies have strived to achieve greater coordination and collaboration among supply chain components in an approach called "supply chain integration".

Information technology, and in particular, the internet, play a key role in furthering the goals of supply chain integration. While the most visible manifestation of the internet has been in the emergence of electronic commerce as a new retail channel, it is likely that the internet will have an even more profound impact on business-to-business interaction, especially in the area of supply chain integration. The Internet can redefine how back-end operations or product design and development, procurement, production, inventory, distribution, after-sales service support, and even marketing are conducted, and in the process alter the roles and relationships of various parties, fostering new supply networks, services and business models. The different dimensions of supply chain integrated in this changing environment is given and explained on next page.

Dimension	*Elements*	*Benefits*
Information	Information sharing and Transparency	Reduced Bullwhip effect
Integration	Direct and real-time accessibility	Early problem detection
Synchronized planning	• Collaborative planning, forecasting, replenishment • Joint Design	• Reduced Bullwhip effect • Lower cost • Optimized capacity utilization • Improved service
Workflow coordination	• Coordinated production, planning and operations • Procurement, order processing, engineering change and design • Integrated automated business success	• Efficiency and accuracy gains • Fast response • Improved service • Earlier time to market • Expanded network
New business models	• Virtual resources • Logistic restructuring • Mass customization • New services • Brick and Mortar models	• Better asset utilization • Higher efficiency • Penetrate new markets • Create new products

INFORMATION INTEGRATION

Information integration refers to the sharing of information among members of the supply chain. This includes any type of data that could influence the actions and performance of other members of the supply chain. Some examples include: demand data, inventory status, capacity plans, production schedules, promotion plans, and shipment schedules. Ideally, such information can be accessed by the appropriate parties on a real-time, on-line basis without significant efforts.

SYNCHRONIZED PLANNING

Planning synchronization refers to the joint design and execution of plans for product introduction, forecasting and replenishment. In essence, planning synchronization defines what is to be done with the information that is shared: it is the mutual agreements among members as, to specific actions based on that information. Hence, members in a supply chain may have their order fulfilment plans coordinated so that all replenishment are made to meet the same objective – the ultimate customer demands.

WORK FLOW COORDINATION

Work flow coordination refers to streamlined and automated work flow activities between supply chain partners. Here, we take integration one step further by defining not just "what" we would do with shared information, but "how" to utilize this information for effective integration and efficiency. For example, procurement activities from a manufacturer to a supplier can be tightly coupled so that efficiencies in terms of accuracy, time, and cost can be achieved. Product development activities involving multiple companies can also be integrated to achieve similar efficiencies. In the best-case situation, supply chain partners would rely on technology solutions to actually automate many or all of the internal and cross-company workflow steps.

NEW BUSINESS MODELS

Adopting e-business approaches to supply chain integration promises more than just incremental improvements in efficiency. Many companies are discovering whole new approaches to conducting business, and even getting new business opportunities, which were not previously possible. E-business allows partners redefine logistics flows so that the roles and responsibilities of members may change to improve overall supply chain efficiency. A supply chain network may jointly create new products, pursue mass customization and penetrate new markets and customer segments. New rules of the supply chain management can emerge as a result of integration fuelled by the Internet.

The Central Theme of SCM is Around Integration Cooperation: Integration cannot be complete without a tight linkage of the organizational relationships between companies. This linkage must take place on many planes.

(a) Channels or communication must be well defined and maintained, with roles and responsibilities clearly articulated.
(b) Performance measures for members of the supply chain also need to be specified and monitored. A member of the supply

chain may be held accountable for some performance measures of another member.

(c) Incentives must be aligned for all members in order for supply chain integration to work. Incentive alignment requires a careful definition of mechanisms in which the risks and associated gains of integration efforts are equitably shared. Moreover, the incentive for each member must commensurate with his investment and risk.

E-BUSINESS AND ELECTRONIC INFORMATION INTEGRATION

The term "e-business" as distinct from "e-commerce" can be used to describe this exciting adoption or the Internet to accelerate the goal of supply chain integration. In this context, e-business specifically refers to "the planning and execution of the front-end and back-end operations in a supply chain using the Internet". In fact, e-business has already had a significant impact on supply chain integration, but it is safe to say that we have only scratched the surface. New models are continuously being developed. By adopting e-business approaches for supply chain integration, companies can realize dramatic returns through efficiency improvements, better asset utilization, faster time to market, reduction in total order fulfilment times, enhanced customer service and responsiveness, penetrating new markets, higher return on assets, and ultimately, higher shareholder value.

The success of any supply chain integration effort is predicted on close cooperation inspired by a perception of mutual benefit and can go a long way toward fostering the necessary level of trust and commitment. For e-commerce the most significant aspect of the World Wide Web is its provision of a single, universally accepted standard for communication between corporate business systems. Proliferating Web-based integration between major organizations, their customers and their suppliers is driving explosive growth in business-to-business integration which is conservatively forecast to grow from a total value of $ 40 billion in 2001 to some $ 550 billion by 2008.

The Internet has transformed this archaic process into something closer to an exact science. An Internet-enabled supply chain may have just-in-time delivery, precise inventory visibility and to the minute distribution-tracking capabilities. With technology advances, supply chains have moved from the paper-heavy adventure noted earlier to a strategic weapon that can help avoid disasters, lower costs and make money. Automating a supply chain requires careful planning, and must start with an excellent understanding of relationships with partners and customers. With Web technology, all the components in the chain simultaneously manage inventory, control manufacturing schedules and deliver an order on time to a customer.

Supply chain management projects should also rethink the chain. Most businesses establish their supply chains around product lines. But today, customer orders touch multiple product lines and multiple channels of distribution. Modern supply chains focus on the customer — and on delivering one order at a time rather than moving one product line at a time. The focus has to be on tilling, delivering and managing inventory for every order that a customer places. Every order should penetrate the same system that manages inventory and connects to suppliers and distributors.

To utilize opportunities offered by business-to-business e-commerce, organizations need to adapt to an environment in which the supply chain management is the principal source of shareholder value. This transition is led by companies, mainly in the communications and computer sectors, who understand the technology and its implications and choose to work only with others among the 'best'. As a group they are characterized by their ability to:

- Grow at 25% per year,
- Operate on a global scale without excessive levels of people and assets, and
- Achieve levels of profitability 20% or higher than their nearest competitors.

As e-commerce has evolved, companies have been changing the way they do business in several areas: through new products and channels to re-invent customer interactions, development of entirely new business models, new access to critical capabilities, and new methods for customer-supplier relationships based upon the relative power of each party. The design of this new business model is based on the concept of digital supply chain to achieve both supplier customer satisfaction and company profitability. It is fast and flexible system that is align with and driven by new customer choice mechanism. SCM in e-Economy offers new opportunities as well as impose challenges. That is why companies need to manage increasing levels of complexity; extended hours; an increased workload in parts of the value chain by virtue of smaller; more frequent ordering and delivery; an expanded geographic base; shorter time names; and a higher emphasis on time accuracy and excellence in service delivery.

Traditional effective management practices may not transfer directly to an e-commerce environment. It is volatile, widely entrepreneurial and technically complex, generally calling for a new leadership style and corporate culture. The electronics and high-tech industry is one that has the foundations and leadership dynamics that are most aligned with the characteristics of successful e-economy leadership. Leaders in this industry have embraced a hand-off leadership style and succeeded in embedding the spirit of innovation, entrepreneurial, calculated risk-taking and continuous innovation into their cultures. Furthermore, connectivity between partners is the key element of new management practices. Without connectivity there can be no effective use of electronic interface and no seamless information, money and physical product flows. Hence, at the advent of the Internet and amazing growth of e-commerce in the e-economy, there is gradual change in the value chain of supply chain management mainly due to addition of digital value. The value chain activities involve the creation, processing, and communication of information, so, information technology has a pervasive influence on the value chain. The special advantage of the Internet is the ability to link one activity with others and make real-time data created in one activity widely available, both within the company and with outside suppliers, channels, and customers. By incorporating a common, open set of communication protocols, Internet technology provides a standardized infrastructure, an intuitive browser interface for information access and delivery, bi-directional communication, and case of connectivity—all at much lower cost than private networks and electronic data interchange or EDI.

In this new supply chain process, every organization interacts on a daily basis with three major entities: customers, suppliers, and partners. With the advent of digital markets, electronic supply chains and virtual partnerships, organizations must now look at these entities through a virtual cloud of sub-entities. Often referred to collectively as the "new Net connections", this cloud becomes like a junction box for reaching customers, suppliers, and partners. The junction box permits an amplified and simultaneous entry to these new market places may be called as Customer Net, Supplier Net, and Partner Net.

This new value chain of SCM ensures seamless flow of goods,

information, value as well as cash within the supply chain on a real time basis facilitating best and consistent quality, minimum costs, quick response. Availability or goods in time without stock-out and consistency and reliability or services. The Web-based supply chain system ensures collection, organization, selection, and distribution of information to the point of uses on real-time basis for hyper responsiveness capabilities of the firm as information have been shined from secondary function to enable of primary functions. Thus, Web-based SCM further empowered corporate enterprises to have competitive effectiveness in global market place.

CONCLUSION

The Internet has changed the management or whole supply chain dramatically. The advent of open real-time communications among manufacturers, suppliers, distributors, and customers has redefined the whole process. Linked through cyber space, any partner in the group can take the lead, and all of the participants lend their support, creating a complicated pattern or interactions. Well-executed Web-based supply chain implementations can drive significant business improvement across the entire value chain, reducing costs, increasing profits, and enhancing competitive advantage through dynamic collaboration among partners. Furthermore, speedier mutual information flow enables them to understand problems and trends in the market coupled with finding out ways and means for the best solution to the problem. That is why, in the supply chain relationships, more collaborative communication strategies are used. Relationships cannot be developed without two-way exchange of information concerned with the parties respective goals, wants, issues, inputs and priorities. Since relational exchanges are characterized by higher level of independence, supply chain partners need to interact more to make relationships alive, working and conflict free. True Web-based supply chain and logistic initiatives expand the view of a company's supply chain beyond its own four walls to include the inner workings of several tiers of suppliers, distributors, and other corporate partners, even when those partners are halfway around the world.

Using Information Technology advantage, strategic issues have been analysed and a model has been created for e-Synchronized SCM by thinking on the subject of e-business and supply chain management achieved by answering to the relevant questions by an empirical method. The impact of e-business on supply chain integration, with particular emphasis on three key areas: information sharing, synchronized planning, workflow coordination, help in the evolution of new business models. It offers real-world examples of how companies large and small have adopted e-business approaches to achieve the significant benefits of supply chain integration. It illustrates the power of e-business with innovating technology solutions. Cross-supply chain performance monitoring will be a critical success factor in achieving the advantages inherent in supply chain integration.

By carefully choosing e-Synchronized solutions and by implementing "hands-free" procurement, a company can achieve great savings and benefits. The key success factor for e-Synchronization is the change in business processes. E-Synchronized supply chain, and virtual office are soon to become a reality and to be incorporated in the business practices.

For electronic supply chain management to be successful, the crux is whether a company has created processes to cover its entire business and is implementing them by means of an appropriate IT arrangement. By looking at the systems in use in the individual fields of industry, one can see how the various value-added chain partners are integrated into planning and also what is the relationship regarding information systems and their content between those partners.

REFERENCES

Aggarwal, D.K. and S. Sharma, "Supply Chain Management in E-economy—A Value Chain Prospective".

Agrawal, D.K. (2001), "7 Ms to make Supply Chain Relationships Harmonious", Proceedings of NCPPO, PMIR, Indore, Excel Book, New Delhi, pp. 405-12.

Assem Kumar and S. Shodangi, "E-synchronized Supply Chain Management in Global Economy".

Davis, T. (1993), "Effective Supply Chain", *Management Review*, 34(4), p. 64.

Verma, S.B., *Information Technology and Management*, Deep & Deep Publication Pvt. Ltd., New Delhi.

25

Electronic Trading Analysis: Trade Index Approach

ALOK SRIVASTAVA

The modern era is of electronic trading between modern electronic digital economies across the world under the existing global electronic digital trade environment. Most of the world's traditional economies have been transformed into the modern electronic digital economies and the sustenance of traditional economies is likely to be at stake in the near future. The major business organizations, industries and individual firms of the developed modern, electronic digital economies have already imbibed the modern electronic digital communication system i.e., global internet/world-wide website system (www) of electronic digital communication system on a large scale and are carrying out global trading transactions through this modern electronic digital communication system across the world. This system is based upon the application of developed latest information communication technology which is based on the applied electronic digital science of communication. This system has enabled the developed modern electronic digital economies in promoting their very large number of global trade transaction very fastly and safely with prompt maximum efficiency at the optimal trading cost within possible shortest duration irrespective of their distances and locations in the world.

Under aforesaid global electronic digital trade environment the demand for software computer programmes for global electronic digital trade transactions, foreign trade relations, terms and agreements of foreign trade relations, etc. regarding the trading partner countries across the globe has increased very significantly. There is a big question as how this herculean task is to be accomplished? To meet this end there is a need for considering trade index approach towards quantitative analysis of electronic trading transactions between modern electronic digital economies which assumes that the whole world market is a single market and acquisition of their globalization status through mass customization operation as their top priority goal to achieve their accruing of maximized total trade gains at the optimal cost of their global trading transactions across the global market without sacrificing their long-term trading interests and goodwill in the world market and also meeting the general interests of consumers at large across the globe during specified period. This trade index approach refers to the measurement of export and import intensities of a country which is carrying out the trading transactions with, any other trading partner country of the world. There may be two types of trade intensity index which are briefed as follows:

(a) Export Intensity Index (E_{ij})

The export intensity index of exporting country i to trading partner country j of the world is a ratio between the ratio of exports of country i to trading partner country j of the world and total world exports of country i and the ratio of total imports of country j and excess of total world imports over total imports of country i. It may be expressed in mathematical form as follows:

$$E_{ij} = \frac{[x_{ij}/X_i]}{[M_j/(M_w - M_i)]}$$

where

E_{ij} = export intensity index of exporting country i to trading partner country j of the world,

X_{ij} = exports of country i to trading partner country j of the world,

X_i = total world exports of country i,

M_j = total imports of country j,

M_w = total world imports, and

M_i = total imports of country i.

The range of value of E_{ij} is $0 \leq E_{ij} \leq 1$. It's possible results may be as follows:

(i) $0 \leq E_{ij} < 0.50 \Rightarrow$ insignificant export intensity of country i to trading partner country j of the world.
(ii) $0.50 \leq E_{ij} < 0.75 \Rightarrow$ significant export intensity of country i to trading partner country j of the world.
(iii) $0.75 \leq E_{ij} \leq 1.00 \Rightarrow$ very significant export intensity of country i to trading partner country j of the world.

(b) Import Intensity Index [I_{ij}]

The import intensity index of importing country i from trading partner country j of the world is a ratio between the ratio of imports of country i from trading partner country j of the world and total world imports of country i and the ratio of total imports of country j and excess of total world exports over total exports of country i. It may be expressed in mathematical form as follows:

$$I_{ij} = \frac{[M_{ij}/M_i]}{[x_j/(x_w - x_i)]}$$

where

I_{ij} = import intensity index of importing country i from trading partner country j of the world.,
M_{ij} = imports of country i from trading partner country j of the world,
M_j = total world imports of country i,
x_j = total exports of country j,
X_w = total world exports, and
x_i = total exports of country i.

The range of value of I_{ij} is $0 \leq I_{ij} \Rightarrow 1$. It's possible results may be as follows:

(i) $0 \leq I_{ij} < 0.50 \Rightarrow$ insignificant import intensity of country i from trading partner country j of the world.
(ii) $0.50 \leq I_{ij} < 0.75 \Rightarrow$ significant import intensity of country i from trading partner country j of the world.
(iii) $0.75 \leq I_{ij} \leq 1.00 \Rightarrow$ significant import intensity of country i from trading partner country j of the world.

The aforesaid results of the two types of trade intensity index being E_{ij} and I_{ij} computed on the basis of collected data of involved economic variables in their respective formulae are useful for analysing the nature of electronic digital trading transactions of a country with any other trading partner country of world particularly in quantitative terms. The quantitative analysis of aforesaid subject matter provides valued economic conclusions which are important for determining foreign trade relations, terms of global trade, foreign trade policies and policy-measures, forward foreign trade planning – management-decisions, etc. of any country with other country/countries of the world. To meet this end, the computation work-out is possible by developing software computer programmes with the help of derived formulae of E_{ij} and I_{ij} and using these programmes through the employed developed sophisticated business computers on a large scale. Thus, the conclusion is that the future prospects of application of trade index approach towards electronic trading analysis of a country with the rest countries of the world are indeed very bright under the existing global electronic digital trade environment.

References

Gupta, Dr. Nidhi, Thesis Abstract on the topic being, "India's Trade Relations with SAARC during the Nineties", Rohilkhand University, Bareilly, 2003.

Kojima, K., "The Pattern of International Trade among Advanced Countries", *Historical Journal of Economics*, Vol. 5, No. 1, 1964.

26

Electronic Marketing Analysis

MADHU

Modern era is an era of information science. Information technology is getting wide popularity nowadays. Electronic marketing is one of the most important aspects of the Internet to emerge. It allows people to exchange goods and services immediately and with no barriers of time or distance. E-marketing is a process of creating, developing and maintaining electronic presence on the Internet facilitating thereby on-line advertisements, other promotional campaigns, obtaining orders, spreading informations, etc. through e-mail and web-sites.

With the increasing use of internet e-marketing has grown with a great pace. The number of commercial (.com) sites has increased to 6,10,000 in 1996 as against 130 in 1993. Organisations of the world over now accept the fact that notwithstanding the demise of many netpreneurs, the web is here to stay and is closely the medium of the future. It serves as an intermediate channel between mass media and personal contact and extends advantages to both buyers and marketers.

BENEFITS OF BUYERS

Convenience

Customers can do online marketing 24 hours a day anywhere in the world sitting in their homes or offices. They don't have to find extra time for going to market.

Information

Substantial information about companies, prices, products, etc. can be availed easily in very small duration of time.

Fewer Troubles

Customers don't have to face sales persons. Hence, there is no persuasion or emotional factor involved. The services are quick and customers need not wait in a queue.

BENEFITS TO MARKETERS

Quicker Adjustments

Companies can quickly change prices or add products according to the prevailing market conditions.

Reduced Costs

The expenses on maintenance of stores, rent, insurance, etc. are very low and can be avoided. The ads have very low cost because of no printing, no postage, no envelope and no stationery. Digital catalogues can be maintained.

Audience Singing

Marketers can get an idea regarding number of people visiting on-line site and the number of persons stopping at different places on the site. This may further help in improving offers and advertisements.

That is why marketers worldwide have been trying to locate the keys to successful marketing on the web. Being a new medium many of the initial moves were based on the trial and error method. This resulted in a lot of hindrances in the path of e-marketing and its slow growth. Hence, to face the challenges and overcome the hindrances some basic points need to be kept in mind. Fabmart, one of the renowned websites on shopping has given some suggestive guidelines on online marketing which are as follows:

Watching the Nail

Since customers have many doubts about Internet transactions the first crucial issue to be tackled is trust. The websites need to build a strong customer response mechanism where every e-mail is responded to quickly. This will retain the trust of the customers and make them come back again and again.

Balancing Business and Creativity

Websites need to have commercial reasons to exist and this must be based on strong business logic. A website designed must keep the business objective in mind and should not take more than 30 seconds to load. On the other hand, a drab and dull website full of text is unlikely to attract visitors. So, there must be a fixed balance between drab text, attractive images, technical design and site performance.

Staying Fresh

While on content, the importance of freshness cannot be over-emphasised. When a website builds up a steady community of regular visitors, it is important to make them feel that there is something new for them to check out every time. Websites which are not updated regularly send out a clear message to customers that nothing much is happening here.

Maintaining Good Customers' Relationship

Many websites insist on cumbersome registration before allowing visitors to browse. The registration forms ask for so much data to be filled in that 8 out of 10 visitors probably go away. The registration form should merely consist of name, address, phone number and e-mail ID which is required to execute the orders. Once a customer has transacted several times then he/she can be asked for more personal data.

Offline Promotion

It has now been proved quite conclusively that promoting an online brand only online severely restricts the reach to audience. There is no choice but to use also offline media like print, T.V., etc. to promote an online brand and create awareness.

Bringing Changes in Banner Advertising

Banner advertising is not working well because agencies and brand managers creating online advertisements are just not comfortable enough with this medium. The medium is still at its infancy in India, somewhat akin to where T.V. advertising was in the mid-1970's

So, agencies and brand managers need to allocate separate online budgets, and develop independent creatives aimed towards utilising the interactive potentials of this medium existing messages and creatives developed for print or T.V. can't be used online without changes.

Building Loyality

A website need to provide genuine value to build loyality. Amazon is a clear example of present, over time, customers continue to shop with it even if the same product may be listed at a lower price at other websites. It has developed a strong brand loyality over its customers.

Follow-up

Brand on the assumption that e-marketing is an entirely new medium, we must keep trying different things regularly and keep measuring them very closely. If something works then it should be continued and if it doesn't work then it should be forgotten and next better idea should be approached.

PROBLEMS OF E-MARKETING

In spite of the benefits provided by e-marketing to the marketers, there are certain drawbacks which are as follows:

Limited Exposure

Only computer literates who are more upscaled and technically oriented than the general population are on-line users. But, generally web users do more surfing then buying. Only a few among them, regularly go for e-shopping.

Confusion and Chaos

The internet offers millions of web sites and a wide range of confusing informations. People on net get irritated very quickly and navigating a large range of web-sites may be frustrating which may result in many unnoticed web-sites.

Security

Information regarding the consumer's credit card number, personal account number, etc. can be misused by unscrupulous interlopers. Certain companies fear that others may invade their computer system for sabotage purposes.

Ethical Concerns

Personal information of the customers are there in the registration form. Customers fear that it may be misused by the companies in an unauthorised way.

Misleading Information

Sometimes for sales promotion and targeting customers web merchants may misguide the customers. They may advertise misleading statements or may even omit relevant informations which may affect the potential purchaser's impression about a product or service.

Web Advertising

The success of web advertising is not up to the mark due to the two major reasons:

(a) It is difficult to measure and charge for site from visitors because multiple measurements are prevalent on the web. So, there is no consensus on the standard for advertising charges.

(b) Most successful advertising on the web is targeted to cover a very specific group. To determine whether a given web site is attracting a specific segments or not one needs demographic information from the visitors, but the visitors are reluctant to provide the informations due to privacy concerns.

CONCLUSION

As we know that revolutions don't happen overnight. So, craving the charm between early adopters and the critical masses will take some more years in the future. But, by following the suggestive guidelines and keeping in mind the basic points for growth and developments we may do wonders in the world of online marketing. Our government should be encouraged to play creative role in promoting e-marketing in the country. And, it may do so by producing supportive legal and regulatory environment. In the age of liberalisation, privatisation and globalisation information has become a life blood for proper functioning of each organisation. So, fields like e-marketing, e-business, etc. need to be developed at a rapid speed.

27

Communication: Skill for Success

PANCHALI SINGH AND HIMANSHU SEKHAR SINGH

A biological living organism continues to live so long as its brains communicate with different part of body, similarly an organisation cannot survive without proper communication, Communication is like blood passing through the human body. Its proper circulation maintain proper health. Thus we can say that communication is one of the most important function in an organisation, organisational activities are base on communication.

Communication is a variety of behaviours, processes and technologies by which meaning is transmitted or derived from information. To be effective in any area, we need a proper communication out there. It is ways by which we transfer our ideas to somebody else. The term is used to describe diverse activities as—conversation.

Data exchange between computers.

Counting behaviour of birds.

The emotional impart of a work of art.

The network of nervous and metabolic sub-system that make up the body's immune system.

DEFINITION

The word communication is derived from Latin word communis, which means common. It is a process of exchange of facts ideas, opinions and as a means that individuals or organisation share meaning and understanding with one another. Communication has many definitions; according to one study the number is above hundred. Here we will look into some of them:

In 1828 – English literary critic and author I.A. Richards offered one of the first definition.

"Communication takes place when one mind so acts upon its environment that another mind is influenced, and in that other mind an experience occurs which is like the experience in the first mind, and is caused in part by that experience." The *Oxford English Dictionary* defines communication as "the imparting, conveying or exchanging of ideas and knowledge whether by speech, writing or signs." The *Columbia Encyclopaedia of Communication* it is defined as "the transfer of thoughts and messages as contrasted with transportation of goods and persons."

According to American Society of Training Directors: "The interchange of thought or information to bring about mutual understanding and confidence or good human relation", Pfiffner defined communication as "heart of management".

According to Millet it is, "Shared understanding of shored purpose." Ordway Teed, "composite of information given or received; learning experience in which certain attitudes knowledge and skills change; listening efforts by all involved; sensitive interaction of point of view leading to a higher level of shared understanding and common intention."

MODELS

Two US mathematicians, Claude Shannon and Warran Weaver, gave one of the most productive schematic models of communication in late 1940's.

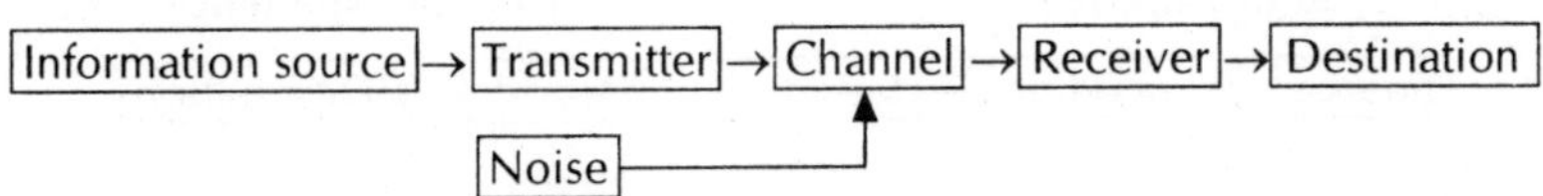

Their revised model contained six elements – a sourced (the speaker); an encoder (the vocal system); a message (language and visual clues); a channel (sound waves in the air); a decoder (the listener's ears); and reviver (the listener). A noise source (static on a radio background noise in force to all communication) later formulation comes to be known as Entropy.

Norbert Weiner also a mathematician, the so-called father of the science of cybernetics, advocated the principle of feedback, a construct be deduced from observation about interaction between human, animals, and the physical environment. Weiner used the term Homeostatic to describe the ability to detect a deviation from a desired state and a feedback mechanism by which the discrepancy is noted and fed back for the purpose of modifying behaviours.

The only real hope of an improvement in our communication system is for the sender to assure himself that his communication has been thoroughly understood by the receiver. Feedback is the yardstick, which measures the effectiveness of communication and is used for evaluation and review and to amend the message in the light of response. Efficient managers have reliable feedback and they succeed in their effective communication. Feedback is a two-way process and is probably the most importance technique of improving communication. Feedback may be—

- Positive when it is given promptly and with interest in it.
- Negative—In the case of negative feedback there is always some resistance and some degree of unwillingness in its acceptance.

Another ground for effective communication, it is essential that the commonness must be there between the sender and receiver. This commonness depends a lot on the field of experience of the two. If the field of experience is absolutely different between receivers and sender, the establishment of commonness becomes difficult. The source can encode and the destination can decode only in terms of experience each has.

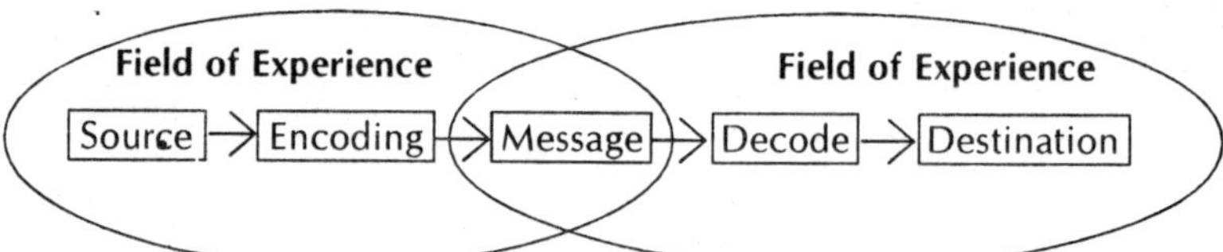

The communication process is not static rather it works in a cycle in which each individual is functioning as the encoder, interpreter and the decoder of information.

What we have discussed so far was one to one communication process involving one source and one destination. However in real life we may be faced with different types of situation like one source and more than one destination and various other situations, the sharing of a channel by several signals is known as multiplexing.

TYPES OF COMMUNICATION

Communication can be grouped in to different types as vocal, non-vocal, verbal, non-verbal, intrapersonal, interpersonal, group, mass, formal or informal.

Vocal communication is the form of communication that uses vocal cords of human being living organism. It is basically an intellectual process where you are able to express your thought or desires, etc. with the use of vocal system and brain.

Non-vocal communication consists of signs, signal, symbols gestures, etc. The common experience is very important to interpret this form of communication. The interpretation might differ from culture to culture but this form of communication is present and is widely used in all the societies.

Verbal Communication

Verbal communication is the use of words to communicate. This form of communication developed with the development of words. Many a times the words facilitate the communications process and many a time they act as a restraint to the process. But this is most important development in the modern communication. The development human civilization has made might not have been possible without words.

Non-Verbal Communication by implication, non-verbal communication consist of hidden messages, it is the cues, which convey message. Three major non-verbal dimensions as—

The body, the voice, the environment.

The body language is also known as the kinesics consists of—

(1) Facial expression,
(2) Gestures,
(3) Body inconvenient,
(4) Pastures,
(5) Eye contact, and
(6) Tactics.

The voice on is also known as Paralanguage, i.e. includes tone of voice, power of emphasis, pitch, rhythm, volume pause or break in sentence, speed of delivery, loudness, softness of the environment. Environment, includes-territory and space, buildings, rooms and seating arrangements, artifacts and objects and time.

Intrapersonal

Intrapersonal form of communication is the one when you talk to yourself or you read something. In this form the source and destination is one. A human being might receive a stimulus from his eyes and interprets in his brain and then gives out from his mouth.

Interpersonal Communication between two or more persons. Interpersonal communication could be face to face or it could be at a distance with the help of telephone, letter, etc. Viewing interpersonal relationship from different perspective can increase our ability to understand them. We will discuss here three perspective:

(a) The interpersonal needs perspective,
(b) Transactional perspective, and
(c) The rules perspective.

Willian C. Schutz suggests that three basic interpersonal needs constitute the driving force behind all interpersonal behaviour. These are—

Need for inclusion—Refers to the need to associate with others, to be a member, to be accepted and to accept others.

The need for control—Represents the need to exercise power and authority, also varies in different people.

The affection need—Reflects the need for close, personal positive feeling between people.

Each of the three needs inclusion, control and affection has two aspects. One aspect is what the person expresses towards other people. The other aspect is what the person wants from other people.

THE TRANSACTION PERSPECTIVE

Interpersonal behaviour is not only pushed by interval need. People also pull behaviour from each other. Clinical psychologist Timothy Leary called this phenomenon the interpersonal reflese.

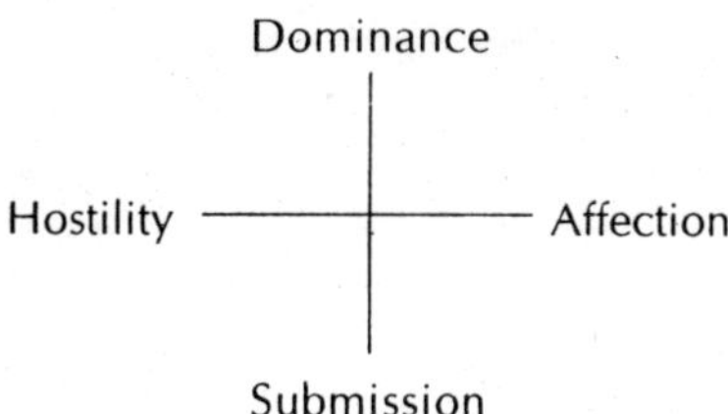

The dominance-submission axis is comparable to the control area in Schutz's framework, while the hostility-affection axis maybe been as a combination of Schutz's inclusion and affection categories. According to Leary's scheme, interpersonal actions are located around these axes. The centre point emotional neutrality, emotional intensity becomes greater as the distance from the centre increases.

TRANSACTIONAL ANALYSIS

Eric Berne, who developed the model, identifies three ego states—

(a) Parent,
(b) Adult, and
(c) Child.

Berne classifies three types of transactions:

(1) Complementary

May involve the same ego states in both parties or different ones.

(2) Crossed

Occur when an ego state that is active in one party is not the ego state being addressed by the other party.

(3) Ulterior Transaction

Differ from the other two in that they contain a hidden agenda.

In Interpersonal communication, it is necessary that the participants act to improve; their knowledge of each other and of themselves. A model known as the Johani window symbolizes this process.

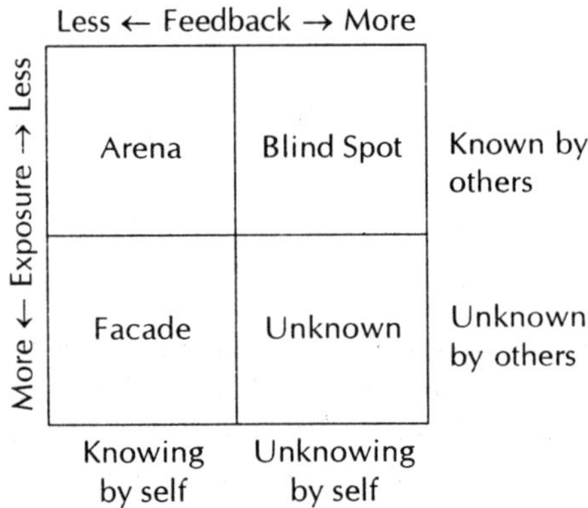

Commutation Rules

Communication rules are tacit understandings that allow people to interpret behaviour in similar ways and that specify appropriate ways to communicate with others in given roles and context. There are two principal kinds of rules—constitutive rules and regulation. Constitutive rules tell as what a certain behaviours means. Regulative rules tell us what we should do and should not do.

Group Communication

Group communication is of the type where several people are involved. A group can have positive or negative effect on its members. A group passes though different stages, i.e. forming, storming, norming, performing and adjourning as given by S.P. Robbins. In a group communication the roles of the speaker and listener are shifted among the members of the group. A group is more than one person working together but to maintain cohesiveness in organisation the number in a group is usually not more than 25. But with the development in communication technology larger groups can also maintain cohesiveness.

Mass Communication

Mass communication, also known as public communication has become possible with the represent development of technology. The technology of modern mass communication results from a confluence of many types of inventions and discoveries. A large-scale sharing of information, disseminated by the media, print, broadcasting, film or the new electronic networks to large audiences, is considered to be public or mass communication.

Formal Communication

Formal communication is the form of communication, which follows the lines of authority within the organisation. It finds its roots; in scalar chain advocated by Henry Fayol in his 14 principles of administrative management. The formal communication are of three types mainly upward, downward and horizontal.

Informal Communication

Informal Communication was studied by Keith Davis, basically it has been observed the members within an organisation form their own informal group based on various factors. He studied this informal communication and characterised them into four categories, they are single strand grapevine, gossip, probability, and cluster. Informal group if utilised properly can raise the performance of the organisation. It can work as uniting force, can give accurate information at a rapid rate, encourages co-operation, fill the gaps of formal structure, etc. That is if handle properly the manager can make best use of informal groups within the organisation.

Communication Skills

Communication if not been received properly is useless. It has been seen that to successful you need to have proper communication in the organisation. A manager has to make many decisions every now and then and the basic ingredient of the proper decision is the communication. So a manager who has to communicate with other members of the organisation has to develop certain skills to be successful.

Terry has given a set of points for proper communication. A speaker must develop these skills:

1. Inform yourself fully.
2. Establish a mutual trust in each other.
3. Find a common ground of experience.

4. Use mutually known words.
5. Have regard for context.
6. Secure and hold the receiver attention.
7. Employ examples and visual aids.
8. Practice delaying reaction.

S.P. Robbins believes that good communication skills take considerable effort to learn and years to practice. He has suggested two most critical skills for effective communication – active listening and provide feedback.

- Behaviour related to active listening.
- Make eye contact.
- Exhibit affirmative head nods and appropriate facial expression.
- Avoid distractive actions or gestures.
- Ask question.
- Para phrase.
- Avoid interrupting the speaker.
- Don't over talk.
- Make smooth transition between the roles of speaker and listener.
- Behaviour related to providing effective feedback.
- Focus of specific behaviours.
- Keep feedback impersonal.
- Keep feedback goal-oriented.
- Make feedback well timed.
- Ensure understanding.
- Direct negative feedback toward behaviour, i.e. controllable by the recipient.

A manager has to make large number of decisions and to be successful his decision has to be correct. To make accurate decision he has to be efficient in communication. That is he has to develop communication skills in all types and finally to master his abilities. A successful communicator is a successful man and is a successful manager who will be heading a successful division or a successful organisation.

REFERENCES

C.S. Rayadu, *Communication*, Himalaya Publishing House, 2001.

Dalmar Fisher, *Communication in Organisation*, Jaico Pub., 1999.

D.N. Agrawal, *Organisational Communication Management*, Deep & Deep, 1989.

F. Luthans, *Organisational Behaviour*, McGraw-Hill, 1981.

Harold Koontz, Heinz Weihrich, *Essentials of Management*, Vth edition.

James A.F. Stoner, Freeman, Gillbert, *Management*, 1997.

K. Davis, *Human Behaviour at Work*, Tata McGraw-Hill, New Delhi.

K.R. Balan, C.S. Rayadu, *Effective Communication*, Castle Books, 1994.

L. Brown, *Communicating Facts and Ideas in Business*, PHI, New Jersey, 1982.

M.T. Myers and G.E. Myers, *Managing by Communication*, McGraw-Hill, 1982.

S.P. Robbins, *Organisational Behaviour*, Prentice Hall, 1991.

28

Electronic Media for Agricultural and Rural Development

SHANTANU KUMAR, UMA SAH AND AJAY KUMAR SAH

The rural agricultural scenario in India has undergone spectacular changes since independence. From the begging bowl image, it has acquired the stature of a food grain exporting country. Still, there is a wide gap between the potential agricultural yield and the actual yield obtained at the farm level. There may be several reasons for this. In addition to many constraining factors, most important is the lack of awareness of the latest developments in the field of agricultural science among a large number of farmers. Therefore, it will be a gigantic task for the extension personnel to make agricultural knowledge and information available to the farmers spread throughout the country.

On the other hand, owing to the breakthrough in science and technology, there is virtually an information explosion. The world today has gone far ahead in the use of electronic communication systems. The electronic media has revolutionised the communication process, resulting in the emergence of many new communication devices. Besides, they have improved the old technologies such as radio broadcasting and other devices already playing an important role in communicating agricultural technologies to farmers, and in this way they help escalate the process of development. The electronic media like, computers, etc. could also play a major role in transfer of hi-tech agriculture from global pockets to the Indian farmer's field.

These modern communication technologies play a crucial role in the transfer of improved agricultural practices to the farmers at different stages of the adoption process. These technologies have the potential to ignite the flame of interest in the farmers. The communication media became further important to the farmers living in remote, far flung areas which are less accessible to extension functionaries. In the field of agricultural extension, the impact of electronic technologies is already well established in India through extensive use of mass media like radio. Now television broadcasting has made rapid strides in the training of extension personnel in India during the last five years. Among the new electronic technologies, computers, video-tapes and Interactive Computer Video Technology (ICVT) deserve close scrutiny for their use in training extension personnel and in other areas of agricultural extension duration.

An attempt is made here to highlight the current status of the use of these electronic media with particular reference to their application in the field of rural and agricultural development of India. Their scope for further utilisation has also been deliberated upon. For convenience in discussion, the available electronic media are categorised in three broad groups as simple electronic media, advanced electronic media and other modern electronic media, and they have been discussed in terms of their status, performance and scope under the sub-heads below:

SIMPLE ELECTRONIC MEDIA

Electronic media like radio, television and video-tapes are placed under simple electronic media because of the lower complexity involved in their operation and maintenance as compared to others.

Radio broadcasting in India started in 1927 and All India Radio (AIR) was established in 1936. It was renamed 'Akashwani' in 1957. Technically, the radio signals cover almost the whole country. However, on an average, there are only 4.4 radio/transistor sets per 100 people, that is, only one radio is catering to the requirement of about 25 persons in India.

In 1965, 10 intensive farm and home units were established at selected AIR stations to feed factual technical information and utility announcements to the farming community. In these programmes, farmers and experts are invited for deliberations, keeping in view the local agricultural problems.

In order to extend the reach, effectiveness, popularity and acceptability of radio, the concept of 'local radio broadcasts' has been observed to be more effective. Local radio stations are ideally suited to the dissemination of farm technology according to the different agro-climatic regions. All India Radio started this type of local radio station first at Dageroli in Kanyakumari district of Tamil Nadu in October, 1984. The concept of 'radio forum' that is working in many countries could be operationalised in the Indian context also. It will synergise the mass media with interpersonal communication which, in turn, would be helpful in generating greater awareness, creating conviction and developing a positive attitude among farmers and rural youth about innovative farm technologies. However, for increasing the effectiveness, radio programmes must be flexible and spontaneous to enable radio to function as a mouthpiece of the local community. The programmes should satisfy the local aspirations of the people whom such stations/forums serve.

Television is yet another powerful electronic communication medium. Though television has been in India for the last 40 years, it has been utilised mostly for entertainment; however it can be used both for motivation and instructions. Doordarshan (the national television service of India) has now become one of the largest broadcasting organisations in the world. Presently, Doordarshan covers over 87 per cent of the country's population.

An instructional programme for farmers, Krishi Darshan, was stared on January 26, 1957, through an agricultural television pilot project. The main objectives of the project were to communicate the latest scientific know-how in agriculture, dairying and animal husbandry to the farmer and to assess the effectiveness of TV as a medium of farm communication. The regular farm telecast of Krishi Darshan commenced from February 2, 1967, with a frequency of one telecast per week. Impressed with its effectiveness and realising the urgency for bridging the 'knowledge gap', from 1976 the frequency of the Krishi Darshan programme was extended to five days a week from Monday to Friday.

A promising experiment in decentralised television broadcasting was the Kheda communication project. This project was undertaken by the Indian Space Research Organisation (ISRO) with Doordarshan. Programmes were produced on hardcore areas like agriculture, animal husbandry, health as well as on social issues. This medium was extensively used for problem solving by recording the problems and taking them to the decision-makers or by bringing the villagers and the decision-makers together to discuss the problems.

Video is another suitable medium for generating and promoting interaction. It can be easily handled and, at the same time, it is easy to carry. Experiments with small format videotape have recently aroused the interest of farmers in developing countries. Videotapes are seen as an ideal medium to promote motivation, attitudinal changes, behaviour reinforcement, community participation and entertainment. The National Dairy Research Institute (NDRI) in collaboration with the Memorial University of Newfoundland, Canada, took a rural development action research project to the village of Taparana at Karnal in Haryana, extensively using video in various contexts.

Videotapes have tremendous utility in the training of extension personnel. The present array of training activities in extension in India covers a wide range from Fortnightly Training Sessions (FTSs) and Monthly Workshops (MWs) to specialised or special courses of extension training institutions. Some videotapes can be recorded on successfully conducted FTSs and MWs. They can be a lesson for others in conducting successful FTSs and MWs and pinpoint pitfalls. Different 'success stories' can be of great practical use to our trainers. Yet another very promising area of videotape utility is technology training. The most successful 'mixes' of training methods and technologies can be video taped and sent to the Directorate of Extension (DOE). The DOE can multiply and send them to the States and training institutions. Such an exchange programme will enhance the training capabilities at the national, regional, State and even divisional level. The extension training institutions like MANAGE, EEIs and others can themselves undertake this valuable exercise.

ADVANCED ELECTRONIC MEDIA

The advanced electronic media includes Interactive Computer Video Technology (ICVT), computer-aided systems (CAS) and the Internet. These media could be said to be advanced owing to the relatively higher degree of technicalities involved in their operation and maintenance.

Interactive computer video technology is the result of advancements in computer technology, video technology and laser technology. It is an amazing device for the storage and retrieval of audio and video information. ICVT fulfils the need for interaction in the communication process. In it, the learners control the system through computers for their interaction with video recorded material chosen for learning.

This provides the opportunity for remediation as well as reinforcement of learning and individualisation of instructions.

The ICVT is rapidly emerging as an important educational communication device, especially in private industry. The potential also exists for widespread use of video discs in formal education. For the first time in India, in the agriculture sector, the Department of Electronics has decided to take up a pilot project on the use of Interactive Computer Video Technology system at a cost of above Rs. 1.5 crore. The system was installed at MANAGE, Hyderabad on a pilot project basis. The overall objective of this project, in a nutshell, is concerned with adopting, testing and evaluating ICVT methodologies and technologies in Indian conditions. To fulfil these objectives and open a new chapter in training of extension personnel, National Informatics Centre, a New Delhi firm, has been given a contract. This is believed to be the first centre of its kind in any developing country in the agricultural sector.

The Chennai Dialogue on Information Technology (1992), chaired by Dr. M.S. Swaminathan, resulted in the proposal for the establishment of a Computer Aided Agricultural Extension (CAEx) and Information Village (IV) which will complement and sustain each other. The key to these schemes is the concept of blending traditional and recommended technologies to create a paradigm where technology development results in the creation of new or skilled jobs. The purpose of CAEx is to generate and disseminate information relevant for a locality, such as a development block or village cluster. Here, local specificity is important. The CAEx system centres around a value-adding programme which receives information from various sources such as the universities, the relevant State departments, regional or sub-regional meteorological centres, and KVKs and input agencies using different electronic media. Value-addition of the received information takes place through the creation of databases with multimedia features (integrating audio/video, still images and text in one application).

Computer Aided Agricultural Extension (CAEx) can generate and disseminate information relevant for a locality in different areas, namely, meteorological information, pest/disease information, marketing price information, remote sensing data (weather), general scientific information and information on different enterprises like aquaculture, apiculture, water harvesting, etc.

Internet—another advanced electronic medium, used today by

over 40 million people – is growing at a fantastic speed of 10-15 per cent per month or about 200 per cent a year. It can be possible to use it at a lower cost compared to fax and telex. For the scientific and research community, the Internet is an essential and indispensable tool. Through the Internet, a scientist can gain instant access to the world's most advanced research facilities and discuss research problems with others working in the same field. It can be very useful for governmental and non-governmental organisations/agencies. Some of the other potential applications of the Internet for agricultural development purposes are:

- The extension agencies functioning at the district or State headquarter level can create their own home pages. Here, all information regarding new improved technologies can be displayed. All the practices can be supported by graphics to make it easy for the users to understand.
- Sharing of relevant information can be done all over the country. This will enhance the knowledge of the participating users. They can discuss their problems and arrive at solutions for them by sharing and utilising their experiences.

OTHER MODERN ELECTRONIC MEDIA

Electronic media such as video text, teletext and video conferencing have been placed under this head. They represent further development and application of simple as well as advanced electronic media.

Video text refers to an information system in which text and graphic information is transmitted and received either by a videotext television or on an ordinary television set with an adapter unit. The concept has been developed to provide a method of low cost information delivery. A videotext system coupled with a microcomputer permits editing as well as retrieval of information on a videotext page. The videotext that is transmitted *via* telephone cables, data lines or a private network is called interactive video text. It has certain attributes which make it a potential teaching medium. It can be effectively used in training and in distance education.

Video text transmission based on broadcast signals is called teletext. Thus, teletext is a system that links a computer to a television by which text and graphic information can be transmitted on a one way basis to home viewers. Indian television joined the advanced nations when, in 1985, it started the teletext, known as 'Intex Service', to telecast the latest news and information in different areas like weather information, share rates, etc.

Video conferencing can be defined simply as any form of two-way conferencing for two or more people in two or more sites that helps in meeting and discussing issues in real time, or on an *ad hoc* basis. A video meeting involves sending slides, playing video tapes using white boards and the fax facility and highlighting three-dimensional objects. Even computer conferencing and video is supported by some systems. It has vast potential application in the scientific world and can be used for educational purposes. It aids quick and efficient decision-making by involving more people and resources in easily arranged meetings.

THRUSTS FOR THE FUTURE

In the near future, all concerted and co-ordinated efforts have to be made to direct the thrust of these electronic communication media more towards the rural areas. A uniform system of centralised directed programming cannot fulfil the multi-dimensional needs of variegated local communities. Therefore, in the near future, there is need to decentralise local transmitters which can make it possible to produce relevant programmes dealing with local issues in the local language and dialect. Thus, better understanding of local problems, timely delivery of information, coupled with compatibility and applicability of information, will increase.

Intensive and extensive research in respect of media and their programmes to ascertain which media mix should be used for what purpose and what strategies could be more relevant or appropriate, are to be undertaken. Further, a responsible electronic communication medium has to be honest and unbiased. It has to be comprehensive, just, courageous, clean, competent and should present basic information. With these few directions and urges, it may be possible to activate a multimedia-based pragmatic and solution-oriented system of balanced and free communication at the village or regional level.

Television, video, radio, etc. have become relevant for rural India but they should follow the participatory model in problem finding and making solutions. Radio is more easily manageable. Therefore, the full potential of radio, including radio fora in all aspects and its operation in relevant fields must be explored and strengthened.

Thus, the entire endeavour demands the planned use of media and technology.

CONCLUSION

The emergence of new electronic media has revolutionised the communication process. These modern communication technologies can play a crucial role in the transfer of improved agricultural innovations. An array of these new electronic technologies is already in use or has tremendous potential for use, in agricultural development. Interactive Computer Video Technology fulfils the need of the interactions in the communication process that undoubtedly increase the quality of the extension process. The potential use of video tapes in agricultural development has been exploited by various institutions. Information obtained through satellite on crops, soil and water resources can enable us to plan for integrated land use development. The National Dairy Development Board (NDDB) is also planning to exploit the tremendous potential of the electronic media in the dairy field. Computer networking at the international, national and local level may establish a good linkage for information dissemination and sharing. The Indian Council of Agriculture Research (ICAR) has also contemplated computerising the whole system to carry out research more effectively. For this purpose, Agricultural Research Information System (ARIS) cells have started working most of the ICAR institutes, directorates, centres and also State agricultural universities. The use of radio and television in agriculture and dairy development has already been established in India. However, other new communication technologies, namely, Internet, videotext, teletext, etc. need further scrutiny and emphasis for their potential use. In the near future, the concerted and co-ordinated efforts of these media with their appropriate combinations could be effectively used in disseminating newly-developed agricultural and dairy innovations to the prospective beneficiary farmers.

PART III

INTERNET AND ONLINE BUSINESS

29

Cyber Crimes and Internet Security Concepts

TRIPTI SINGH

When Charles Babbage struck upon the idea of linking mathematical calculations to the stream of events he had hardly imagined the Computers in its present form.

Today computers do more than simply compute, supermarket scanners calculate our bills while keeping store inventory, ATM let us conduct banking transactions from virtually anywhere in the world and of course the amazing Internet. The Internet actually embodies all forms of communication one to one, one to many and finally many to many.

One of the greatest manifestations of Internet and world-wide web has been Internet and E-Commerce. It refers to all forms of commercial transactions involving both organisations and individuals that are based upon the Electronic processing and transmission of data, including text sound and visual image. It may be B2B, B2C, C2C and E2S.

With the spread of E-commerce, several questions were raised on how secure government business and private computers really are.

Hacking started with telephones technology. Institutions like research centre, defence organisations, financial networks and educational networks are ideal targets for hackers. Individuals can suffer the consequences of malicious hackers when they trespass and damage computer systems that regulate our lives or access personal and confidential information.

As more money moves on the Net, it would become more appealing to the crooks. A survey by a US-based Science Applications Corporations reported that computer break in at 40 Corporations resulted in losses exceeding $ 800 million last year alone.

WEAPONS USED BY CYBER TERRORIST

Due to their anonymity so many cyber terrorists are out with so many lethal weapons.

Viruses

Viruses are the oldest and the best known software weapons which come in all shapes and flavours. According to Mcafree Associates, a maker of virus detection and protection software, around 10,000 viruses are currently in circulation and about 300-400 new viruses are being created and circulated per month. Some viruses may infect your PC boot sector, some may infect the file, erase your computers CMOS set-up tables, and some may make subtle but detrimental changes in your data and finally false virus warning may deter you to take extreme steps.

Worms

Worms are breeder programs, reproducing themselves endlessly to fill up memory and hard disks.

Logic Bombs

Logic Bombs are embedded pieces of destructive code that detonate on preset data source when specified set of instructions is executed, unleashing destructive actions throughout a network.

Bots

Bots are pieces of codes designed to save the Internet and perform specific actions.

Syn

Syn attacks involve sending a torrent of connections request which creates a major Traffic jam at the site, cutting it off.

Extortion

A mere threat can be as effective as an actual attack.

Another major threat on the Internet is Impersonation where a person tries to act as someone else and conduct transactions and correspondence on his behalf. Digital signatures are an immediate solution, but a person may submit different signatures for different transactions. However, Generation of Public Key and Private Key are a good options. But a Man in Middle Attack may be generating, fake keys intercepting messages and reading and altering it.

Cyber Terrorism can take many forms, from disabling a country's defence system or Power grid or threatening a bank, to using laptops with satellite uplinks and heavily encrypted messages to liaise across national boarders with Global underground network as being done by Osama Bin Laden.

Terrorist can also come in the form of misinformation or may involve changing medical or financial records or starting passwords. Cyber Terrorism are many times interested in gaining publicity. In one of the most shocking cases computer was used to change the medication files of the patients which led to wrong medication and ultimately his death. The files were later on corrected to cover their tracks, so that the nurse would be blames for the accidents.

INTERNET SECURITY CONCEPTS

Internet technology is driving a genuine business revolution and so the Internet security has become all important. Some of the reliable concepts and techniques are:

Firewalls

Firewalls are systems designed to prevent unauthorized access to a firm or a private network. They act as filters for messages entering or leaving the system.

Security threats can be further counteracted by either an identification or authentication. The person can be identified and authenticated by what he knows (e.g. a password) or by human characteristics (biometrics) or by what he owns (smart cards)

There are two categories of Biometrics Techniques:

- Physiological based techniques which include—
  Finger print analysis,
  Iris analysis,
  Hand geometry vein pattern analysis,
  Ear recognition,
  Odour detection, and
  DNA pattern analysis and sweat pore analysis.

- Behavioural based techniques include
  Hand written signature verification, and
  Keystroke analysis and speech analysis.

A digital signature is superior to handwritten signature that it is nearly impossible to counterfeit plus it attest to the contents of the information as well as to the identity of the signor.

The IT Act further gives extensive responsibility to the Controller of Certifying Authority appointed by the Central Government, for prescription of security procedures. He has to verify the nature of and volume of transactions level of sophistication of parties and the cost of availability of alternatives, in spite of standardisation of procedures and forms, human error and biases cannot be ruled out.

An overview of the IT Act 2000, strongly hints on issues like Copyright violations on the net, or tampering and theft of internet usage hours. The penalty amounts to Rs. 1 crore but it cannot ignore the fact that keeping a watchdog on the Cyberspace is an impossible mission. Moreover, most of the website actively solicited viewers to their site either for the purpose of enlightening prospective customers about their product and/or their services.

ELECTRONIC PAYMENT SYSTEM

The increasing power and decreasing cost of computers coupled with advancement in computers, now on an average consumer has the technology capability to use electronic transfer in any of the meaning-ful ways. E-Commerce has become an increasingly Commercial area, and Electronic payment has become a central part to Online business between buyer and seller.

Electronic currency is essentially a system that allows a person to pay for goods or to computer. Thus it is a digital currency.

Using Electronic Commerce is like using a virtual ATM. The user logs on to the Internet, goes to website, verifies the ownership of the account, and withdraws the desired amount of currency. The bank issues a unique number which is the serial number of the coin signed with the bank private key and is stored in the hard disk. The user when requires sends them to the digital bank upon receiving the coin the bank verifies the serial number of the coin against the list of spent coins. If the coins have not being already used, the bank credits the account of the vendor and the vendor ships the product to the user. However, these payments have both advantages and disadvantages.

Advantages

Confidentiality/Privacy.

Security – Some experts worry about the security of Electronic Commerce but RSA Cryptography makes it almost impossible to break the code of digital signature. Additionally the enacted digital signature statutes requires a certification authority to use trustworthy system.

Disadvantages

Fraud – If a consumer somehow misplaces his private key and a perpetrator uses it to withdraw funds the bank would never know and the consumer would be liable. Additionally if the security code is broken and the message is intercepted, the hacker will be able to perpetrate fraud on the recipient of the message.

Peer to Peer Double spending – There is always a possibility of Double spending of digital signatures in case of peer to peer transactions. Thus a consumer always has a choice of including intermediary bank in the transactions.

Illegal activity with Electronic Currency.

Nowadays smuggling millions of dollars in a suitcase are over. Electronic payment systems as Montex and Mark Twain would give less visibility and transparency and transfer and storage of money from the comforts of ones own home to offshore banking account in a matter of seconds. Electronic commerce is anonymous, portable and easy to handle.

TAXATION ISSUES

E-Commerce also becomes a major concern when use for Tax Evasion. To find an effective solution to the problem of E-Commerce, following issues need to be resolved.

Residency of individuals Section 6(1) (a) of the Income Tax Act emphasizes on the physical presence of the person for 182 days or more in a year and presumes that person a taxable resident of that year. But in the context of the Internet the test becomes even more untenable. A person could effectively make thousands of 'trips' per year *via* the Information highway to another jurisdiction without ever being subject to a broader control mechanism. The same applies to corporate residency.

Traceability

Stored value cards could also be used for transactions over the Internet but could be internationally negotiable for goods and services in a real world. Whereas in real world cross-border transactions are regulated by customs and postal services the internet offers no enforcement mechanism.

Cross-border shopping on a global scale. For cross-border transactions a customer is liable to pay customs duty and sales tax. But suppose a company is operating a commercial website, i.e. hosted by a computer in a tax haven country, the company would not be liable to pay any taxes, these ramifications would be very serious for government revenue. But the IT Act 2000 seems to have very little solutions for it.

Banking

Similarly cyber banks would be issuing untraceable currency that would be negotiated internationally.

E-COMMERCE AND THE IT ACT

Section 6 of the IT Act recognises the means for payment or receipt by electronic form but has not made prescriptions for payment or receipt by electronic form.

CONCLUSIONS

Definitely a legislative vacuum exists when it comes to the regulations of the E-Commerce. Various manifestations of the Cyber Crime and Cyber Terrorism have further added to these grey areas.

REFERENCES

HYPERLINK http://www.asianlaws.com
HYPERLINK http://www.ecommerce.com
HYPERLINK http://www.internet.com

30

Legal Dimensions in Cyber Transactions

V.K. AGARWAL

Rapid developments in information technology have empowered both individuals and enterprises to interact and transact business through the electronic mode, shrinking the influence of time and geography. It is estimated that some 300 million Internet users were participating in electronic commerce at the turn of the century, an activity that could amount to more than US $ 300 billion.

Electronic commerce, production, advertising, sale and distribution of goods and services *via* telecommunications network can be divided into three broad categories:

1. The searching stage where producers and consumers, or buyers and sellers, first interact;
2. The ordering and payment stage, once a transaction has been agreed upon; and
3. The delivery stage.

Electronic commerce is a boon for both producers and consumers as it helps them to overcome the traditional barriers of distance from markets and provides market information and access to explore opportunities. Businessmen are no longer required to maintain physical establishments or hunt for prime locations. Virtual shops, contact points and networking through the Internet, in most cases, may enable storage near to the production site and distribution can be made directly to the consumer. Global access helps even small industries and businesses to reach the customer anywhere, which, in the traditional mode of business, is not easily possible. E-commerce eliminates dependence on the middlemen for procuring raw materials or selling goods and services.

LEGAL DIMENSIONS IN CYBER TRANSACTIONS

Doing business through cyberspace is exhilarating, but it can be frustrating for want of rules, without which business cannot be conducted. The global reach through the Internet is fraught with the risk of exposure to a multitude of legal puzzles which promise to plague the regulation of online trading and virtually every other cyberspace activity.

Given the unique nature of this emerging mode of trade, many questions need to be answered. A number of legal issues arise when trade and business communications are carried out through electronic means. For instance, if a service was sold over the Internet across countries, in which geographical location can the transaction be deemed to have been effected? Once the order is placed, electronically, when and where does the transaction take place? This question may be important form the point of view of consumer protection and establishing jurisdiction. Furthermore, electronic transactions require electronic contracts and electronic signatures, which will have to be provided for in the contract laws. Indeed, how do you know who you are dealing with in cyberspace? Thus, it is all the more important to understand the various legal aspects involved in cyber transactions, such as how a contract could be electronically formed, the acceptance and use of digital signatures, security of electronic records, authentication and non-repudiation of a transaction and the confidentiality of commercial transactions.

Risk of Exposure to Various Jurisdictions

Simply by establishing a web site on the Internet, a business is able to offer its products and services to a global market at a modest expense. With this global reach comes the risk of exposure to a multitude of legal jurisdictions.

The risk of exposure to legal actions from different jurisdictions can be minimised by including on the web site a statement clarifying that it is only intended to target customers in specific countries. In doing so, the company will have to ensure that the web site complies with the laws of such countries. Although this may not necessarily restrict the persons in other jurisdictions from accessing the web site, it will certainly protect the company concerned against litigation in jurisdictions in which the company does not want to deal/ transact/ conduct business, as clarified by the statement.

There may be a situation where companies involved in particular industries may be prohibited to deal with customers in certain jurisdictions or companies are not allowed to conduct business in a country which is subject to trading sanctions or for any other reason. It is desirable that software is so programmed that it allows customers from only approved jurisdictions to make contact with the company. If the web site contains information commonly regulated by governments, the company must ensure that a disclaimer is put on the web site, which the user must first accept before proceeding further. However, this may not be necessarily sufficient.

Advertisement to Conform to Law

The restrictions on advertising on conventional media also apply to advertising in cyberspace. Indian law entitles a customer to claim damages if he is induced to enter into a contract to buy goods or services through a misleading advertisement. Many jurisdictions have similar consumer protection laws; therefore, it must be ensured that all the information contained on the web site is accurate and conforms to the law in force and is regularly updated.

Business to Customer Transactions

Where the company's web site makes a world-wide offer for its goods and services, it may be obliged to deal with a customer in a jurisdiction in which it does not want to conduct business or may be obliged to deliver the order even if it does not hold sufficient stock. To deal with such situations, the company will have to ensure that its web site constitutes an 'invitation to treat' which will allow companies to provide that no contract is made until a confirmation is sent to the customer.

Generally, companies wish to trade under their own standard terms and conditions. It is, therefore, suggested that the company should include a statement in its web site clarifying that any offer made by the customer will only be accepted on the company's usual terms and conditions as set out on the web site.

It is also essential that the terms of any contract concluded through this medium contains the applicable law. The obvious choice for an Indian company should be Indian law to be applicable to the transaction but issues beyond familiarity and convenience must be considered. The location of the customer must be taken into account and it must be ensured that, in the event of a dispute, a judgement of the court, under jurisdiction of applicable law is enforceable in the jurisdiction in which the customer is based.

Business-to-Business Transactions

In the case of business-to-business transactions, the situation is a little complex because both the entities would like to deal with each other on their own terms and conditions. As both will be placing the orders on one another through e-mail, the communications between the parties may constitute a series of offers and counter offers. In situations where the transactions take place regularly on an informal basis, it may be unclear between the parties which terms and conditions are finally accepted and applied to the transaction; this may not become apparent till a dispute arises. To avoid any future misunderstanding and also to have a cordial relationship, it may be suggested that both the companies enter into an agreement containing terms and conditions on which they wish to transact business. Such an agreement may also include a clause specifying that any dispute between the parties shall be settled through arbitration or other alternative dispute resolution process.

Protection of Intellectual Property Rights

Problems relating to IPRs in cyberspace are more difficult to resolve than those in the real world, because cyberspace is not territorial in scope, whereas IPRs are necessarily protected independently in each jurisdiction. While an Indian company's web site may comply perfectly with Indian law, the global reach of the Internet may subject such a company to violations of the laws of any other country from which it can be accessed. This may be particularly true in the case of intellectual property law – the use of a trademark on a web site may be perfectly lawful within India but may infringe the rights of another party in a different jurisdiction where another company uses the same mark.

Apart from ensuring that companies do not infringe the intellectual property rights of other parties, they should ensure that their trademarks and other intellectual property rights are adequately protected in the newly expanded market in which they may be operating.

A new dimension has been added to the protection of well-known marks with the rapid spread in the use of the Internet for electronic commerce. One aspect of domain name relates to trademarks. Domain names are the user-friendly form of Internet addresses that generally end up with .com, .org, .net or with a country code. These names also have a secondary use as identifiers of businesses or their products and services on the Net. Domain names are usually registered with minimal procedures, on a first-come-first-serve basis. Many problems have arisen with regard to the enforcement of trademarks with the increasing use of domain names. Famous and well-known marks are the particular target of 'cyber squatting' and misleading use. These problems are found even in developing countries that have begun their use of the Internet more recently. Therefore, companies are advised to register their trademarks in the principal countries with which they conduct business.

As commerce on the Internet also involves the sale or licensing of intellectual properties, the growth of e-commerce depends on adequate protection of intellectual property rights and copyrights and the viability of e-commerce depends primarily on the confidence of sellers on the mechanism that ensures the protection of intellectual property rights.

REGULATIONS OF E-COMMERCE

1. Initiatives at National Level

Realising the importance of e-commerce and to curb malpractice, various countries, namely, the U.S.A., the U.K., Japan, Germany, Singapore, Canada, Hong Kong, Australia, Denmark and Switzerland have enacted laws to deal with electronic transactions. India has also prepared a draft of the Information Technology Bill, 1999 dealing with electronic records, digital signatures and computer crimes and the Draft Electronic Commerce Act, 1998, to facilitate a secure regulatory environment for electronic commerce by providing a legal infrastructure governing electronic contracting, security and integrity of electronic transactions, the use of digital signatures and other issues related to electronic commerce.

The draft bill has been divided into 13 parts and deals with electronic records and digital signatures, regulation of certifying authorities, digital signature certificates, duties of subscribers, penalties and adjudication, cyber regulations, computer crimes and exemptions relating to network service providers. The Draft Bill also proposes to amend the Indian Penal Code, Indian Evidence Act, Banker's Book Evidence Act and Reserve Bank of India Act.

The Draft of the Electronic Commerce Act deals with electronic records and electronic signatures, the integrity and authentication of secure electronic records and secure electronic signatures; issues of electronic contracting including legal issues related to the use of digital signatures. The Draft also deals with the acceptance and use of electronic records and electronic signatures by government authorities. The liability of network service providers and criminal penalties are also dealt with by the draft.

2. Global Initiatives

Products which are bought and paid for over the Internet but are delivered physically would be subject to existing WTO rules on trade in goods. But the situation is more complicated for products that are delivered as digitised information over the Internet, as a variety of issues arise relating to the appropriate regulatory regime.

Both the supply of Internet access services and many of the products delivered over the Internet fall within the ambit of the General Agreement on Trade in Services, but there is a need to clarify how far particular activities are covered by the members' market-access commitments.

WTO has started examining all trade-related issues of e-commerce including its effect on trade and economic prospects, financial implications, treatment of e-commerce in the GATS legal framework and intellectual property issues, etc. The United Nations Commission on International Trade Law (UNCITRAL) adopted a Model Law on e-commerce in 1996 intended to facilitate use of EDI, e-mail, telecopy, etc. by providing standards by which their legal value can be assessed. The Model Law on e-commerce establishes norms that validate contracts formed through electronic means, sets default rules for contract formation and governance of electronic contract performances. It also defines the characteristics of valid electronic writing and an original document. Besides, it provides for the acceptability of digital signatures for legal and commercial purposes and supports the admission of computer evidence in courts and arbitration proceedings.

WTO and WIPO both are also involved in discussions of IPR issues in respect of global e-commerce. WTO has brought out a specific study on the TRIPs provisions and electronic commerce and WIPO initiatives resulting in new obligations in relation to issues arising out of electronic commerce on copyright and related rights and may result in further disciplines in the area of trademarks.

A WTO study entitled *Electronic Commerce and the Role of the WTO* examined the potential trade gains from the rapidly increasing use of the Internet for commercial purposes. The report outlines the complexities as well as the potential benefits of trade *via* the Internet, provides background information for the 134 WTO members who are now engaged in the process of developing policy responses to this new form of commerce which is growing at a staggering rate.

The study also emphasises the extraordinary expansion of opportunities that electronic commerce offers, including for developing countries, but noted that much remains to be done by way of improving access to the necessary infrastructure and user skills if these opportunities are to be realised.

Among the policy issues identified in the study are the legal and regulatory framework for Internet transactions, security and privacy questions, taxation, access to the Internet, market access for suppliers over the Internet, trade facilitation, public procurement, intellectual property questions and regulation of content.

The World Intellectual Property Organisation (WIPO) has also prepared a Digital Agenda, setting out guidelines and screening solutions to problems raised by the impact on electronic commerce and intellectual property. The 10 points of the WIPO Digital Agenda are as follows:

1. Broaden the participation of developing countries through the use of WIPONET and other means for:
   - access to intellectual property information;
   - participation in global policy formulation; and
   - opportunities to use their intellectual property assets in electronic commerce.
2. Entry into force of the WIPO Copyright Treaty (WCT) and the WIPO Performances and Phonograms Treaty (WPPT) before December 2001.

3. Promote the adjustment of the international legislative framework to facilitate electronic commerce through:
   - the extension of the principles of the WPPT to audio-visual performances;
   - the adaptation of broadcasters' rights to the digital area; and
   - progress towards a possible international instrument on the protection of database.
4. Implement the recommendations of the Report of the Domain Name Process and pursue the achievement of compatibility between identifiers in the real and virtual worlds through the establishment of rules for mutual respect and the elimination of contradictions between the domain name system and intellectual rights.
5. Develop appropriate principles with the aim of establishing, at the appropriate time at the international level, rules for determining the circumstances of intellectual property liability of Online Service Providers (OSPs) which are compatible and workable within a framework of general liability rules for OSPs.
6. Promote adjustment of the institutional framework for facilitating the exploitation of intellectual property in the public interest in a global economy and on a global medium through co-ordination and, where desired by users, the implementation of systems in respect of:
   - the inter-operability and interconnection of electronic copyright management systems and metadata of such systems;
   - the online licensing of the digital expression of cultural heritage; and
   - the online administration of intellectual property disputes.
7. Introduce and develop online procedures for the filing and administration of international applications for the Patent Co-operation Treaty (PCT), the Madrid System and the Hague Agreement at the earliest possible date.
8. Study and, where appropriate, respond to a timely and effective manner to the need for measures designed to improve the management of cultural and other digital assets at the international level by, for example, investigating the desirability and efficacy of:

- model procedures and forms for global licensing of digital assets;
- the notarisation of electronic documents; and
- the introduction of a procedure for the certification of web sites for compliance with appropriate intellectual property standards and procedures.

9. Study any other emerging intellectual property issues related to electronic commerce and, where appropriate, develop norms in relation to such issues.
10. Co-ordinate with other international organisations in the formulation of appropriate international positions on horizontal issues affecting intellectual property, in particular:
    - the validity of electronic contracts, and
    - jurisdiction.

References

Bajaj, Kamlesh Kumar and Nag, Debjani, E-commerce, the Cutting Edge of Business.

E-commerce, A Survey of Business Households in India (June 1999), prepared by Business Industrial Research Division of Indian Market Research Bureau.

Focus—*WTO Newsletter*, Aug.-Sep., 1998.

Focus—*WTO Newsletter*, June, 1998.

Mukherjee, Anjan E., Business Evolution, paper published in the backgrounder of the 26th National Management Convention of AIMAF held on August 18-20, 1999 at New Delhi.

"Spread of E-governance Needed", *Business Standard*, November 6/7, 1999.

UNCTAD, Trade and Development Report, 1999-2000.

Watar, Jayashree, TRIPs and the WTO Millennium Record, 1999, Some Reflections on Future Issues related to IPRS in WTO and the Way Forward for Developing Countries.

World Development Report, 1998.

WTO, Annual Report, 1998.

31

Internet in India: An Overview

SATYANARAYANA PATNAIK AND A. SARAVANAN

Advances in scientific research have given rise to most of the sophisticated new technologies in the information and communication fields that are now drastically changing the concept of a large size diversified world to a global village. In the new millennium, the information revolution is heading towards digitised communication channels in cyberspace. Knowledge informed, entertained and educated as a result of the free flow of information and sharing of data with the help of advanced technologies though television and the personal computer at home, we are witnessing a quantitative transformation in our social, economic and political sectors. The networking of people through innovative communication and information technology is creating limitless access to all available forms for social learning and intelligence. The breakthrough is the result of advancement in information technology and progressive merging of telecommunications with the world of computers both at the technology and policy levels.

One of the biggest achievements of the 21st century is the introduction of an advanced communication network, namely, the Internet, that connects millions of computers through a network. This is a process of linking end-to-end digital source and receiver. The Internet can be broadly defined as a worldwide network of computers communicating *via* an agreed upon protocol (rules for exchange of information). It provides access to the most diversified sources of information hosted by individuals and various organisations worldwide on a vast network of servers. Presently, the Internet gives access to the World Wide Web, or just Web, which interconnects thousands of servers created by various organisations, commercial establishments, industrial units, academic institutions, common or targeted groups and even private individuals. The web pages loaded on servers provide various types of information such as plain text, pictures, animation and multimedia either free of cost or for a modest fee. Besides, the web pages offer services like e-mail, conferencing, electronic publications and other commercial facilities. It is a new mode to trade text or information from one point of the globe to another quickly, cheaply and easily. It is not only a one-way communication process; it also receives information in the opposite direction and performs as an interactive medium *par excellence*. Though it is not interactive by itself, the amount of control the users have is due to the computers themselves and it enables the users to send and receive information to and from the network.

Information in the net flows from the source to the destination through intermediate nodes. These nodes have sufficient intelligence to route the information to the appropriate destination. The information packets between source and destination are routed through different paths as they move towards the final destination. For the information to reach the destination, a common set of rules and procedures, called protocols, is followed by all Internet-based systems. These are well known as the transmission control protocol and Internet protocol mechanisms. The characteristics of the Internet are:

1. Point-to-point communication;
2. Ability to locate/search huge amounts of data;
3. Hyperlinking from one server to another; by clicking on the highlighted word the user is directly switched to another data source, perhaps on the other side of the globe; and
4. Instant and interactive community creation on a global basis.

As considerable research on the new information medium is being continuously added on, it is becoming user-friendly, reliable and faster in providing maximum benefits to its clients.

Initially, the Internet was primarily used for research purposes due to its fast exchange of information, cost effectiveness and availability in digitised mode. Now, researchers around the world are using this medium to work together, exchange ideas and results and many even carry out joint experiments or simulations without being in the same place. The Net brings them much more opportunities by reducing the communication and distance gap through cheaper and faster interaction.

A NEW ERA

Until the Nineties, the Internet was relatively limited and mostly confined to the academic and military communities. In the U.S.A. the Internet has been used extensively as a new communication medium and the people are heavily dependent on it for the past two decades or more for electronic mail and for getting valuable information on politics, elections, business and State affairs. Towards the end of the last and the beginning of the present decade several world incidents such as the Gulf War, disintegration of the USSR, conflict in the former Yugoslavia, disturbances in China and Iran and similar events virtually changed the flow of information.

In the world of communication, the Internet is undoubtedly a significant new development. In the past 10 years, the Internet network has grown on a compound annual growth rate of more than 100 per cent, says Dr. Henry Chasia, Deputy Secretary-General of the International Telecommunication Union. By July 1997, there were more than 19 million Internet host computers in the world, compared to 2.2 million hosts in 1993. Today, the Internet service users are estimated to range from 40 to 60 million worldwide. A recent estimate indicates that this powerful source has added another four per cent a year increasing the total worldwide users to more than 10 million by 2000. Though the rapid penetration of the Internet is visible, not all countries or regions of the world are benefiting equally from its development. It is found that out of the total Internet connections in the world, about two-thirds are registered in North America. Developed countries with 16 per cent of the world's population have more than 90 per cent of Internet hosts. Around 50 developing countries still do not have direct Internet facility and the African continent is the most backward in terms of Internet penetration.

In India, the Internet service has drawn attention mainly in metropolitan cities and large urban areas. However, the Government's efforts and newly formulated Information Technology Policy envisages that Internet services are spreading to all district headquarters. This is a significant step in revolutionising the information sector in the country.

INFRASTRUCTURE IN INDIA

The last few years have seen a sea change in the areas of information and communications, particularly after the penetration of the Internet and has undergone transformation of a different kind wherein the availability of information has played a key role. Presently, several millions have access to all kinds of information resources to enrich their knowledge base. India stands among the highest Internet subscribers in the developing world. There are two main reasons that support and enhance Internet penetration in India. One, English is the universal communication language on the Internet. A sizeable part of the Indian population is well versed with the English language and those who have access to the Internet prefer communicating in English than in other languages. The other reason is the rapid spread of the computer network, growing telecommunication infrastructure and flourishing computer software industries. Besides, the liberal approach towards the Internet subscribers and the Government's enhanced support for the development of the IT and communications infrastructure in the country is also another reason for the growth of the Internet in India.

Since the late 1980s, Internet service was available in India on a non-commercial basis, only for educational purposes, by the Educational Research Network (ERNET). The service was the first joint venture of the Indian Government and the United Nations Development Programme in establishing an Internet infrastructure in the country and it opened the Indian Internet service for global accessing. Presently, the service has eight nodes at different locations and has access to more than 10 countries; its subscribers number about 0.5 million in approximately 600 organisations. The commencement of SatwanHub initiated the access of the ERNET service through the VSAT network. The main sites of the ERNET are interconnected through terrestrial links whereas access to overseas gateways is through 64 kbps (kilobytes per second) links. It also has links with two local networks in the U.S.A. The ERNET subscribers are mainly academic and research institutions, non-governmental organisations and, to a limited extent, private and international organisations. The ERNET is planning to launch several multimedia-related programmes such as video conferencing, document retrieval mail facility and is targeting a broader subscriber base.

GIAS

The Gateway Internet Access Service (GIAS) is a full-featured Internet available from 20 nodes operated by VSNL and DoT. Access to GIAS is available *via* dial-up lines up to 33.6 kbps or *via* leased lines at 9.6 kbps to 2 mbps or higher and provides full Internet access through normal telecom services. Commercial Internet services were started in 1995 by Videsh Sanchar Nigam Limited (VSNL), India's international telecom carrier, using GIAS, in Mumbai and Delhi. When the service was launched, VSNL had only 703 customers, 64 access lines, four Internet nodes and Internet connectivity up to 64 kbps. Since its inception, the service provided by VSNL has spread to many Indian cities and towns and it was estimated that up to mid-1997, the VSNL's Internet subscribers were around 15,000. Viewing the sluggish growth of its subscriber base, VSNL has adopted several strategies, including reducing the subscription fee.

Presently, VSNL has 12 Internet nodes operating at different locations in the country. Statistics show that up to June 1998, VSNL and the Department of Telecommunication (DoT) had over 150,000 subscribers, 8,000 access lines, 40 nodes and adequate capacity for two million customers and international connectivity up to 70 mbps. VSNL is connecting its main Internet nodes located at Mumbai to the U.S.A. through satellite and to Europe through submarine cable. It has Internet nodes at several Indian metro cities which are connected to the main Internet node though the inter-city links of DoT. Its subscribers vary from individuals to corporate organisations.

The National Informatics Centre Network (NICNet) service was started with the assistance of the Planning Commission in 1988 and it provides exclusive service to government organisations in the country. It uses the satellite-based data communication of NIC for its functioning. It has around 700 micro earth stations (MES) located in various parts of the country while the master earth station is located at Delhi which is connected to the MES. The network is the first established web server in India and is presently connected to over 200 overseas networks in 160 countries. It has been providing Internet access through a direct highspeed link to Spinternet in the U.S.A. Nicnet provides electronic mail facilities to research and educational networks (RENNIC). It also provides service in the area of management information for rural development schemes, medical literature and analysis and retrieval systems and the National Library of

Medicine. Its subscriber base was estimated at about 10,000 in 1997.

The Department of Electronic's Software Technology Park (STP) has launched an Internet service, Softnet, in collaboration with Sat Comm Services, India. The six STP centres are located at Bhubaneshwar, Tiruvananthapuram, Hyderabad, Gandhinagar, Noida and Bangalore, each with an international gateway and facilities to provide high speed data communication links and direct Internet access. The Softnet offers a dedicated leased line service ranging from 9.6 kbps to 2 mbps for interactive applications. The network is also planning to provide services such as video-on-demand, bandwidth-on-demand, authoring web pages and setting up web servers.

IT ACTION PLAN

Since the mid-1980s, the Indian information technology (IT) sector has extensively revolutionised and placed India on the forefront of the global information technology scenario. The country duly recognised IT as an agent capable of changing every facet of human life, bringing in a knowledge-based society in the 21st century. Recognising its importance, the Approach Paper to the Ninth Five-Year Plan emphasised several measures for development of information technology and communication infrastructure in the country. As the basic necessity for developing an appropriate national information infrastructure, many inter-related facilities are required such as satellite communication facilities with digital telephone exchanges, expansion of the telephone network and computers. The Plan laid emphasis on providing telephone facilities in all villages by 2000. The recently formulated Information Technology Action Plan (IT Task Force), a major initiative by the government, emphasises setting up a world class info-infrastructure including an extensive spread of fibre optic networks, satcom networks and wireless networks for seamlessly interconnecting the local informatics and national informatics infrastructures and global informatics infrastructure to ensure a fast, nation-wide onset of the Internet, extranets and intranets. The Action Plan Report envisaged that DoT will open Internet nodes and authorised ISPs at all district headquarters and local charging areas. No licence fee is necessary for setting up of ISP operations by companies for the first five years, and after this a nominal fee of Re. 1 will be charged.

Promotional measures would be undertaken to encourage

technologies that bring IT and Internet to the masses through a vast network of cable TV houses and authorised cable TV operators. They would be permitted to provide Internet access without taking additional licence. Mega websites would be created on the Internet for promoting, marketing and encouraging Indian software products and packages under multiple initiatives. Similarly, creation and hosting of web sites on servers located in India would also be encouraged. The Plan paid due attention for IT for all by 2008 where it envisages accelerating the rate of PC/set top box penetration in the country from the 1998 level of 1 per 500 to 1 per 50 people, along with universal access to the Internet with a flood of IT to be a frontier area of knowledge. A plan, Operation Knowledge, is being proposed with the aim to universalise computer literacy and also to spread the use of computers and IT in education. Under the proposed plan, computers and the Internet would be made available in every school, polytechnic, college, university and public hospital in the country by 2003, whereas all universities, engineering and medical colleges, R&D organisations and institutions of higher learning would be networked for a supplementary programme of distance education for improving the quality of education.

CONCLUSION

With the fast growing global technological revolution in the information and human resource development sectors, India has initiated several strategies for its active participation to provide the most sophisticated Internet communication to people at the rural level. The Ninth Five-Year Plan has indicated that by 2002, Internet subscribers in the country would be around one million while the recent Indian policy on the Internet forecasts the number could be around two million within a period of two to three years. To achieve the target results, there is need for a careful assessment by our information planners and policy makers on the inter-related infrastructural requirements necessary for the growth of the system and how the new information dissemination technology would provide optimum benefit to a maximum proportion of the country's population. Certainly, rapid diffusion of the Internet depends on proper telecommunication and computer networks. India's telephone density is hardly 1.3 per cent (telephones per 100 population) against the world average of 11 and our computer density is around 1.5 (per thousand population) against the world average of two. Certainly, to make the Internet a popular information medium in India, there is need to strengthen the growth of both teledensity and PC infrastructures. Presently, the ratio of telephones to PCs in developed countries ranges between 1:3 to 1:5 and India if initiates strategic measures in the next two to three years to improve PC penetration to one per 100, the ratio would be 1:6. Besides, the level of education of the general population of a country and local diffusion of the Internet is closely related. To make the Internet a popular information medium in India, considerable efforts have to be initiated at different levels of our educational system. The other aspect is affordability of the service charges for connecting to the Internet. The new generation of Indian software professionals are well recognised for their technological skills by the world. A low cost Internet facility for people in the country by these professionals may be explored.

The Task Force on Information Technology and Software Development, to realise the objectives in bringing India on to the information super-highway, should collectively look to overcome the basic problems for the rapid diffusion of the Internet in India and ensure that the country will not miss the opportunity of the global communication revolution.

32

Internet, XBRL, and Online Business Reporting: Challenges and Opportunities

V.K. VASAL AND RAJENDRA P. SRIVASTAVA

Information Technology (IT) with a bouquet of tools including Internet has radically transformed the decision-making processes and business environment. As a 'decision-support system' to internal management, it has enabled business managers to collect, process, store, transmit, retrieve, and use data/information with enhanced speed and greater efficiency. And, also, it has provided businesses with a new (electronic) media in the form of Intranet and Internet (in simple terms, a worldwide network of computer systems) for communication both within and outside the entity. As an electronic media for communication, Internet has provided businesses with a capability to deliver financial and other business information to the external users for a period ranging from the usual annual, to quarterly, to theoretically, real-time. In fact, use of Web for information reporting purposes, commonly termed as 'on-line reporting', has gained immensely in importance in recent past. For instance, e-Bay is supplying such business information as the latest auction prices for various products through its web site in real time. These auction prices can be accessed by the 'public at large', in a transparent manner and without much cost, in realtime. It is reported that some companies like Cisco, with the necessary support of IT and Internet, have already acquired the capabilities for supplying financial statements to the external users on a daily basis.

However, the aforesaid spectacular growth in electronic information delivery capabilities of companies has been accompanied by some problems. Two of such problems are, first, a variety of incompatible languages in which electronic information is currently being encoded, and, second, a whole range of incongruent platforms through which this electronic information is being collected, processed, disseminated, retrieved, and analysed along the information-supply-chain. These problems, as a consequence, impair the speed and efficiency of decision-making processes. At times, reliability of information communicated under the prevalent system may also be doubtful. As an aid to the decision-making processes, therefore, a need (and an opportunity) exists to evolve a language or a support technology for making electronic exchange of business information faster, efficient, and reliable across different software and varied computing platforms. And, herein lies the genesis of eXtensible Business Reporting Language (XBRL). As a technology, XBRL has been (is being) developed for standardising, enhancing, and improving the content and capabilities of information reported electronically, for both internal and external users. In fact, parallel to accounting being labelled as the 'language of business', XBRL has been hailed as the 'digital language of business'.

In the above background, the primary objectives of the present paper are two-fold. First, the paper has examined the regulatory aspects and corporate reporting practices of Indian companies with respect to supply of electronic annual reports through the Internet. And second, based on the findings for the first, the paper has built-up and argued a case for (preparing and) supplying electronic information in XBRL. While arguing a case for XBRL, some advantages accruing from the XBRL environment to the management in general are also discussed.

INTERNET AND EXTERNAL INFORMATION REPORTING

The current business trends show that companies all over the world are using Internet as a medium for electronic delivery of business information. In this regard, India is no exception. A search launched on the Internet for this study has shown that each of the 'Top-10' Indian companies (ranked in terms of sales revenues), in both private and public sectors, is currently maintaining a web site. In fact, companies like Reliance Industries, Hindustan Petroleum and several others are supplying an electronic version of their respective annual reports, besides other business information, to varied stakeholders through their respective web sites. It is envisioned that, with time, almost every publicly traded company shall be supplying information on all dimensions of reporting—mandated/voluntary, financial/quantitative/textual—through the Web. This indeed marks beginning of a new era in faster, cost-effective, and adequate delivery of financial and other business information to various stakeholders of businesses. Though, it may be stated here that studies published by FASB and IASC a few years ago have raised some pertinent questions on the qualities of electronic information delivered through the Internet.

Like elsewhere in the world, Securities and Exchange Board of India (SEBI) has already taken some initial steps in introducing, mandating, and regulating the supply of electronic information by companies listed on the Indian Securities Market. In this direction, SEBI has institutionalised a system called Electronic Data Information Filing And Retrieval (EDIFAR) since July 2002. This system is modelled on the lines of EDGAR (Electronic Data Gathering, Analysis and Retrieval) system of the US, and SEDAR (Systems for Electronic Document Analysis and Retrieval) in Canada, and is being hosted on the SEBI web site (www.sebi.gov.in). And, like EDGAR and SEDAR, EDIFAR system is a repository of business information for listed Indian companies. The system makes mandated business information available at a unique site for all kinds of users, including the investors. This regulatory environment is discussed further in the following Section of the paper, followed by an examination of the electronic reporting practices.

ELECTRONIC BUSINESS REPORTING—INDIAN REGULATIONS

As stated above, SEBI has created a repository of information called EDIFAR system in India. This repository is an electronic information filing system that aims at centralisation and accelerated dissemination of business information on listed companies. This system promises to enhance transparency and to bring greater efficiency in the Securities' Market, thus, benefiting various market participants including investors. The system is being implemented in a phased manner by amending the listing agreement of the listed companies with the Stock Exchanges (Clause 51). EDIFAR seeks to replace physical filing of the business information with the stock exchanges for all actively traded companies, over a period of time.

Till now, SEBI has notified names of the companies covered under the EDIFAR system in three phases. In the first phase, effective July 2002, 200 companies were required to file online, among others, the full version of their respective annual reports. Companies covered in the first phase are the ones constituting the BSE Sensex, S&P CNX Nifty, and BSE 200 indices. In the second phase, effective September 2002, a total of 700 companies were covered for submitting electronic information at the web site. And in the third phase, effective December 2002, 1196 companies are covered under the system. That is, one-out-of-seven listed Indian companies is required on date to electronically file its financial and other business information (including annual reports) with the EDIFAR system. Though still in its nascent stage, ever growing number of companies covered in the EDIFAR system proves the point that electronic information reporting through Internet has come (is coming) of age in India.

ELECTRONIC ANNUAL REPORTS—INDIAN EVIDENCE

In this section, first, an attempt has been made to explore the reporting practices of companies with respect to electronic annual reports (e-annual reports) filed by them under the EDIFAR system. For this purpose, an experiment has been conducted on the electronic reporting practices of 100 companies, two samples of 50 companies each, as at the end of calendar year 2002. Analysis of findings for this experiment, besides generating some preliminary evidence on the reporting practices of Indian companies, has provided inputs for conducting the second experiment arguing a case for supplying of XBRL coded information through Internet.

As already stated, for the first experiment, electronic annual reports of 100 companies constituting two samples of 50 companies each have been examined. The first sample consists of companies included in the NIFTY Fifty index, and the second sample consists of companies covered in the NIFTY Junior index. Findings of this experiment have led to drawing of the following inferences.

For 50 companies constituting the NIFTY Fifty index, first, it is found that 26 (52%) companies have filed electronic documents with the EDIFAR system. Since all of these companies were included in the first notification of SEBI in July 2002, non-supply of electronic information by 48 percent companies even after a lapse of half-a-year reveals a lack of seriousness, and laxity on the part of these leading and most actively traded companies. This finding has serious regulatory and policy implications. Second, out of 26 companies reporting through EDIFAR system, only 16 (32%) have filed substantial or complete electronic copies of their annual reports. That is, 10 (20%) companies have filed some electronic documents but these are other than their annual reports. Third, an interesting finding is that electronic annual reports of all the 16 (32%) companies are in 'pdf' format. Fourth, it is observed that size of the electronic annual reports filed with EDIFAR system has varied widely, between a minimum of 234.9 KB for Indian Petrochemicals Corporation to a maximum of 17.68 MB for Shipping Corporation of India. In terms of size of the electronic annual reports, top three ranks are occupied by Shipping Corporation of India (17.68 MB), Sun Pharmaceuticals (11.16 MB) and Bharat Petroleum (9.61 MB). It is an accepted fact that, for a given software, time taken to access, scan, and process an electronic document varies directly with its size.

On the other hand, for the 50 companies constituting the NIFTY Junior index, the findings are as follows. First, only 20 (40%) companies have filed some electronic documents with the EDIFAR system. Since 47 of these 50 companies were included in the first notification of SEBI in July 2002, non-supply of electronic information by 27 (57%) of the required companies even after nearly half-a-year indicates a lack of seriousness and laxity on the part of these leading and most actively traded companies. This finding is similar to the one noted above for NIFTY Fifty companies, and has associated regulatory and policy implications. Second, it is found that out of 20 companies filing electronic documents, only 10 (21%) have filed substantial or complete copies of their electronic annual reports. In other words, the other 10 companies have filed some electronic documents but these are other than their electronic annual reports. Third, electronic annual reports of all the 10 (21%) companies are found in 'pdf' format. Fourth, like the NIFTY Fifty companies, the empirical analysis for NIFTY Junior companies shows that size of the electronic annual reports filed with EDIFAR system varies widely, between a minimum of 336 KB for Merck to a maximum of 4.00 MB for Madras Cement. While wide enough, this range is less than that observed for the NIFTY Fifty companies. Among the NIFTY Junior companies, top three ranks in terms of size of the electronic annual reports are occupied by Madras Cement (4.00 MB), Ashok Leyland (2.82 MB) and Global Trust Bank (2.27 MB).

As stated earlier, bigger is the size of an electronic document, more is the time taken to access, scan, and extract information out of it by a given software. This is true in general. However, as against an existing software, it is possible to design a new language or software that could save on the time required to harvest electronic data from the Internet. If accomplished, new language or software should be termed as more efficient compared to the former. In this background, the second experiment has been conducted. The experiment appraises current practices of supplying electronic annual reports in terms of an efficiency (time-) metric, and, thus, argues a case for XBRL coded business reports.

Under the second experiment, three biggest sized electronic annual reports (as found from the first experiment) in the two samples of companies are accessed once again. But, this time the experiment is performed as follows. First, a time-metric recording the time taken (in minutes) to access electronic annual reports is introduced. And, second, in order to control external environmental factors, reports of the companies are accessed in one sitting. Results of this experiment have shown that, partly due to the fact that electronic annual reports of five of the six companies are in colour, a total of nearly seventy minutes (approximately twelve minutes on an average) are used for merely displaying the annual reports from the EDIFAR system. Add to this, the time required in searching a data item (say, the amount of 'R&D expenditure') in a 'pdf' file, and extracting and assembling it in a work-file for further analysis. And the whole exercise has taken about one-and-a-half-hours (on an average, approximately fifteen minutes per company). Obviously, fifteen minutes per company is too much of time for preparing data for financial analysis in this electronic age. However, this finding should be read along with the following fact. Since inputs for a query at the EDIFAR system are demanded (and accepted) in three sequential steps (one on completion of the other), a slice of the total time — approximately fifteen minutes per company — can be apportioned to the sub-optimally designed querying method of the EDIFAR system.

As against the findings of the second experiment, observers opine that, if data-items are coded in XBRL, a specially designed financial reporting browser can access, extract, and organise information on a data-item(s), say the amount of 'R&D expenditure', into a spreadsheet for, say, 100 companies in less than a minute (a small fraction of an-hour-and-a-half). This would be so because XBRL coded electronic annual reports (called XBRL Instance Documents) are, in a loose sense, akin to data kept in a database that is uniformly structured and applied across the firms. The efficiency (both in terms of speed and cost), reliability and thrill of information management of this kind can be experienced with the model XBRL coded data for select companies that NASDAQ has made available through its web site. In this perspective, an elementary discussion on the XBRL technology is attempted in the following sections.

XBRL—BUILDING BLOCKS

XBRL is variously envisioned as (i) a consortium of persons, XBRL International, or (ii) a programming language/software, or (iii) a technology for exchange of information. It is in the second and the third senses that XBRL is defined in this chapter.

As a language and a technology, XBRL aims at increasing the usefulness of business information delivered in an electronic form, say through Internet. Accordingly, XBRL has been widely acclaimed and endorsed as the 'digital language of business' by various professional bodies like the AICPA (American Institute of Certified Public Accountants) of the US on the west-end and the Institute of Chartered Accountants of Australia on the east-end of the world map. As an e-technology, XBRL is based on the eXtensible Markup Language (XML), very much like EBXML (Electronic Business XML), CML (Chemical Markup Language) and AIML (Astronomical Instrument Markup Language). A discussion (alphabetical) on some of the key concepts that form the building blocks and background to the development (and understanding) of XBRL is given below.

(i) eXtensible

The first key term in XBRL is the property of 'extensibility'. This property is alternatively termed as 'expendability' of the language. Conceptually, extensibility refers to the capability of the XBRL in permitting incorporation of new language elements. This capability of the language allows users to enrich the language by introducing new features and modifying the existing ones.

To illustrate, let 'Current Liabilities' in the balance sheet be divided into seven items with 'Sundry Creditors' being one (see Schedule VI of the Companies Act, 1956). Now, let it be presumed that two additional items dividing the amount of 'Sundry Creditors' into (i) 'Total outstanding dues of small scale industrial undertaking(s)'; and (ii) 'Total outstanding dues of creditors other than small scale industrial undertaking(s)' are additionally required to be presented (see Companies Act (Amendment) 1999). The extensibility feature of XBRL permits linking-up of the instructions for the two new items to the XBRL instructions already written for the earlier set of items (called XBRL taxonomy). That is, XBRL taxonomy (accounting concepts and their inter-relationships) need not be written once again for the enlarged list of data-items. Rather, linkbase feature of the XBRL allows linking up of the accounting concepts and relationship(s) of the new items (defined in an independent supplementary taxonomy) with the accounting concepts and relationship(s) defined in the earlier taxonomy.

The property of extensibility is very handy in situations when list of items reported for various elements of the financial statements are not the same across firms, industries, and countries. For example, many an items constituting non-current assets in Oil and Gas Industry (items like rigs, exploratory oil and gas wells) may not be applicable to companies in general. In a situation of this kind, XBRL may prepare a taxonomy called a 'Global Common Document' (GCD) for items common to all the firms, industries, and countries. And, any country-specific, industry-specific, and firm-specific variations (extensions/limitations) can, then, be written as independent taxonomies that can be imported and incorporated with the GCD. This blended set of instructions is then used for validating an 'instance document' (an XBRL coded electronic business report), say a balance sheet or a profit and loss account or a cash flow statement. Such an arrangement is illustrated in Figure 32.1 with reference to the taxonomy framework proffered by the International Accounting Standards Committee Foundation (IASCF).

(ii) Markup Language

The second important feature of XBRL is that it is a markup language. In simple words, a markup language is a collection of codes (or tags). These tags may refer to the 'structure' and 'format' of an electronic document as well as 'context' of data. Notably, the source of all markup languages is the Standard Generalized Markup Language (SGML).

Two popular and widely used markup languages are 'Hyper Text Markup Language' (HTML) and 'eXtensible Markup Language' (XML). Notably, HTML uses tags that govern appearance — size, shape,

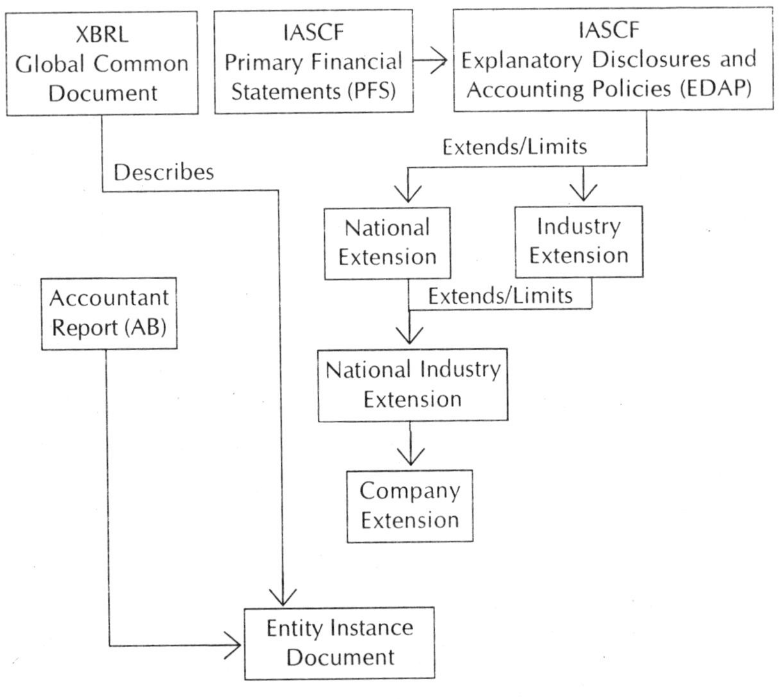

FIG. 32.1

International Accounting Standards Expressed in XBRL for Electronic Financial Reporting.

Source: International Accounting Standards Committee Foundation (IASCF) and XBRL International.

colour, etc. – of data on the Web. These tags are generally used in pairs and are enclosed within angle brackets, with tag in the closing angle bracket preceded by a slash. To illustrate, HTML uses tags '<H1> and </H1 >' through '<H6> and </H6>' for headings, with former for the most important heading and the latter for the least. Similarly, tags '<B> and </B>' are used by HTML for displaying data, say a number '4233390000', in boldcase.

As against HTML, XML is a markup language that 'describe' data. In describing data, XML offers the feature of flexibility. For instance, to describe data for amount owed to a supplier, a company may adopt the tags '<seller> and </seller>'. However, to describe the same kind of data, another company may choose some other tags, say '<vendor>

and </vendor>', or '<creditor> and </creditor>'. Since XBRL is based on XML, it too offers the flexibility in devising the tag names. Hence, to describe data on, say, 'Current Liabilities', two different bodies developing XBRL taxonomies may devise different tag names. But, as is obvious, for achieving comparability of business data across different taxonomies, an interface equating two different sets of tags would be required.

It may be stated in the passing that Charles Goldfarb, one of the inventors of SGML, has likened HTML, to use a simile, to a 'word processor', i.e., concerned with display or presentation of information, and XML to a 'database', i.e., concerned with providing context to the data. Since XBRL is based on XML, business data coded as per XBRL, thus, carry all the advantages of data kept in a typical database.

(iii) XML

As XBRL is based on XML, some additional important features of XML are discussed here. Since XML (and hence XBRL) describes data, it is a technology that is aptly designed to store, carry, and exchange data. XML (and XBRL) achieves this capability by storing data in plain text files with the addition of markups or tags. And, storing of data in plain text files, in turn, permits smooth and efficient exchange of data amongst incongruous operating systems (say Windows, Unix and GNU/Linux) and other software, and incompatible computer systems (say Macintosh and IBM PC). This is arguably one of the important reasons for several companies converting their HTML coded business information into XML coded ones (as reported in recent years through the print media) for delivering them electronically, both through the Intranet and Internet.

To continue with the example discussed earlier under the second building block (Markup Language), as against HTML tags governing the appearance of a number in 'boldcase', XBRL describes a number '4233390000' as follows. That the number is: (i) monetary data, (ii) in rupees, (iii) on 'Current Liabilities' (actual), (iv) of ONGC, and (v) for the year ended as at March 31, 2002. This is achieved in XBRL by using appropriate tags. Once coded, and validated against the applicable XBRL taxonomy, movement of this number along the information supply chain, regardless of the application software or computing platform used, shall always carry the description associated with it. This description or contextualising of data is a cutting-edge feature of XML (and hence XBRL) over HTML. And, it is a property that not only enables 'talking' of computers with each other, but is also at the root of designing and operationalisation of intelligent software such as FRAANK (Financial Reporting And Auditing in Network-enabled Knowledge).

XBRL—PROCESS

The major building blocks of XBRL are discussed in the previous section. In this section, first, a synoptic review of how XBRL conducts itself is done and, second, a case in favour of XBRL is argued, with reference to the said building blocks.

As stated in the preceding section, XBRL is a technology that describes business information in a manner such that, irrespective of the operating systems and computing systems involved in the information supply chain, information can be exchanged with greater speed, higher efficiency, and improved reliability. In fact, XBRL enables gathering (and analysis) of business information to match precisely to the needs of the users. This is accomplished in XBRL with the help of following two instruments: an instance document and an XBRL taxonomy. These two instruments of the XBRL are discussed in the following paragraphs.

Instance Document

In simple terms, an electronic version of the XBRL-tagged business report is called an 'instance document'. That is, an electronic (digital) version of each of the financial statements (such as a balance sheet, a profit and loss account, or a cash flow statement) and other business reports (such as a budget) created within the XBRL environment. This instance document essentially contains the factual data.

In operational terms, an 'instance document' is created through the active intervention of the preparers of financial and other business reports. These preparers, in the initial stage of information supply chain, assign contextual meaning to individual items of business data (both numerical and textual) in terms of the XBRL tags. It may be stated here that some software packages are currently available for accomplishing the task of coding business data with the XBRL tags. In the next stage, XBRL-tagged business data contained in an instance documents are validated against the relevant XBRL taxonomy(ies). This validation is done with a view to ensure that accounting concepts and inter-relationships among them, and other business rules have been duly observed in constructing an instance document. An 'instance document' pertaining to summarised balance sheet of ONGC for the year ended as at March 31, 2002, conforming to the International Accounting Standards Committee Foundation (IASCF) taxonomy, may appear as illustrated in Appendix-1 (upper portion). The instance document in raw XML is also given in the lower part of the Appendix.

XBRL Taxonomy

At the root of an instance document is the core XBRL technology in the form of XBRL taxonomy(ies). XBRL taxonomy is essentially an XML Schema document. And, as an XML Schema document, taxonomy is an extensible dictionary or vocabulary of financial and business terms. It maps and pre-defines various accounting concepts and inter-relationships amongst them (each accounting concept is referred as an 'element' in taxonomy). For instance, XBRL taxonomy may pre-define the accounting concepts (termed elements) 'Receivables' (Gross), 'Provision for Doubtful Debts', and 'Receivables (Net)' and establish inter-relationships amongst these elements in terms of XBRL tags. A computer, in turn, accesses this XBRL taxonomy for validating and understanding factual data on various elements that constitute an 'instance document' (say, amounts of assets, liabilities and equity in a balance sheet coded with XBRL tags). In short, XBRL taxonomy enables a computer (program) to talk to the business reports.

It may be emphasised once again that an instance document might be governed by two or more XBRL taxonomies. For example, an instance document (say a balance sheet of an Oil and Gas company) may be governed by the following. A 'global common document' (GCD) taxonomy of IASCF (for items common to all firms worldwide), a national taxonomy (for items unique to a country), an industry taxonomy (for items unique to an industry, say Oil and Gas), and firm-specific taxonomy (for items voluntarily disclosed, and, hence, unique to a firm). Thus, validation of an instance document may require a referencing to multiple XBRL taxonomies. This is exhibited in Figure 32.1.

In building an XBRL taxonomy, due examination of the authoritative literature is done. To illustrate, development of an XBRL taxonomy for the balance sheet of Indian companies should refer such authoritative literature as the relevant provisions of the Companies Act, 1956, accounting standards issued by the Institute of Chartered Accountants of India (ICAI), and best accounting practices. Based on this examination, a detailed checklist of XBRL elements (various accounting concepts), and their inter-relationships, should be prepared. These elements and their inter-relationships should, then, be incorporated in a taxonomy with XBRL tags (as per norms and conventions generally accepted and endorsed by an authoritative body) such that computers are able to understand and interpret these tags. XBRL tags can be written as description for an element name only (say, 'liab-cur-total' for '(Total) Current Liabilities'), or as description in terms of two element names related with one another as a parent and a child (say, 'currentLiabilities.sundryCreditors' establishing that element 'Current Liabilities' is a parent to the colloquially named element 'Sundry Creditors'). Appendix-1 illustrates the former convention for naming the accounting concepts in an XBRL taxonomy.

The recent versions of XBRL taxonomy(ies) published by various authoritative bodies around the world have very widely used a tool called Xlink (linkbase) for representing the accounting concepts and their inter-relationships. These linkbases make XBRL taxonomy document (main) appear more manageable and neat by placing information on each of the attributes — labels, reference, definition, presentation and calculation — of elements into separate documents. With the help of linkbase tool, these separate documents are then linked to the main taxonomy document. An extract from the XBRL taxonomy document developed by IASCF and using the tool of linkbase is illustrated in Appendix-2.

XBRL AND ELECTRONIC FINANCIAL REPORTING

As discussed above, XBRL taxonomy contextualises or describes business data (elements) and their inter-relationships at a conceptual level in terms of several attributes. But, an 'instance document' also adds further context to the data. In specific terms, an instance document describes data in terms of the following attributes — entity (name of the company), segment (business segment within the entity), scenario (budget or actual), period (as at a date or for a period), unit (currency), and precision (for numerical data). Taken as a whole, contexts to the data (contained in both the taxonomy and the instance documents) enable computers to perform a contextual search on the Web. Theoretically, data on an item (say 'Current Liabilities') from XBRL coded business reports (say a balance sheet) can now be harvested and profiled for 'n' number (6, as for the experiment conducted in Section 2 above) of companies by simply clicking a few buttons! This is so because XBRL-enabled software locate and assemble the required business data (textual, quantitative or monetary) into a spreadsheet by executing a simple command.

The aforesaid capabilities of XBRL deserve to be recognised against the findings for the time-metric experiment performed in Section 3 of this paper. Accordingly, findings of the second experiment are considered once again here. As discussed, the experiment has shown that approximately one-and-a-half-hours were taken for locating, extracting and assembling of data on a single item (amount of 'R&D expenditure') from the 'pdf' files of 6 companies from the EDIFAR system, the repository of electronically filed annual reports in India. As against this, no more than a minute may be required in the XBRL environment to complete the said experiment. This comparison clearly highlights the efficiencies (in terms of both time and cost) that can be achieved in the decision-making processes of the external users while using electronic annual reports from the Internet.

XBRL AND FUTURE DIRECTIONS

In addition to introducing efficiencies in the decision-making processes of the external users, XBRL environment also yields tremendous benefits to the management in general. Figures 32.2(a) and 32.2(b) highlight these benefits graphically by comparing the overall processing and dissemination of information under the conventional *vis-a-vis* the XBRL environments. Figure 32.2(a) exhibits that the traditional reporting system may identify, mine, and assemble accounting data from the accounting system and other sources a number of times, each time specific to a purpose. Obviously, this is not the most efficient approach to information management. On the other hand, Figure 32.2(b) shows that under the XBRL reporting environment, once accounting data from all the sourrces has been coded in XBRL, various accounting reports can be generated for multiple uses in a very efficient manner.

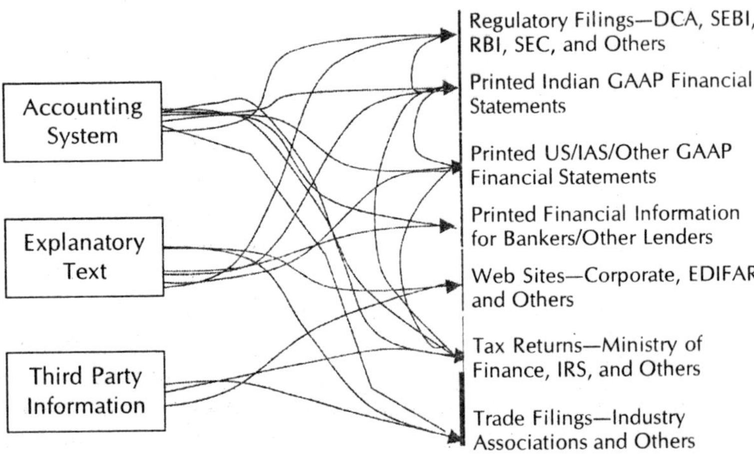

FIG. 32.2(a)

Flow of Information in Traditional Reporting Process.

Source: Adapted and modified from Haffman and Stand (2001) and Vasal and Srivastava (2002).

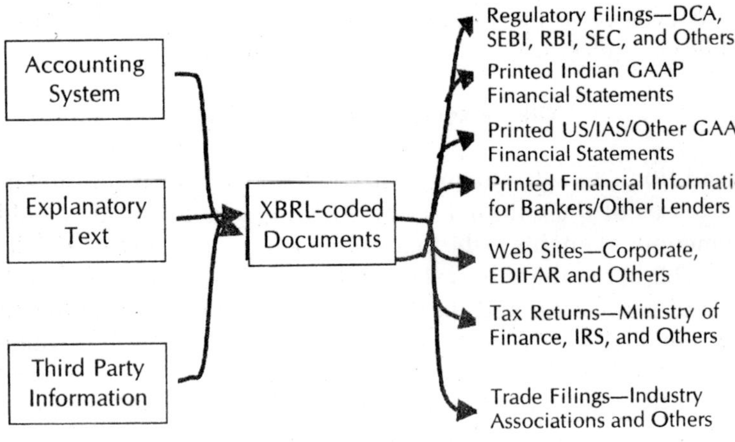

FIG. 32.2(b)

Flow of Information under XBRL Reporting Process.

Source: Adapted and modified from Haffman and Stand (2001) and Vasal and Srivastava (2002).

In fact, XBRL coded information provides viable opportunities, both to management and external users, for designing and implementing intelligent agents such as FRAANK (Financial Reporting And Auditing in Network-enabled Knowledge) for not only assembling but also analysing and interpreting the business information. That is, with XBRL coded data, the intelligent agents enable the computer (programs) to talk and understand the information contained in the published financial statements (such as a balance sheet and/or a profit and loss account) and other business reports. These intelligent agents locate, extract, assemble, analyse, and draw inferences for the decision-makers. Thus, XBRL environment offers vast opportunities for achieving higher speed, greater efficiency, and enhanced reliability in exchange of business information, and, thus, benefiting decision-making by various user-groups (both internal and external to an entity). Even for the auditors, XBRL environment offers several new opportunities such as rendering assurance services (like continuous auditing) for the XBRL coded business data that enters and moves along the information supply chain, both through Intranet and Internet.

In terms of adoption of XBRL, it is worth noting that at the level of an economic unit, some prominent bodies are already experimenting with the XBRL coded business data. These include entities (alphabetically) like the Australian Prudential Regulatory Authority (APRA), Bank of Tokyo Mitsubishi, Microsoft, Mitsui Banking Corporation, Morgan Stanley Dean Witter, Reuters, and Wacoal. In the domain of external reporting, the Morgan Stanley Dean Witter has taken a pioneering lead. The company has achieved the singular distinction in 2002 by becoming the first company to file an XBRL coded electronic document with the SEC in the US. In this regard, it is also worth noting that, beginning Spring 2003, Tokyo Stock Exchange has asked companies to file the highlights page of their financial statements in terms of XBRL.

Adoption of XBRL technology by a variety of entities and its endorsement by the Securities Market suggests that both the accountancy profession and SEBI in India should initiate steps for experimenting with this new technology, perhaps on the lines of Tokyo Stock Exchange. It is suggested that, to begin with, some of the most actively traded companies may be asked to file XBRL coded quarterly reports with the EDIFAR system on an experimental basis. This would, as a pre-requisite, require formation of a taskforce with members representing the disciplines of accountancy, IT, and others. The taskforce should deliberate and lay down a roadmap for implementation of the XBRL. This is considered highly desirable not only to keep pace with the evolving technological scene in the world, but also to realise such objectives as investors' protection, better corporate governance by making performance of public entities more transparent, and ensuring faster and cheaper supply of business information for decision-making purposes.

SUMMARY AND CONCLUSION

In the background of growing importance of Internet and online reporting by companies, as also the SEBI requirement to file electronic copies of financial and other business reports, the paper has first, examined the practices of Indian companies with respect to supply of their electronic annual reports through the EDIFAR system. For a sample of 100 companies, the paper has inferred that a large proportion of actively traded Indian companies are yet to begin complying with the SEBI requirement to supply electronic annual reports through the EDIFAR system. In this regard, the paper has highlighted several weaknesses in the prevalent practices of corporate reporting through the Internet. Second, in terms of a time-metric (average number of minutes taken to locate, extract, and assemble information per company), the paper has argued a case in favour of XBRL-coded electronic annual and other business reports. It is inferred that XBRL-coded electronic documents would bring faster, cheaper, and more reliable information to the decision-making processes of both the external (as well as internal) users. In this regard, building blocks of the XBRL technology are also discussed and illustrated in the paper. Some policy recommendations for establishing the XBRL environment are also made.

REFERENCES

Financial Accounting Standards Board (FASB)—Electronic Distribution of Business Reporting Information, FASB, 2000.

Financial Accounting Standards Board (FASB)—GAAP-SEC Disclosure Requirements, FASB, 2000.

Hoffman, C. and Strand, C. XBRL Essentials, *AICPA*, USA, 2001.

Hoffman, C., Kurt, C. and Koreto, R.J. The XML Files, *Journal of Accountancy*, May 1999.

International Accounting Standards Committee (IASC)—Business Reporting on the Internet, *IASC*, November 1999.

Vasal, V.K. and Srivastava, R.P. eXtensible Business Reporting Language—The Digital Language of Business, *Indian Accounting Review*, June 2002.

Zarowin, S. and Harding, W.E. Finally, Business Talks the Same Language, *Journal of Accountancy*, August 2000.

Appendix-1
(A Sample Instance Document—for Illustration Purposes only)

ONGC Limited

Balance Sheet as at March 31, 2002

	(Amount in Rupees)
Sources of Funds	
Shareholders' Funds	297221750000
Loan Funds	88579000000
Total	385800750000
Application of Funds	
Non-Current Assets, Cost (Net)	274933490000
Current Assets	176658990000
Less: Current Liabilities	65791730000
Net Current Assets	110867260000
Total	385800750000

Line-items presented in the above instance document could appear in raw XML as given below (tagged with XBRL codes as per IASCF framework):


```
<group xmlns:xml = "http://www.w3.org/XML/1998/namespace"
xmlns = "http://www.xbrl.org/2001/instance"
xmlns:xsi = "http://www.w3.org/2002/XMLSchema_instance"
xmlns:ias = "http://www.iasb.org.UK/xbrl/2001-08-16/"
xsi:schemaLocation = "http://www.iasb.org.UK/xbrl/2001-08-16/ias.xsd">

<ias.bs>
<ias:eq-total numericContext="C1">297221750000</ias:eq-total numeric
    Context= "C1">
<ias:liab-nonCur-total numericContext="C1">88579000000</ias:liab-non
    Cur-total numericContext="C1">
<ias:liab-total numericContext="C1"> 385800750000</ias:liab-total numeric
    Context="C1">
<ias:asset-nonCur-total numericContext="C1">274933490000</ias:asset-
    nonCur-total numeric Context="C1">
<ias:asset-cur-tot numericContext="C1">176658990000</ias:asset-cur-tot
    numericContext="C1">
<ias:liab-cur-tot numericContext= "C1">65791730000</ias:liab-cur-tot
    numericContext= "C1">
<ias:asset-total numericContext= "C1">385800750000</ias:asset-total
    numericContext= "C1">

</ias:bs>

</group>
```

Appendix-2
An Extract of XBRLTaxonomy (IASCF Framework)

```
<schema xmlns:xml="http://www.w3.org/XML/1998/namespace"
xmlns:xhtml="http://www.w3.org/1999/xhtml"
xmlns:link="http://www.xbrl.org/2001/Xlink/xbrllinkbase"
xmlns:xlink="http://www.w3.org/1999/xlink"
xmlns:xbrli=http://www.xbrl.org/2001/instance
xmlns:ias="http://www.iasb.org.UK/xbrl/2001-08-16/"
xmlns="http://www.w3.org/2002/XMLSchema"
targetNamespace="http://www.iasb.org.UK/xbrl/2001-08-16/"
elementFormDefault="qualified">
<annotation>
<appinfo>
<link:linkbase    Ref xlink:type="simple" xlink:href="linkbase\ias_presentaion.xml"
                  xlink:actuate="onRequest" xlink:role="http://www.xbrl.org/
                  linkprops/linkRef/presentation" xlink:arcrole="http://www.w3.org/
                  1999/xlink/properties/linkbase">
                  <xhtml:p>links for presentation relationship</xhtml:p>
</link:linkbaseRef>
<link:linkbase    Ref xlink:type="simple" xlink:href="linkbase\ias_reference.xml"
                  xlink:actuate="onRequest" xlink:role="http://www.xbrl.org/
                  linkprops/linkRef/reference" xlink:arcrole="http://www.w3.org/
                  1999/xlink/properties/linkbase">
                  <xhtml:p>links for references</xhtml:p>
</link:linkbaseRef>
<link:linkbase    Ref xlink:type="simple" xlink:href="linkbase\ias_label.xml"
                  xlink:actuate="onRequest" xlink:role="http://www.xbrl.org/
                  linkprops/linkRef/label" xlink:arcrole="http://www.w3.org/1999/
                  xlink/properties/linkbase">
                  <xhtml:p>links for Labels</xhtml:p>
</link:linkbaseRef>
<link:linkbase    Ref xlink:type="simple" xlink:href="linkbase\ias_definition.xml"
                  xlink:actuate="onRequest" xlink:role="http://www.xbrl.org/
                  linkprops/linkRef/definition" xlink:arcrole="http://www.w3.org/
                  1999/xlink/properties/linkbase">
                  <xhtml:p>links for definion relationship</xhtml:p>
</link:linkbaseRef>
<link:linkbase    Ref xlink:type="simple" xlink:href="linkbase\ias_calculation.xml"
                  xlink:actuate="onRequest" xlink:role="http://www.xbrl.org/
                  linkprops/linkRef/calculation" xlink:arcrole="http://www.W3.org/
                  1999/xlink/properties/linkbase">
                  <xhtml:p>links for calculation relationship</xhtml:p>
</link:linkbaseRef>
</appinfo>
</annotation>
</schema>
```

33

The Internet

VIJAY MUKHI AND K. PANDYAN

The Internet is a network of computers all over the world, connected to each other through telephone lines. It is estimated that there are over 50 million such computers worldwide and they are growing at a rate of 10 per cent per month. Using the telephone network, these computers can communicate with each other. These connections can use the regular dial-up telephone lines or dedicated higher capacity lines to connect a user to the nearest Internet Service Provider (ISP). The ISP makes Internet access available on a local telephone line and helps the user avoid direct long distance or international calls to connect to computers in other parts of the world.

But since the Internet has grown to a phenomenal size, it has also become complex for users. To help the growing number of users who are not computer professionals, various developments have occurred. First is the setting up of online services like CompuServe, America Online, etc. These online services operate on one powerful computer connected to the Internet. Users from any part of the world can connect to this computer and avail various facilities there, including access to information from databases, software libraries, news, bulletin boards for various interest groups, online chat facilities, e-mail, etc.

A recent but revolutionary development on the Internet is the World Wide Web (WWW). The computers on the Internet have addresses to identify them. Many of the computers on the Internet provide information, specialising on a topic or subject. There is a large number of such servers on the Internet. When a user is looking for some information, it may be necessary for him/her to look for such information from more than one server. WWW links the computers on the Internet like a spider web, facilitating users to go from one computer to another directly. When the computers with related data are linked, the user can connect from one to another. When a user keeps hopping from one computer to another, it is called 'surfing'.

The Internet facilitates 'many to many' communication. Modern technology has, so far, made possible communication 'one to many' as in broadcasting, 'one to one' as in telephone, 'a few to a few' as in telephone conferencing and 'many to one' as in polling. In addition, WWW works on 'multimedia', and information can be accessed and transmitted in text, voice, sound and/or video. Graphics and interactive communication are two distinctive features of the Internet and the WWW.

Internet's uses are many and depend on the innovation of the user. The common uses of the Internet can be classified into three primary types, namely, Communication, Data Retrieval and Data Publishing.

Communication on the Internet can be online or offline. When some users connect to a single server or on an online service at the same time, they can communicate in an 'online chat'. This can be truly 'many to many' as in a room full of people talking to each other on a peer to peer basis. Alternatively, the users send mail to each other and it can be read by the receiver whenever he/she finds the time. This is offline communication, but 'one to one' or 'one to many'. Similarly, it is possible for users to get together electronically with those sharing common interests in 'usenet' groups. The users post messages to be read and answered by others at their convenience, in turn all of which can be read and replied to by others and so-on.

For meaningful data retrieval, availability of data that has been compiled from various sources and put together in a usable form is an essential prerequisite. On the Internet, a large number of databases exist. These have been put together by commercially run data providers as well as individuals or groups with special interest in particular areas. To retrieve such data, a user needs to know the addresses of such Internet servers. Then, depending on the depth of information being sought, different databases have to be searched and the required information compiled. The work involved is similar to a search process in a large library, except that the Internet 'library' is immense and dynamic because of regular updating and entirely electronic. While some skill is required for searching, the user will be able to access, search and check a large collection of servers. Conceivably, the Internet will have the latest information available because all data is transmitted electronically world over. For corporate users looking for latest information on products, markets and strategies, such sources are welcome.

Data publishing is a new opportunity that the Internet has made possible. Information that needs to be made available to others can be either forwarded in a usenet site or kept on display in a special site. Internet discourages, by social pressure, the sending of unsolicited e-mail.

BUSINESS USE OF INTERNET

Business has taken to the Internet only recently. Though the Internet has been in existence for many years, mostly the research and education sectors have been the primary users all this while. The Internet has developed references on what is acceptable and unacceptable practice. For example, the Internet is open and anyone can communicate with anyone anywhere on the Internet, but the prevalent custom prevents unsolicited e-mail and promotional communication on the Internet. Hence, business has to use the Internet innovatively but within the norms and mores of this fast growing world community.

The world is shrinking. That was what everyone believed when steam engines and other transportation means changed the way people lived. Then again, global communication facilities made the world appear even smaller. Now the Internet is affecting humans more than any other change that the world went through. If living styles change, business methods and practices also have to change.

This is already happening in the economically advanced countries led by the U.S.A. The telephone and fax are things of the past. No one is able to conduct any worthwhile business unless the business communication occurs on e-mail. An e-mail address is the basic facility that anyone on the Internet gains. The communication is quicker and more convenient than any other mode ever used. It is reliable and provides easy identification of the sender. Electronic mail works similarly to paper mail through the postal system but is entirely electronic.

Through the Internet, users can conduct online interactive communication. This is another major facilitator for any business. Most businesses need a lot of interaction internally among executives and externally with business associates when many persons have to contribute to discussions. This is done by planning and arranging meetings and conferences for which people travel from different locations to come together in one place. This 'many to many' communication can be handled on the Internet quite effectively, without the people needing to travel. At pre-defined times, those who have to communicate together can be online through the Internet and hold electronic conferences. This is truly 'many to many'. Similarly, many discussions can be held through a forum where people post messages to each other and respond to them periodically. This is similar to having a bulletin board on which everyone posts messages.

Businesses require a lot of external information in various functions regularly for taking decisions. For this, a lot of time is spent in searching and getting information. The Internet is a storehouse of information and is able to cater to a very wide range of information needs. This is possible since users are able to electronically identify common interest groups and share information. It is easy to create databases and make information accessible to other users on the Internet. Users have to only search for information sites, qualify and retrieve useful information.

When businesses need to make information on their products and services available to others such as their clients, the Internet provides a very convenient vehicle. Such businesses can set-up their own web sites or home pages. When the potential clients and others visit the site or the home pages, they will have the option to send an e-mail immediately to indicate their interest or queries. For a business, such queries are not preliminary but qualified enquiries. It will also be possible to monitor the number of visitors to the home pages periodically.

Very often, in a marketing situation, a number of preliminary queries are received and they are responded to with brochures and literature, mostly sent by ordinary mail because of the amount and quality of material and the distances involved. The Internet presents an alternative scenario in dealing with such a situation. Particularly, international queries can be attended to by advising the potential clients to access this information at their website at their convenience. This website cannot only surpass the brochures on presentation quality, they are also dynamic and give the latest information. It is easy to update the home page electronically and regularly. The potential customer can also complete a query form and forward it electronically by clicking a few choices on-screen.

COST YOURSELF ON THE INDIAN INTERNET

Different cost structures exist for different ways in which the Internet can be accessed in India. First, the basics. Currently, Videsh Sanchar Nigam Limited (VSNL) is the major Internet Service Provider (ISP) in India. To connect to the Internet, the user, however, has still to reach VSNL from his place. This is through the local telephone facility, Mahanagar Telephone Nigam Limited (MTNL) in the metros and Department of Telecommunication (DoT) in other locations. Those in the metros have two options for connecting: one is dial-up and the other is through leased line.

Currently, VSNL charges Rs. 25,000 to corporates and Rs. 15,000 to individuals for TCP/IP and Rs. 5,000 for shell account facility, for 250 hours of usage or one year, whichever ends earlier. There are also other categories of users. The cost of telephone usage is currently about Rs. 1.25 per call and the calls are metered every three minutes in digital exchanges. Within the metros, it is expected that connection speeds of 9600 bps can be achieved most of the time, especially from the newer digital electronic exchanges.

The alternative to dial-up is the leased line. DoT charges for leased telephone lines depending on the speed required—9.6 Kbps, 64 Kbps or 2 Mbps, and the distance to be covered. Typical costs for a 9.6 Kbps would be Rs. 1.5 lakh and for 64 Kbps line, Rs. 3.75 lakh. In addition, VSNL charges Rs. 8 lakh for one year for a 9.6 Kbps line and Rs. 15 lakh for a 65 Kbps line. Unlike the dial-up connection, the user is permanently connected on the leased line. For a corporate user with multiple terminals within the organisation, the leased line can work out to be more economical.

The Internet is a new opportunity that is sweeping the world and, unlike any other technological development so far, it offers a level playing field to everyone, irrespective of location. On the Internet, there are no barriers of gender, professional background or time and place. There are only two kinds of users, those who provide information and those who use the information. It is also necessary to use and experience the Internet to be able to appreciate its potential and then exploit it.

34

Internet and Rural Development

DON RICHARDSON

Ian Smillie in his book, *Mastering the Machine: Poverty, Aid and Technology*, notes that:

> From the beginning of time, technology has been a key element in the growth and development of societies. But technology is more than jets and computers; it is a combination of knowledge, techniques and concepts; it is tools and machines, farms and factories. It is organisation, processes and people. The cultural, historical and organisational context in which technology is developed and applied is the key to its success or failure.

The Internet is not a panacea for development, but it can and does bring new information resources and can open up new communication opportunities and challenges between people and their organisations, institutions and governments. By providing an open and uncontrolled means for interaction, dialogue and information sharing, the Internet offers intriguing opportunities for bridging the gaps between development professionals and the stakeholders they serve. The source of the Internet's "obsessive appeal is not technology or information, but people. In fact, it is really an interpersonal medium in which information plays a supporting role" (Smolan, 1996). It can enable bottom-up articulation and information sharing and its use increases daily.

Unfortunately, in today's knowledge-based economies there are 'information-haves' and 'information-have-nots' and there is a large gap between them. The Internet is not responsible for this gap. But, unless we can make the tools of the Internet and other basic telecommunication services like the telephone more widely available, especially to the rural poor, the expanded use of the Internet among the 'information-haves' will widen the gap.

The process of globalisation and the transformation of industrial and agricultural economies into economies based more and more on information and knowledge infrastructure, require us to devote considerable energy to enabling the 'information have-nots' to gain access to information and knowledge infrastructures. Without this access, the 'information have-nots' will be at the mercy of external forces, with little or no ability to understand, respond or direct the forces that affect their lives. It is imperative to find ways to access the Internet to intermediary peoples' organisations and local agencies that serve the poor. Rural and urban families that are struggling to achieve prosperity through learning and knowledge no doubt would embrace use of the Internet if it were available to them.

BENEFITS OF THE INTERNET

The Internet's most important benefit is probably its use as an interpersonal communication tool that is the foundation of participatory communication. The term 'participatory communication' is used to describe processes to two-way dialogue and expression that encourage the sharing of feelings, desires, beliefs and experiences. Together with problem analysis, people communicate with one another to search for solutions to their problems and engage in bottom-up communication which raises the awareness of decision-makers to those problems (Bessette, 1996). The basic tenet of participatory communication is that the communication process is more important than the production of media products or their content. Participatory communication within the field of communication for development tends to involve facilitated interventions and media used to catalyse two-way communication, dialogue and problem-solving (Richardson, 1997).

DRAWBACKS

The Internet, like its sister media, the telephone, fax and postal system, opens up entirely new channels and options for use to stay in touch with friends, family and peers. It enables us to communicate, instantaneously, inexpensively, reliably and globally. Benefits to development include increased efficiency in the use of resources. It can open opportunities to reduce duplication of efforts and promote collaboration. Reduction of communication costs, global access to information and human resources used for planning, consultation, decision-making and action can be outcomes of the use of this technology. The Internet's biggest drawbacks are dependency on largely urban-centred telecommunication infrastructures and the availability of computers that are affordable. Generally, poor levels of Internet service exist in countries—both developed and developing—which have monopolistic, expensive, State-run telecommunication systems.

In spite of the Internet's drawbacks, there has been a rapid increase in the use of the Internet in developing countries (Richardson, 1997). But, none of the potential development benefits of the Internet will be fully realised by the technology alone. Its potential development benefits can be realised only when people, including development planners, development beneficiaries, private sector telecommunication providers and other stakeholders work together to plan, implement, use and evaluate Internet applications. Projects that fully involve intended beneficiaries in planning, design and implementation and meet their needs at the same time tend to focus less on telecommunication infrastructure and computers and more on basic communication and information applications that meet people's needs. Thus, access to and use of Internet services are more likely to be sustainable.

There is a tendency among Internet advocates to see the Internet as the single most important Information Communication Technology (ICT) on the planet. This presents a danger to development planners and stakeholders who might be seduced by the Internet's tremendous capabilities. In many cases, the Internet is simply not an appropriate tool for providing the communication and information applications that meet peoples' needs. The Internet is only one medium among thousands, and there are other electronic media such as the telephone, the fax and the photocopier whose development potential has never been fully tapped by development communication specialists. There are traditional communication systems, folk communication processes and simple printed media as well that have powerful communication advantages.

COMMUNICATION FACILITATOR

As a rural development and participatory communication facilitator, I see everyday how rural people benefit from the Internet. Five years ago, I made a decision to devote much of my career to helping rural people and farmers 'get online'. Since then, my work has taken me across the rural areas of Canada, Chile, Egypt, Mexico, the Philippines, Senegal, South Africa, Zambia and Zimbabwe to assist rural organisations and farmers' groups to help their members access the power of rural telecommunication systems, telephones and the Internet. I have seen first-hand how farmers in rural Chile get better prices for their crops because they use the Internet to gain up-to-the-minute farm market information from the website of the Chicago Board of Trade. I have seen how rural development practitioners in Senegal communicate across their country by e-mail, bypassing a terribly inefficient postal service. In Canada, I have seen how rural people in my own area use the Internet to sell hay and advertise free kittens to their neighbours.

I was not always an Internet enthusiast and I am all too aware of the Internet's faults. As someone who really does not like computers, I can remember arguing vehemently that e-mail is a tool for computer 'geeks'. I refused to use an e-mail system that had been installed in my university office. With pressure from my students, however, I eventually relented and let my students teach me how to use e-mail and how to 'surf' the World Wide Web. After finding some very useful information and discovering that I could actually communicate with an old friend in northern Labrador, I was hooked. I quickly realised that this tool could revolutionise communication in the rural areas in which I work.

In 1993, with the help and encouragement of some enthusiastic students, I set out to see if we could create a community-oriented Internet service in the country surrounding my university. At that time, there were very few non-computer-geeks using the Internet. However, a few pioneers in Canada and the United States of America were promoting the concept of 'freeness' or free access and community-owned and managed computer communication networks connected to the Internet. My students and I learnt everything we could about the Freenet movement and embarked on a two-year community development initiative to create one of the first low cost, high access rural community networks in North America. Today, the Wellington

County FreeSpace network (http://www2.freespace.net) serves 21 rural municipalities and one city. The lessons learnt from that effort are now being applied in rural communities around the world (Richardson, 1995, 1996a, 1996b). In the process of developing Freespace, I also learnt a great deal about the Internet, its history, its limitations and its empowering nature.

FACILITATING PARTICIPATION WITH INTERNET INITIATIVES FOR DEVELOPMENT

The nature of a participatory communication initiative *via* the Internet is difficult to understand until a person has an opportunity to participate in such an initiative. Organisations that do not have a strong community communication and outreach orientation are prone to scepticism and dismissal because they may fear greater contact with the public, particularly if they are also engaged in community 'turf wars' or 'empire building'. The same is true for Internet initiatives within organisations. If an organisation, or the organisations within a community, are not already functioning with participatory management styles, there may be little value in introducing a communication tool that can optimise communication flow. This is an important factor for facilitators of Internet initiatives to understand. It is necessary for facilitators to spend time in the early days of an initiative in order to get a better understanding of the complex nature of the community, organisational and stakeholder politics, as well as leadership personalities and political manoeuvring.

The keenest participants in participatory communication initiatives involving the Internet are people who are predisposed to participatory communication and participatory management styles. Facilitators during the community organising effort of the Wellington County FreeSpace network reached this conclusion. The facilitators, based at a university, prompted a vision of a community-owned and managed network that would neither be owned nor controlled by the university, but any community organisation.

The facilitators experienced frustration with the lack of leadership, commitment and understanding among county governments, libraries and school board officials. So they found themselves evaluating prospective partners based not on the extent of their profile in the community, but on the prospective partners' existing record for participatory communication, openness and information sharing within the community. The FreeSpace facilitators began holding community information sessions to introduce the community network vision to stakeholders from all corners of the country. Very quickly, they noticed that the people and organisations with the most interest and commitment were organisations that were already deeply involved in various aspects of local community development, or providing meaningful local services.

Eventually, three key leaders of the community organisation came forward to publicly champion the project. The champions of the FreeSpace project were people who required only a minimal introduction to community networking or the technology. They quickly determined that such a network could be a tremendous resource for enhancing their work and helping to solve problems in country communication, outreach and information sharing. Their strong commitments to community development and continuous communication with their clients and members was the primary factor in engaging their support. The legitimacy that they brought to the project did what countless hours of 'preaching' to the country government officials could not. Once the community network began service, their profile helped foster broad public attention and helped bring in the hesitant community organisations (including the country government) to support the project.

LESSONS LEARNT FROM FREESPACE

This experience convinced the facilitators to start keeping track of 'lessons learnt' so that they could share these lessons with other Internet advocates and facilitators of community-owned and managed Internet services. These insights can spare you of at least some struggles and potential mistakes, we hope.

Lesson 1

Start working with community organisation leaders who already see the benefits of community networking—those organisational leaders who are predisposed to collaborative, open and participatory communication approaches to community development. Do not spend time trying to convince organisational leaders predisposed to turf wars or empire building and who demonstrate little regard for public participation processes.

Lesson 2

Real, risk-taking community leadership is not necessarily found within elected bodies and local government bureaucracies where one might normally expect to start looking, and we should expect community champions to come from unexpected sectors of community leadership. The 'obvious' champion organisations, especially local government, may not immediately buy into a community access Internet project.

Lesson 3

Provide many opportunities for women and young people to actively volunteer their time and energy for practical and identifiable tasks. Recognise and reward their efforts at every opportunity and provide mechanisms to ensure that they can participate in key management roles.

Lesson 4

Fast and decisive network implementation yields the desired results of participatory community communications, and a small team of consultative decision-makers is far better than management by networks of committees. Open and participatory community management must be maintained, but a small team of accountable decision-makers will accelerate the organisational process during the creation of an Internet project.

Lesson 5

Provide training in, and human resource development support for, project management, leadership and teamwork.

Lesson 6

At its core, a community network's goal is to enhance community communication, information sharing, help educate people about valuable Internet services and encourage the application of the Internet in support of local development.

Lesson 7

If you desire to use the Internet within your community or organisation to enhance participatory communication, start now. Do not be afraid to start small.

There is a temptation to wait for others to build the network or to wait for money or to wait for more sophisticated equipment. The longer you wait, the longer you will be without the benefits of an electronic network and access to the global information of the Internet. If others build the network for you, there is a very good chance that it will serve their interests and not your community's interests. If you have a computer and a phone line, you can establish a very basic e-mail community network using free software and a $ 100 modem. There are thousands of small community 'telecentres' in developing countries that provide local phone and fax services to citizens in urban and rural areas. Many of these 'telecentres' are beginning to provide access to e-mail and World Wide Web searching. One Internet computer in a small telecentre can provide services to countless individuals and organisations. Some telecentres do a good business simply providing telegram-style e-mail services between families, friends and a small business among communities within a nation or region.

Lesson 8

Start from the bottom-up. Large government initiated top-down networking efforts have a high failure rate, are unsustainable and cost large amounts of money. In areas where expensive top-down solutions have been applied, there has been serious damage to the seeds of local community networking initiatives by three to four years (Sam Lanfranco as cited in *Ontario-Africa Working Group*, 1994).

Top-down solutions fail because electronic communication involves reciprocal exchanges, dialogue and relative freedom, not unidirectional information distribution or elitist information hoarding Bottom-up solutions tend to be less expensive, more practical and intrinsically relevant to the participants who helped to design and create them. According to Tindimubona and Wilson (1992), the spread of FidoNet networks in Africa has spread in a grassroots, non-hierarchical manner and 'top-down' organisational structures have met with resistance.

Lesson 9

The distinction between information providers and information users has little meaning in an electronic commons (Graham, 1994). Everyone is both information provider and user in the midst of a web of human communication and sharing.

What we were trying to do depended upon a human network first. There is no point in promoting the use of computer-mediated communication unless there is a strong human network that underpins that (Richard Labelle, as cited in *Ontario-Africa Working Group*, 1994).

Lesson 10

Build an energetic steering committee. Electronic networks are about people, not technology. Start your initiative by building a team of enthusiastic proponents who come from diverse backgrounds. Do not stack your committee with 'techies' or 'computer geeks'. Actively seek people who know more about communities than computers.

Lesson 11

Always try to work with people who work with community-minded organisations or community development agencies. Their experience and contacts in the community will help ensure that you will find the resources and support you need.

Good organisations with which to begin working include service clubs, health clinics and educational institutions involved with outreach and continuing education initiatives, libraries and non-governmental organisations involved in economic development. When linked together through improved communication systems, the power of such grassroots organisations can be multiplied manifold. At the same time, they can use their Internet connections to enhance inter-agency collaboration, joint service offerings and joint planning.

Lesson 12

Use local expertise whenever possible and provide necessary training and capacity building where the expertise does not currently exist.

Lesson 13

Take a business-like approach.

An electronic community network is often organised as a collectively owned infrastructure. Whatever the ownership model, the community network is still a business and should be run like a business. Thus, it is wise to include a handful of veteran business people on your steering committee. Their advice and knowledge are consistently valuable. However, it is wise to avoid working exclusively with business interests or allowing business interests to dominate the community network.

Lesson 14

Take sustainability seriously.

While you will want to provide free or very low-cost access to the network, you must also find creative ways to generate revenue. Advertising, value-added services and re-selling of network services to government bodies and large organisations are some ways to create the revenue needed to keep the network running. Low-cost or free access is the first step to creating a thriving pool of users. A thriving user base is 'essential in generating sustainability for a network' (Tindimubona and Wilson, 1992-93).

It is also important to recognise that it is more important to address the sustainability of the improved relationships that the Internet helps establish, as opposed to sustainability of an Internet service organisation. The world of Internet service is dynamic and subject to rapid technological change and small organisations that provide Internet services sometimes have a short life span. If they are successful in encouraging users to use the Internet to enhance relationships, those relationships will far outlast any particular Internet service.

Lesson 15

Community ownership is important.

Do not build the network for your organisation alone. Build it with and for your local community. Electronic communication is only valuable if everyone has the opportunity to participate. If it is accessible only to an elite group, the benefits will never be realised. If people have an ownership stake in the network (however small) they are likely to take an active interest in supporting and promoting the network. The consumer co-operative model is a model that operates successfully in many Canadian communities. We concur with Graham (1955):

> "The essential element for community network development is grassroots control. Community networks are not 'infrastructure'. Community networks are caretakers of electronic public space created by the community, not providers of something for the community" (p. 3).

Lesson 16

Participatory community management will help a network thrive.

Community members need mechanisms for influencing network management, system and software design as well as acceptable user policies. Democratic structures serve this purpose well. Each user should have the opportunity to become a member of the community network organisation (usually upon payment of a small membership fee) and have a vote in deciding network policies and electing an executive council to oversee the work.

Lesson 17

Provide opportunities for students and young people to learn about the technology and the community development potential of the Internet.

Lesson 18

Strategic marketing brings resources.

Community network infrastructures are built with capital and equipment. A strategic marketing effort can bring many of the resources you need marketing new community networks is difficult to see and touch. Letters, advertisements and verbal appeals are largely ineffective marketing techniques. The only strategy we have found effective is to bring demonstrations of realistic prototypes to where people are – right to someone's office or home, giving them a 'hands-on' experience. Large public demonstrations are useful to create interest and awareness.

Lesson 19

Aim for equitable access.

Try to extend your network services to people who would not normally participate. Create discussion fora for people of diverse ethnic, cultural or linguistic backgrounds.

Lesson 20

Train volunteers to train new users.

Once a network is operational, training becomes the number one priority. A well-supported group of volunteer trainers can provide a low-cost and effective programme for helping new users to configure their modems and navigate the system. Train your volunteers well, provide them with on-going support and advanced training opportunities. Training is needed at various levels: training in planning, installing, promoting, using, managing, repairing and maintaining an electronic network (Tindimubona and Wilson, 1992: 3).

Lesson 21

Share resources, ideas and lessons learnt with other community networks.

Once your network is operational, you can help other community networks by sharing your experiences. The lessons you have learnt will help new networks find their feet faster.

Lesson 22

Enlist the support of 'Respectable Wired Elders'.

Within many nations, regions and organisations there are often Internet enthusiasts with influence or decision-making authority who, by virtue of age, wisdom and established credibility, can lend significant support to specific development initiatives. We call these Internet champions the 'Respectable Wired Elders' because, unlike many of their younger peers, their voices and vision can capture the imagination of 'un-wired' politicians, funding agency bureaucrats and private sector benefactors. They are often an untapped resource but their support can add a fantastic boost to a project.

THE FUTURE OF COMMUNITY NETWORKS

The establishment of community network extension services, regionally, nationally or locally, could provide programmes for enabling communities to develop strong organisation strategies for establishing community networks. They can also provide a mechanism for enabling the regional and national networking movements to share resources and ideas and provide opportunities for collaborative projects. At the same time, they can help focus advocacy efforts on improving telecommunication infrastructure for regions with poor phone services, particularly rural regions.

Ideally, Internet extension services will provide a seed-capital funding mechanism for helping to start community network initiatives. A funding mechanism that involves a peer review process will help ensure that people from within the community networking movement, and not ill-informed bureaucrats, review funding proposals. Internet extension services could also provide public statements of support and encouragement as well as learning opportunities for politicians and policy-makers to provide momentum for the community networking movement.

Around the world, people are working hard to build a vibrant network of Internet services that support community development and general human, social and economic development goals. In the process, we are all learning some valuable lessons. These lessons need to be continuously shared with emerging Internet and development champions, especially those coming up in developing countries. As we strengthen communication and information sharing about means for enabling the Internet to serve developmental goals, we can also share our other ideas, knowledge, dreams and vision, easily and seemingly within the electronic common of the Internet.

35

The Application of Internet

PATRICK KOMMU

Personal computer sales in the Asia-Pacific region totalled 5.3 million units in 1994. In 1999, PC sales totalled 19.2 million units. Advertisement revenues reached $ 42.9 million and are estimated to be $ 1.1 billion in 1997.

Bill Gates, the Chairman of Microsoft, promises that the ubiquitous Internet will bring in 'friction-free capitalism'. Arthur C. Clarke, the science-fiction author, once pronounced that any advanced technology is indistinguishable from magic.

In the *laissez faire* environment, progress will be rapid. By opening new and uncensored avenue for the flow of information, the Internet ushers in growth and prosperity. With the high-speed and low-cost transfer of information, the Internet provides the latest communications technology.

In the present information explosion, tens of billions of words pass through the Internet daily. It has about 50 million users, a figure that is rapidly increasing. The users now constitute a 'global village'. Also, Interactive features are increasing on the Net.

The main characteristics of the Internet are brevity, instant gratification, constant electronic stimulation, channel surfing, short attention spans, fast-moving images and five-second sound bites.

New bandwidths provide information to more people cheaply and faster. Several consortiums are building regional telecommunication networks to avoid congestion. On account of low investment in telecommunications infrastructure, some Asian governments are lagging behind. For Asia, some of the new services on the Net are being provided by the 'Shanghai Home Page', 'Burma Web', 'Sri Lankan Cricket Page', 'Asia Business Directories' and 'Asian Trade Online'.

Lowering of costs made instantaneous international communications possible. At present, a fibre optic cable can carry more than 5,00,000 communications simultaneously. However, the Information Superhighway needs huge investment in fibre optic cables, computers, telephone systems and trained personnel.

WORLD WIDE WEB

Information technology is changing our lives in unpredictable ways. The World Wide Web is steadily swelling with interactive and advertiser-sponsored billboards. It is expected that the Net will eventually allow consumers to bypass middlemen while increasing their choices and finding better bargains. Also in future, it will provide advice about everything from legal problems to new medical treatments.

CompuServe is now providing access to about 2,000 databases. Enthusiastic Netizens, or citizens of the Internet, are counted by the thousands in cities. IBM has developed software and services to link personal computers, workstations, mini-computers and mainframes. Now PC networks can be managed through the Net with a Web Browser.

The possibilities in the new media world include teleworking. Now it is possible to control quality and co-ordinate production without any regard to place or distance. Moreover, surfing could be through Local Area Networks to Metro Area Networks and then on to Wide Area Networks.

In order to prevent hackers from downloading information, security is being enhanced with the 'dial-back' feature. Also the 'Intranet' is expected to provide internal web sites, bulletin boards, e-mail, network communications, client-server products and services to business customers.

Without any physical contact, more games, electronic shopping, video on demand and other services will be available on the Net. In future, wireless, palm-size receivers — a combination telephone, computer, fax and TV — will provide hundreds of video, audio and text channels. Right now, hand-held receivers that link to e-mail, Net services and fax communications are expensive.

Presently, financial transactions are occurring at great speed and in astronomical numbers. For instance, stocks, bonds and currencies traded on world-wide electronic markets amount to $ 3 trillion each day.

At Brown University, U.S.A., students in the Hypertext Fiction Workshop work on the 'hypertext novel', which has no pre-determined beginning, middle or end. Also sales of electronic novels, which will be available on CD-ROM, are increasing.

With increased access to the Net in schools and libraries, more educational opportunities are provided to all. Already sales of electronic encyclopaedias excess sales of printed ones. Shortly 'textbooks' will provide wireless connections to libraries. As the screen technology improves, 'netbooks' will become more popular.

A TEACHING TOOL

The Web is a perfect teaching tool. Microsoft has developed new products for 'electronic schoolhouses' in which students can create 'homepages' for themselves or their schools.

OmniGo, the personal communicator, combines voice, electronic mail, electronic messaging, fax and access to on-line services such as CompuServe and the Net. Credit cards, smart cards, etc. could be used to make payments quickly and securely over the Internet. A few security products are now available on the Net for banks and the military.

Microsoft has offered its Net Explorer software for free to lure customers away from Netscape. In the U.S.A. and the U.K., real estate agents are offering houses for sale on the Net. Further, the National Telephone Directory of the U.S.A. containing about 105 million telephone numbers is now available on the Net.

The world's first airport-based cyber cafe and Internet centre is at the London Heathrow business centre. It allows surfers to review world markets and news, e-mail colleagues and also to relax with an on-line game. Cyber cafes, where people can sign-on and socialise, have become some of the hottest meeting spots all over the world.

Aptech, the computer training institution, is launching software engineering courses, information technology and management programmes on the Net. The Reserve Bank of India has opened a page/site on the WWW where information regarding foreign exchange, etc. will be available.

Nowadays, companies are offering guides to their products, operations, services and information. The Health Online Service allows people around the world to follow medical operations live on the Net. Images are accompanied by a commentary from specialists.

Digital navigation will facilitate sorting and deciphering messages. Hitachi is launching a $ 500 PC, providing modem functions for accessing the Net, along with a CD-ROM device. Sun Microsystems, Oracle and others are also engaged in similar efforts.

The Internet phone products offer virtually free long-distance calls. New technology compresses speech into digital data packages. For this, computers must be equipped with a microphone, sound card and high-speed modem. With customer service, sales support and Web site tours, the Net phone will become more popular. Surely, the convergence of communication, will be a new and exciting phenomenon.

In the present-day world, computers could be considered 'thinking tools'. They assist humans in acquiring meta qualifications necessary in the increasingly complex world. One day computers may mimic human reasoning and sensory perception. In the present information economy, quick adaptation to new technologies is essential for survival and growth. Open institutions and rapidly available information nurture democracy.

36

Internet and Related Issues

S.K. MANGAL

The term Internet has been coined from two terms interconnection and network. A network is simply a group of computers that are connected together for sharing information and resources. Several such networks have been joined together across the world to form what is called the Internet. Thus, it is a network of networks. The Internet comprises of thousands of computers connected together by different means.

HISTORY OF INTERNET

In 1969, the ARPA (Advanced Research Project Agency) created ARPANET to help the researchers communicate with each other. ARPA's task was to develop a geographically dispersed, reliable communication network for military use that would not be disrupted in case of partial destruction from a nuclear attack. Other private networks came up soon after ARPANET, such as BITNET, CSINET, etc. In 1990, the ARPANET was dismantled and other networks substituted it. Although the Internet was originally meant for research purposes, it has now changed drastically and is used mainly for commercial purposes.

APPLICATIONS OF INTERNET

1. E-mail

The most common use of Internet is electronic mail. Using e-mail, a user can send text, pictures, programs or even movies to any other person on the Internet anywhere in the world. Each user has a unique address. This address helps in identifying a user to whom you wish to send e-mail.

There are two main advantages of e-mail over normal mail (now called snail mail). The first is at the speed at which delivery takes place (almost instantaneously) and the second is that it costs almost the same regardless of you are sending mail to someone next door or someone living many kilometres away.

2. Internet News

Another way of communicating on the Internet is so called Internet news. There are a number of news groups on the Internet. These news groups are different from e-mails. The messages sent to a news group are simply posted on the electronic notice board. Anyone can see these messages. There are thousands of news groups, organized by their content type. For example, the COMP groups are computer-related while REC groups are recreational in nature.

3. Chatting and Conferencing

Yet another way of communicating on the Internet is known as Internet Relay Chat (IRC). Using IRC you can speak to the other users around the world virtually in real time as though you were in the same room. Using the appropriate software you can chat. For example, through MIRC you can join any channel you want.

Apart from chatting software there are messengers (e.g. Yahoo messenger or Rediff bol) where you can send messages to your friends or relatives in text or voice form and chat to them if they are on-line, i.e. if they are also connected to the net.

4. Getting Information

Internet provides a tremendous wealth of information. With thousands of systems connected to the Internet, there are millions of programs (software) and data that have been available to the users. These files may be text files, graphic files, sound files, full motion video files or even program files.

There are number of ways in which you can obtain the desired information to make it easier to locate and transfer information when needed.

TOOLS AND TECHNIQUES OF INTERNET

1. Getting Connected

To excess internet at first one should get connected. There are two ways two get connected, namely:

(i) *Dial-up Access*

It is the most common method of getting connected. You can get connected through a modem and a telephone line. It comes out be less expensive as it requires very modest hardware and software. It's disadvantages being that it is very slow and less reliable. It is also busy during peak hours.

You need a browser software like Netscape Navigator or Internet Explorer and some other software like WS–FTP, MIRC, ICQ, etc.

(ii) *Direct or Dedicated Connection*

Dedicated connections on the other hand are much faster and reliable. You are connected to the INTERNET all the time. This type of connection provides you the opportunity of becoming a service provider. You can also join your network to the net. This connection is complex and difficult to maintain. Moreover, the cost involved is also very high.

2. Internet Explorer

In 1995, Microsoft released the Internet Explorer, a Web browser that works with Windows. Internet Explorer is very tightly integrated with Windows which lets users combine it with other Windows programs, e.g. other programs can launch Internet Explorer when the user selects a URL in the other programs' documents. Further, Internet Explorer can cause other Windows to be launched when particular Web documents are accessed.

3. Netscape Navigator

On 18th September, 1995 Netscape Communications released the Netscape Navigator. It has various features:

(i) It can be configured for mail and news;
(ii) It can be used to read mails;
(iii) File transfer support for both sending and receiving files;
(iv) Context-Sensitive help both on-line and through the Netscape Web Pages;
(v) Native AU and AIFF sound support (AU and AIFF are sound file formats);
(vi) It also gives bookmark facility; and
(vii) Provides dynamic documents, where a server can push new data to a Netscape Navigator window for continuously or regularly updated information, such as stock quotes and weather maps.

4. FTP

FTP stands for File Transfer Protocol. It is used for copying computer files from one computer (FTP server) to our computer (downloading) or for sending files from our computer to another computer (uploading). The executable files to be uploaded or downloaded can be compressed or not. FTP contains rules for uploading and downloading. There are over 10,000 servers in the world. You can log-in with password or as "anonymous".

5. Archie

The best way to sort through millions of files available by anonymous ftp is with archie, the gigantic database of all the files that are known to be publicly available. The archie database system is maintained by many universities and networking organizations. Most of them run the same software, and all share information on the best ways of making the database available to the widest audience.

6. Gopher

Developed by University of Minnesota, Gopher is Client/server menu-driven interface. There are about 1800 Gopher servers in the world. Most of them are run by Universities. Some advantages of using Gopher include the following:

(i) Directory trees are shown as lists,
(ii) Links can be to files on other computers,

(iii) Gopher can link to other services, e.g. you can have an entry that automatically starts a link to another computer through the telnet program,
(iv) Most of the Gopher clients are customizable,
(v) It is designed to handle any kind of information, and
(vi) Combined with veronica you can quickly search on all known Gopher servers for particular information.

7. Veronica

This tool is proven effective for years. Windows version of it tried to simplify things for naive users. It still remains hard to use for non-computer professionals.

8. World Wide Web

The World Wide Web (WWW) is the universe of network-accessible information, an embodiment of human knowledge. A technical definition of the World Wide Web is, "All the resources and users on the Internet that are using the Hypertext Transfer Protocol (HTTP)." A broader definition comes from the organizations that Web inventor Tim Benerse-Lee helped found, the World Wide Web Consortium (W3C). The W3C can be defined as, "The World Wide Web Consortium (W3C) exists to realize the full potential of the web."

The W3C has taken over what was formerly called the CERN httpd or Web server. You can find some useful information at the W3C website—

http://www.w3c.org/

9. URL (Uniform Resource Locator)

A URL (Uniform Resource Locator) is the address of a file (resource) accessible on the INTERNET. The type of resource depends on the INTERNET application protocol. Using the World Wide Web, Web's protocol the Hypertext Transfer Protocol (HTTP), the resource can be an HTML page, an image file, a program such as CGI application or Java applet, or any other file supported by HTTP. The URL contains the name of the protocol required to access the resource, a domain name that identifies a specific computer on the Internet, and a hierarchical description of a file location on the computer. On the Web an example of a URL is:

http://www.projects.com/c++

This describes a Web page to be accessed with an HTTP (web browser) application that is located on a computer named www.projects.com. The specific file is in the directory named/c++ and is in the default page in that directory.

HTTP URL can be for any Web page, not just a home page, or any individual file, e.g. the following URL would bring you the whatis.com logo image—

http://whatis.com/whatisanim2.gif

10. URI

To paraphrase the World Wide Web Consortium, Internet space is inhabited by many points of content. A URI (Uniform Resource Identifier) is the way we identify and of those points of content, whether it be a page of text, a video or sound clip, still or animated image, or a program. The most common form of URI of the Web page address, which is a particular form of URI or subset of URI, called a Uniform Resource Locator (URL). A URI typically describes:

(i) The mechanism used to access the resource;
(ii) The specific computer that the resource is housed in; and
(iii) The specific name of the resource (a file name) on the computer.

On the Web an example of URI is—

http://www.w3 org/lcns/www/w3c_main.gif

It identifies a file that can be accessed using the Web protocol application, HTTP, ("http://") that is housed on a computer named "www.w3.org" (which can be mapped to a unique Internet address).

In the computer's directory structure, the file is located at—

lcons/www/w3/w3c_main.gif

Character strings that identify FTP addresses and e-mail addresses are also URIs (and, like the HTTP address, is also the specific subset of URI called a URL).

Another kind of URI is the Uniform Resource Name (URN). A URN is a form of URI that has 'institutional persistence', which means that its exact location may change from time to time, but some agency will be able to find it.

LAYERS OF TCP/IP

There are seven layers in what is officially called the ISO OSI Reference Model. The layers are:

1. The Physical Layer.
2. The Data Link Layer.
3. The Network Layer.
4. The Transport Layer.
5. The Session Layer.
6. The Presentation Layer.
7. The Application Layer.

1. The Physical Layer

The Physical Layer is pure hardware, including the cable, or other connection medium and the network interface card. This is where the electrical signals move around.

2. The Data Link Layer

This is the layer that splits the data into packets to be sent across the connection medium. Here's where the wiring, such as Ethernet of token ring gets involved. After this the information is on the wire, the data link layer handles any interference. If there is a heavy sunspot activity, the data link layer works hard to make sure the interference doesn't garble the electric signals.

3. The Network Layer

IP is the TCP/IP protocol that works at this layer. This layer gets packets from the data link layer and sends them to the correct network address. If more than one possible route is available for your data to travel, the Network Layer figures out the best route.

4. The Transport Layer

Although the Network layer routes your information to its destination, it can't guarantee that the packets holding the data will arrive in the correct order. That's the job of the Transport Layer. **TCP** work at the **Transport Layer**. This layer ensures that you packets have no errors and that all the packets arrived are reassembled in the correct order.

5. The Session Layer

The other protocols that make up TCP/IP sit on layer 5 (Session) and above layer establishes and coordinates a session, which is simply the name for a connection between two computers. You have to have a session before two computers can be even think about actually moving data between themselves.

6. The Presentation Layer

The Presentation Layer works the operating system and file system. Here's where the files get converted from one format to another, if the server and client use different formats. Without the presentation layer, file transfer would be restricted to computers with the same file format.

7. The Application Layer

This is the layer where you do your work, such as sending e-mail or requesting to transfer a file across the network. Without the application layer, you couldn't create any message or data to send, there would be no Web browsers, and your computer wouldn't know what to do with any data that someone else sent you.

INTRANET, ETHERNET AND HTML

Inter-based technology has now migrated to what are called Intranets. These networks are corporate networks, basically portions of or overlays to traditional enter prose networks, which use the same lower-layer and application-level protocols as the Internet, specifically WWW related technology. Companies are deploying Intranet technology in increasing numbers corporate networks. Intranets use same protocols and locally based web servers. It provides vast amount of corporate information. Documents are stored in HTML, and clients need Web Browser software.

Ethernet is the name given to the popular packet-switched LAN technology developed at Xerox PARC in the early 1970s. It's a 10-Mbps broadcast technology. It's a 10-Mbps-broadcast bus technology. Each computer in the Ethernet has a unique 48 bit no. called Ethernet (MAC) address Data transmission on Ethernet occurs in frames of size 64 to 1518 bytes. Ethernet frames are *self-identifying*.

WWW is based on files having special formatting instructions in HTML, i.e. Hyper Text Markup Language. HTML documents are SGML documents with generic semantics that are appropriate for representing information from a wide range of applications.

References

CIStems, *Internet: An Introduction*, Jaipur.

Daniel Mioli, *Internet and Intranet Engineering*.

Paul E. Hauffman, *The Internet Instant Reference*, 3rd edition.

37

Role of Internet in Strengthening Democracy

J.V. VILANILAM

The outstanding features of the 20th century have been identified by several scholars of political science as democracy and telecommunication technology, including interactive communication technologies such as the Internet and Electronic Mail (e-mail). These are likely to continue as the most outstanding features of the 21st century. This article attempts to examine the role of the new technologies in strengthening democracy.

What is interactive communication? How does it differ from mass communication?

Communication is a term derived from the Latin root of *communis*, which means 'sharing', 'commonness', 'commonality', etc. Although communication is defined in several ways, all scholars agree that it is a process that takes place mostly at two levels: interpersonal (interactive) and mass. Most of us tend to forget that the highest incidence of communication occurs at the interpersonal level. Many people mistakenly equate communication with mass communication because of the ubiquity, perseverance, regularity, familiarity and global character of mass media products.

But communication between persons (interpersonal), inter-group, members of the family, organisations, between managers and supervisors, between supervisors and workers, among personnel at various levels, among people in general, between political leaders and their followers—all these are examples of interactive, interpersonal or inter-group communication. It is not difficult to see that such communication is at the very root of society. Without it, there is no society. Society functions through communication and feedback.

Then what about mass communication?

Mass communication is different because there is little or no feedback from the audience or the persons who receive mass mediated messages. The communicator and the communicatee are anonymous as individuals, although we can identify the organisation that communicates and the group (children, adults, women, workers, etc.) that receives the communication. The nature of mass communication, however, is such that there are extraneous elements such as the technical appurtenances (the media), principles of sound and signal transmission through electric and electronic means, wired and wireless networks. There is also the need for training the communicators. There is no one person to whom a message is directed, it is directed to a very large, anonymous and heterogeneous audience consisting of masses of people in their thousands or even millions. They belong to different socio-economic, political and cultural groups. In other words, the recipients of the mass communicated messages belong to a heterogeneous mass. And the communicator is not just one person or a small identifiable group of persons.

Democracy is supported by four pillars—the legislature, the executive, the judiciary and the press (here, press is used interchangeably with the media). Modern media is not the same as the small businesses which ran community newspapers in the olden days. The role of the mass media in agenda setting, in general, has been established by many researchers. The media, through association with equally powerful businesses, moulds public opinion in such a manner that people's dissent is suppressed and assent or assumed assent is highlighted depending on the media's own economic interests. Undemocratic and anti-people actions by those who wield power are sometimes de-emphasised if the media's own interests are affected. Since most media is not just in the media business alone but are conglomerates having several other business interests, one cannot be too sure about their independence. Democracy is strengthened by the collective action of the people—a properly informed people. If the media of communication and information is not independent of vested interests, the public is misled. When governments overspend money forgetting the basic needs of the large majority of the people, public action through discussion and frank expression of opinion at town meetings, panchayat samitis and small group discussions in the interactive/ interpersonal mode become essential.

All that the modern media can do is publicise rapidly the activities of the panchayat administration but the essential aspects of communitarian democracy and priorities are interpersonal in practice. The mass media may not generate the people's enthusiasm; they may mobilise people but the people can act only through interactive discussions and collective action for their own benefit. The mass media can cover the events but because of its structure and nature, cannot follow up the processes essential for the redressal of people's grievances beyond a certain limit. The outcome of people's actions will depend on their own interpersonal and inter-group communication and action.

All over the world, the pattern of voting in recent years has clearly shown the people's dwindling interest in franchise despite much discussion in the conventional media. But political scientists and sociologists, communication experts and social leaders are now suggesting that the mass media has to be de-emphasised if the democratic process has to be strengthened. Less than half the voters exercise their voting rights in many established democracies such as the U.S.A.

To rejuvenate the interest of the people in elections and in vital issues affecting the people of a locality, the people themselves have to come together and revive their flagging interest through active discussions. Many political observers and communication scholars are of the view that the Internet and e-mail are the best means to motivate people. In matters vital to their locality or area of residence, local people can consult one another through these interactive devices.

The telex, teleprinter, videotext, teletext, e-mail, Internet — these interactive communication devices can be utilised provided citizens have access to them. Today, these are utilised mostly by big corporations, multinational in origin and operation; big global firms, industries, banks, insurance companies, universities and international and national research institutions. But the average citizens' use of the Internet or e-mail is still very scanty. The ultra-modern communication systems have to reach the stage of popular use if they have to become effective aids to the process of strengthening democracy.

Electronic voting is the first step. Even in India, where the mass media systems as well as the interactive systems are currently confined to the metropolitan cities and large towns, electronic voting machines were used in recent elections. Their use will be extended to other areas in future elections, but can we say that the use of electronic machines alone will ensure modernisation of political democracy?

DEMOCRACY HAS TO BECOME A WAY OF LIFE

Voting is only one aspect of democracy. The democratic way of life will become widely prevalent only when the absolutely poor (some 320 million Indians) become empowered through education and steady jobs. Many modern aspects of life are still out of bounds for these hapless millions. Life is a constant struggle with adversity for them.

Assuming that the poor, illiterate masses will eventually reach a stage where they will have fulfilled the basic needs of food, clothing, shelter, education, health care and, above all, steady employment, we can talk more realistically about the use of the interactive systems.

The benefits of the processes of liberalisation, privatisation and globalisation will have to reach the rural areas. When important decisions affecting the socio-economic political and cultural life of the people are taken in the Panchayati Raj system, are all the people of the panchayat (gram, block and zila) properly informed? Are they getting an opportunity to voice their opinion? Even without going to the panchayat meeting, citizens can express their views electronically. Political leaders can query the people of their constituencies through e-mail. They can also hold tele-conferences with leaders of various citizen groups assembled at a media centre.

Specific issues can be discussed this way and political parties can arrive at decisions based on the people's mailed (and hence, documented) views. When citizens interact through e-mail or the Internet, they do it in a free atmosphere and without fear or favour, within the shortest amount of time.

Information Technology (IT) is revolutionising business and professional communication systems and methods, making the task of communication and exchange of information easier, more effective and more efficient. Sound printers or computers that can directly print dictated words are being tested and developed.

All this will enhance the performance of e-politics, that is, the practice of democracy through electronic means. The convergence of telecommunication and computer technology (IT) can lead to the emergence of a new democratic political culture. But for this to become widespread, the intra-personal information and communication process gong on within the human body has to be strengthened by formal and informal education and the use of modern devices by all citizens. Experience, education and proper equipment will determine the quality of the interactive messages, their transmission efficiency and the action based on such interaction.

THE INTERNET AND DEMOCRACY

The most modern, and by far, the quickest and most effective world-wide system of communication is the Internet. It links subscribers globally through its world wide web (www) and each subscribing person or organisation can be reached within minutes, if not seconds.

The Internet is a huge global network of computer chains. It is, in a way, the nets' net, wiring sources of information on any topic, event or personality under the sun in a global super-computer web or network.

Citizens of countries, regions of countries or those belonging to different political ideologies can communicate through the Internet or e-mail. Telephone, telegraph or the postal service may be ineffectual in certain situations, but e-mail and the Internet can be relied upon. Universalisation and the democratisation of information, a primary requirement of democracy, are made possible by the new devices of interactive communication.

The success of a democratic system depends on decentralisation. Concentrating the power of communication in fewer and fewer hands is the characteristic of the mass media systems. It is responsible for the steady erosion of democratic values. The mass media system, despite its eulogisation by everyone as the Fourth Estate, has proved itself to be anti-democratic because of its heavily concentrated ownership pattern all over the world today. The freedom to inform through the mass media resides in a few hands.

But the Internet and other systems are basically decentralised systems. The user himself can create websites or join the use-net of the news chain already created. Nobody's special permission is needed. Web pages created by the user-citizens themselves can be accessed and utilised by other users living in any part of the globe. All they need is a computer with Internet facility. Even if they do not have such a computer system of their own, they can use the services of a website service agency.

Existing broadcasting and telecasting facilities are controlled from a central point. Those who have something to publicise – data, graphics, pictures, cartoons or ideas – can enter the network at any point when they need to.

Another advantage is that there is no need to remove an old page or site to install a new website. This, too, increases the immense possibility of fostering the communication process. Broadcasting and telecasting technologies do not have this kind of unlimited possibility because their channels have limitations and in the fierce competition for channel facility, many communicators fail. Further, the amount to be spent on channel broadcasting or telecasting is enormous; ordinary citizens cannot afford it. Only big media companies can reach the millions through radio, TV or Cable TV. On the other hand, the Internet empowers even ordinary citizens to disseminate ideas that are useful to the general public. All they have to do is invest a few thousand rupees for home facilities or go to a nearby e-mail Internet kiosk.

PUBLIC OPINION SURVEYS

Surveying and assessing public opinion is an essential part of the democratic system. But it is highly expensive and sometimes a somewhat undependable method, especially when conducted in the conventional manner. With the help of interactive e-systems, citizens can be surveyed in a more dependable and less expensive manner. When citizens with computers at home having web server/web hosting service are surveyed, opinion votes can be collected quickly and decisions implemented on the basis of the survey results. The basic cost of components will include the cost of a personal computer and its hardware, subscription for the Internet/ online service and the cost of connecting the computer with the global service.

More subscribers will mean more widespread service and bigger bandwidth for the network. This will help citizens and their organisations to realise the social, political, economic or cultural objectives.

According to some experts, the world is seeing, for the first time in history, "a medium of mass speech," to which so many millions have access, and yet many millions are still unable to utilise all its immense possibilities to strengthen democracy. Today, there are over 600 crore people on Planet Earth, of whom some 300 crore are in a democratic system of one form or the other. This, too, is a first time phenomenon in human history. Never have so many been under democracy. When the new electronic means of communication and their use become more widespread and universal, more and more people will come under the democratic system. (We cannot ignore the reality that half the world's population has not even used the telephone once in their lifetime).

Using the new technologies, ordinary citizens in different parts of the world can raise their voice against injustice and violence perpetrated on innocent humanity and their voice will be heard quickly by the decision-makers whose conscience will be agitated.

Not only man-made disasters, but natural disasters in different regions of the world can be conveyed effectively by citizens in the far corners of the world. Tragedies can be minimised and, in some cases, totally averted. This is a distinct possibility because there is no national control on cyber space.

38

Use of Internet in the Manufacturing of Products

AMITA SHARMA

The traditional thinking that industrial organisations can boost profits and increase market share by expanding their operations is no longer valid in the 21st century. Though expansion is certainly one of the means but is no longer forms to be the basic means for remaining competitive in the marketplace. In the present context the emphasis has shifted to achieving operational excellence at minimum cost and time. Although this idea of being the best at what one does goes by different names, like business process engineering, total quality management and re-engineering, the theme, always remains the same. Delivering high quality goods and services at lower price, efficiently and quickly to the customer is the crux of success and survival while at the same time trying and achieving and maintaining higher levels of organisational productivity.

The productivity discussions, which started in the 1990's continue till to date. Some experts argue that there is no clear relationship between technology and industrial productivity while others argue that the impact of technology on productivity is so deeply profound, pervasive and intangible that it defies old productivity measures in industry and trade.

Measurement of productivity is a difficult process because the traditional measures of productivity do not necessarily apply to information systems. The information systems provide long-term intangibility benefits like improved customer services, ready availability to timely and accurate data, competitive advantage, leadership in the global market place and high quality of decision-making. Any measure of productivity must be broad. Some new measures like "Slash Cycle times", "delighting the customer", and innovative partnerships are beginning to emerge. The Slash Cycle Times is a term for reduction of the amount of time between product conception and delivery to the customer. These new measures bring together advanced information technologies, intelligent minds and caring business organisations to focus on the customer.

OBJECTIVE

The objective of this chapter is to present real world information systems and their contribution to the evolving concept of organisational productivity, specially manufacturing information system. Although qualitative measures of productivity gains may be hard to come by providing strong evidence that IS help commercial organisations to increase profits, decrease costs, enhance customer satisfaction, sustain competitive advantage in the market place, reduce product life cycles, achieve increased efficiency, hire and retain outstanding people and develop strategic alliances between retailers and suppliers.

MANUFACTURING INFORMATION SYSTEMS (IS)

The world of manufacturing is undergoing significant and rapid changes. Today manufacturing environment looks quite different from the shop floor of a decade ago. Nowadays, mechanical manufacturing has given way to automation and in the coming years computers and information technologies are expected to play an even bigger role in changing the manufacturing landscape. A manufacturing IS is a system that supports the manufacturing. IS applies to both manufacturing and service environments. Production systems specifically address information needs related to acquiring and managing raw materials, scheduling equipment, manpower planning, repair and maintenance and other activities related to production. Now we will discuss the manufacturing IS of Parametric Technology Corporation (PTC) in the following paragraphs.

Methodology

The use of Internet in the manufacturing IS has changed the face of industrial manufacturing. Nowadays Computer Aided Design (CAD) is rapidly replacing 2D. Drafting boards in designing various products. The net enables organisations and suppliers to interact directly with those who really matter, forging, a closer link between them. The catering of the concerned parties is instantaneous, direct, effective and conclusive. PTC develops, markets and supports product designer software solutions. With the help of Mechanical Computer Aided Design (MCAD) and Collaborative Product Commerce (CPC) product can be designed with faster speed and more efficiency in the business organisations.

Today the important challenges are being faced by the manufacturing organisations in two stages as under:

(i) First is the period between the initial conception of the product and growing of specifications for the product from somebody who would like to manufacture it to the stage of getting that product ready for the market.
(ii) Second stage is taking the manufactured product to the market and to the customers.

The first stage, i.e. from the concept to creation of the product is called time to market and the second market related aspect is called time to customer. The two phases are tackled by the IS smoothly, efficiently and effectively to provide the producer what he require most and in a manner, i.e. his complete objective. In the age of globalization, most of the manufacturing organisations have spent huge amounts to address the time to customer aspect with solutions like Enterprise Resource Planning (ERP), Supply Chain Management (SCM) and Customer Relationship Management (CRM) Systems. And the entire: other half of the equation, the Time-To-Market, has really only been addressed by organisations through implementation of MCAD style solutions. However, the major new initiative in the market to increase efficiency is how one can slash the Time-To-Market, which means manufacturing organisations saving the costs competition by getting the product faster to the customer. PTC provides MCAD solutions from Pro/E family with a set of collaboration tools known as Windchill.

Windchill

Efficient and effective use of Information Technology (IT) can keep a producer one step ahead of his competitors and enable him to snatch the lead and be the for runner. It is IT which is fast and can reduce the time lag element to its minimum. It is the powerful and flexible, collaborative technology, owned and developed by PTC, that powers many of PTC's product development solutions. It provides a state of the art, Wed-based, collaborative environment for product development. Its distributed architecture allows organisations to integrate their business processes with geographically dispersed divisions, partners and customers through a proven, powerful data management structure and work flow engine. This in turn enables users to innovative products, while controlling every phase of the process. It also provides capabilities, for data management, configuration management, document management, seamless integration with legacy systems, 3-Dimensional (3D) visualization and design applications. Some important Windchill Technology-based PTC solutions are as under:

1. *PTC Project Link*

A quick-start solution that powers manufacturing-related exchange and enterprises with collaborative Net-native workspaces. It enables project teams to develop innovative products and speed time-to-market.

2. *PTC Parts Link*

A customer-facing B2B solution for suppliers of parts and components that changes the tools of selling from old-fashioned paper catalogues or static Web pages to a dynamic, interactive selling environment.

3. *PTC Dynamic Design Link*

Manufactures who make design-to-order products can now do so more efficiently and at a competitive price by automating their design and engineering processes. This powerful solution speeds the time from concept to production, lowers costs and builds customer relationships.

4. *PTC Product Life-cycle Management*

A tightly focused, multidimensional solution that enables companies to leverage product data both inside and outside their enterprise. It is built using PTC's CAD, product management, visualization, and integration capabilities to provide manufactures with a unique approach to product development.

5. *PTC Contract Manufacturing*

OEMs and contract manufacturers can accelerate a product's time-to-market with the PTC Contract Manufacturing Solution which facilitates the flow of product data, engineering changes, approved vendor information, and RFQ's.

6. *PTC After Market Support*

This solution changes the after market business from offering only product support to delivering a full range of high-income revenue growth services that improve customer satisfaction and retention.

7. *PTC 3D-Products*

Creating the mechanical designs of the future requires an integrated collaborative engineering environment that promotes idea sharing. Mechanical Computer Aided Design (MCAD) focuses on product design drafting and modelling while Mechanical Computer Aided Engineering (MCAE) tests the strengths of these designs by simulation. When both these disciplines are working in concert the final product achieves excellence in both functionality and quality with reduced development cycles. While both these disciplines benefit from a highly reliable integrated networked-based environment MCAD designers typically get their job done on Sun's Ultra systems while most MCAE engineers invest in the speed and power of Suns' Ultra desktops and Ultra HPC servers to run large, multi-threaded simulation and analysis applications.

Sun offers flexible configuration choice for both MCAD and MCAE engineers, from custom fit low cost solutions, to systems that take advantage of multi-threaded multiprocessing applications to process numerically intensive interactive 3-D graphic projects at unprecedented speeds. The high-end visualization graphics ability of Suns' Creator-3D systems combined with very large system memory to give users the power to push the limits of mechanical design. Sun Microsystems is the MCAD, MCAE market leader, and holds this leadership position by consistently delivering high-performance, reliability, and seamless networked processing.

Mechanism of Windchill

The above mentioned Windchill Technology based PTC solutions invigorates product development and slashes Time-To-Market. It provides a robust, collaborative environment where Engineers, Suppliers, Customers, and Manufacturers can meet and exchange information with each other. Pro/E helps in designing, documenting and even managing the product assembly. With MCAD feeding into the collaboration tools, detailed diagrams and drawing can be shared across the organisation, allowing information to be shared automatically all the way through to the ERP, SCM and CRM solutions. At PTC this process known as Create, Collaborate and Control. 'Creation' is where one can create the actual materials of the product, diagrams and drawings. Collaboration and Control is the sharing of information with various organisations or different parts of organisations as well as other suppliers and customers in a mutual and secure environment, all the way through to the ERP and SCM systems.

In the present phase of economic recession, tools like Pro/E and Windchill solutions can assist in reducing the Time-To-market. This can reduce organisations costs by increasing their efficiency while allowing them to maintain quality. This ultimately leads to attainment of better speed by the supply process to enable the product reach and the availability there to those who products have been dominant products in India for the High-End-manufacturing Organisations. The PTC have also come up with two new sets of products that add to the Pro/E family which can address the lower-End requirement of the market. These two products are Pro/E-Desktop and Pro/E-Desktop Express. The first product includes 70% of Pro/E products in terms of functionality, but is considerably cheaper. The second product is designed to be about 70% of Pro/E-Desktop and is available on the website as a free down load product. With the Desktop Express product PTC is making the product available to organisations who have a lower-End requirement. This can further help organisations to move from the first stage to 3-D-Design.

Today, the Internet is being used a lot for communications. The next wave should be complex collaboration which will involve the sharing of complex 3-D-Models in a secure environment between organisations using the Internet. Thus, manufacturer can involve his customers, suppliers and even other departments in the organisation like maintenance in getting real time information on how a product is being developed and designed and also in getting real time inputs. There is a need to ensure that the new systems can have access to all data in the minimum time for utilisation. And one has to ensure it specifically works with all the other major MCAD-Vendors to provide better collaboration and control Windchill can work with CAD tools. To address collaboration and control, Windchill products also have connections available with all ERP systems, the supply chain management systems, CRM system and other systems. Thus, Windchill facilitates MCAD system trade through to the Time Customer solutions. The windchill is built as a CPC solutions from the ground up as an Internet solutions and can be used in both environments. For instance, a manufacturing company can use Windchill for aligned purposes on an Externet or it can be hosted to provide benefits to many organisations. The Indian market has got good MCAD opportunities and has an explosive opportunity in collaboration and control space with Windchill product. In fact, India has the potential to be the largest market for PTC products in South Asia.

CONCLUSION

Information is at the foundation and is the base of creation of a sound structure in any field of activity. Informations is the mother of innovation. Information technology or information system provides if readily. The information technology has revolutionized the world and industrial, business and all other activities. It enables to chisle your production of all wastes and bring it to the minimum of cost concept. It provides your production with design and shape which is most alluring and acceptable by the consumer. It brings together all those who create and generate production, i.e. brings together engineers, industrialists, manufacturers, financiers and advisers of Consumerism to work in close harmony and collaboration. The vast store of information has given birth to various agencies which provide information on different subjects promptly. Information technology performs another function besides providing information, that of communication. With globalisation world has become a one small unit. One who can make it shorter to reach the remotest part scores first and is the winner. Information technology thus provides information for fast communication. Information is providing the product its designing and production in the shortest time, cutting the production period to the shortest time lag. Communication enables to reach with your product without delay any where in the world and therefore, then you are a winner, a leader in your trade and successful.

In short and in substance in modern times you cannot survive without information technology. With it you swim in prosperity without it your are lost in the darkness of doom. Information technology is the latest and most effective new God of modern world. Apply yourself to it, attain it and master it. Success, then, is yours.

References

Bets, Mitch, "Mapping Tools Research Mainstream Market", *Computerworld*, April, 1994.

De Pompa, Barbara, "The Electronic Sales Call", *Information Week*, August 17, 1992.

Earls, Alan, "Manufacturing Finds Firmer Ground", *Computerworld*, February, 1994.

Hildebrand, Carol, "Financial Affairs", *CIO*, March, 1994.

La Plante, Alice, "Faster Factories", *Forbes*, ASAP, October, 1994.

Migilarese, Piero and Emilio Paolucci, "A System for Group Production Planning in Manufacturing", *Interfaces*, May-June, 1993.

Perry Linda, "Handle with Care Net", *Information*, April, 1992.

Ripciardi, Lucy R., "Is your Data Integrated and under your Control?," *Financial Executive*, July-August, 1993.

39

The Cellular Revolution: An Overview

AMIT NEB

Like the computer revolution, the cellphone or the mobile is creating a major revolution across the country. What started as a repple is today emerging as a giant ware bringing about a virtual socio-economic change in the country. The sea change is visible in every aspect of human life. In inter-personal life, business and commerce at the highest and lowest levels and fields unheard of like matrimonial markets, rescue operations, and shockingly enough in the dangerous fields of terrorism too! In the initial stages the possession of cellphones was the privilege of a few, but today with cellular majors vying with one another for the market, it has become affordable for anyone. The changes in a space of less than a decade have been so dramatic that many have come to realize that they cannot contemplate a life without their favourite mobile.

The year 2002-03 was a defining year for the mobile services business. Not only did the mobile services and some 7.75 million subscribers but also registered 50-53 percent growth in revenues, according to the Eighth National Telecom Survey Report, carried out by *Voice E Data* magazine released in July 2003. According to the report, the communication services market in India was worth Rs. 50,358 crores in 2002-03 This is a growth of 5.11 percent over the financial year 2001-02, when the market size was Rs. 47,908 crores. The services covered in the survey include the basic services, the cellular services, national and international long distance Internet services, VSAT services and radio trunking services. As per the report, while basic services contributed 57 percent to the total services industry size of

Rs. 50,358 crores last year, the fast-growing cellular services stood second with 16 percent.

The rapidly growing mobile subscription base has now crossed 16 million as a of August 2003. The cellular revolution has now reached the grassroots. In a few cities like Mumbai and Ahmedabad, you don't have to search for autorickshaws. Some savvy drivers wait for the customers to dial in-on their mobile. "After incoming calls became free, a host of rickshaw drivers, carpenters and plumbers are using our service." Says a CEO of a mobile major. While corporate majors are driving up cell phone revenues in urban pockets, mobile phones are changing the way small entrepreneurs and farmers do business in the interiors of the country. The escort of a disabled patient visiting the Regional Cancer Centre in Thiruvananthapuram uses his cell phone to call the chauffeur (who too possesses a mobile) from the distant parking lot. On another occasion the company driver standing in a queue at the busy reservation counter of the Ernakulam South railway station informs his GM's 'Madame' at home about the late running of a train, for the reservation of a seat in which he was asked to book. He takes an on-the-spot decision on alternatives while still at the head of the queue.

Cellephone companies are now trying to rope in more customers by providing special services to communities like fishermen, farmers and even those seeking life partners. User communities in urban areas are also the new beneficiaries. Many companies are targeting specific user communities even in the countryside for you don't have companies everywhere. In Kerala, BPL was the first to convince fishermen to have mobile. Of the six lakh cell phone subscribers in the state, about 12 percent are fisherman who use their phones while at sea to ascertain the best available rates for their catch at the several markets on the Kerala coast. An empty basket of your favourite fish in the market need not disappoint you: the vender would contact his man on the sea and if his reply is favourable, the seller will ask you to contact him again.

Idea Cellular also provides special schemes for fishermen across the coastal regions of Gujarat, Maharashtra and Goa. "We provide coverage up to 15 kms. into the sea. This allows fishermen to keep in touch with the mainland," says the CEO of Idea Cellular, Gujarat. In the north, Airtel helps farmers sell grains and vegetables in Punjab and Haryana. According to Airtel North India CEO, the organisation provides the latest rates at the five main markets at Jalandhar, Amritsar,

Patiala, Ludhiana and Bathinda. Over 400 local farmers have signed up for the service.

In recent times the over Rs. 500 crores money spinner matrimonial advertisement market has caught the fancy of the cell operators. Mobile First, the consortium of cellular operators BPL Mobile Escotel, RPG Cellular and Spice Cellular launched only July 23, 2003. India's first matrimonial service on mobile telephones. The scheme enables the Mobile First subscribers to find prospective life partners either for themselves or their near and dear ones through mobile phones. According to the managing director of Spice Telecom, Karnataka, which operates in the Punjab and Karnataka circles, the three million pan-India subscribers of Mobile First in 700 urban centres would be able to subscribe to this facility by using their SMS. While registration would be free, the operators will generate revenue through the greater use of SMS.

Even before the national launch of the service in Bangalore on July 23, 2003, trial runs have already led to the data base under the Life Parnter Scheme to jump to over 10,000 profiles in no time. It is indeed a boon when an individual could search for a life partner with greater ease and speed and that too at a low cost option to place a matrimonial advertisement with the reach extending across almost all the states and metros. The Life Partner Scheme is expected to generate over Rs. 250 crores as revenue for various operators.

Who want get tired in the big cities standing in long queue for paying the electricity bills, water bills or for getting cinema tickets. It is the time when tempers run high and when the poor consumers have to wait patiently to get their turn. When some elements try to jump the queue, a hell breaks loose. But some cellular service providers are prepared to come to the rescue of these consumers. They provide personnel who come to your door step, collect the bill and make the payment or even deliver movie tickets. You can also call the service provider or send an SMS to arrange technicians like electricians or plumbers. Even a doctor is on call, as are crucial services like blood banks and ambulances. This kind of service is not a source of revenue for the operators, but it promotes goodwill.

Service providers also allow for payment of cell phone bills electronically. Citibank Suvidha or Citibank Credit over phone by calling the bank through kiosks placed at ATMs or *via* the Internet. Standard Chartered Bank's credit card customers can pay cellphone bills through credit card, while ICICI and HDFC account holders can pay up over the Net. Hutch, with its service Hutch 4 Help has been trying to help customers get in touch with chemists, hospitals, ambulances and bloodbanks. Spice's Disha card enables women customers to access plumbers and electricians for nominal payment of Rs. 7. Airtel enables sourcing of SSLC or CBSE examination results by sending an SMS.

This is said revenues from mobile advertising and marketing (through mobile commerce) will exceed $ 1 billion over the next two years. During 2003-04 alone mobile advertising is expected to surpass online advertising revenues. It is claimed that by 2005, more people would access information on hand-held devices (mobile phones). There could be substantial increase in revenues by promoting mobile commerce (m-commerce).

The m-cash concept uses the mobile phone through SMS mode to conduct transactions. The cellular service provider has prototypes functioning at feed and beverage companies like Pepsi and Kingfisher. Cadbury has already set-up SMS-related vending machines at 35 locations on a pilot basis.

According to cell majors with an estimated 70 percent of the country's population below 30 years category which accounts for 25 percent of the current subscriber base, it is only natural to target the new schemers for the youth.

We have restricted the use of mobile while driving simply because it could create conditions for accidents. But Doctors in Delhi are pressing the Delhi Government to waive this rule just because doctors have to attend to emergency calls while driving. It amounts to injustice to the patients. At present, the traffic cop can slap a fine of Rs. 1,000 if they find you using the mobile while driving.

It is indeed a matter of pride that an Indian engineer, Mr. Arun Sarin, a graduate from the IIT Kharagpur, has taken over as the Chief Executive of the world's biggest mobile phone company, the $ 100 million UK based Vodaphone. This has made Arun Britain's most powerful Asian businessman. Mr. Sarin has been a director of Cisco Systems, the networking switching giant. He was also the CEO of Vodaphone, US and Asia-Pacific operations and Chief Operating Officer of Airtough, a US-based wireless provider. Born in India, he did his B.Tech. at IIT Kharagpur and obtained both an MS and MBA from the University of California at Berkeley in 1978.

Like any other scientific or technological device the mobile is also used for destructive purposes. You can't blame the mobile if the user uses it for committing crimes against humanity. The notorious terrorists Amrozi bin Nurhasyim of Indonesia denoted his car-bomb attacks in Indonesia in October 2002 by using mobile phone.

Even five year olds in England use mobile phones, prompting worries about their health and safety. A new research by the British Government has advised against young children using mobile phones for long calls because of the greater risk of radiowaves penetrating their thinker skulls. Primary school children in U.K. are the fastest growing market for mobile phones. With more than 4,00,000 owning a handset. One in nine children aged five to nine has a mobile phone, double the number two years ago.

Cell phone operators in India have mounted an aggressive market strategy to woo potential customers and their campaigns are yielding rich dividends. Indian society is in a flux and people of all categories are trying to get mobile telephone because they need it. They are no longer going in for it for the heck of it. For most of them mobile has added colour and convenience to their daily life.

40

Perfect Competition: From Myth to Reality

YOGESH UPADHYAY AND S.K. SINGH

In the last two decades, Information Technology has played a key role in transforming the way business is conducted. With each new wave of technology, it has brought about fundamental changes. In all these, the one technology that has truly been an effective agent in changing the fundamental ways of doing business is none other than ubiquitous thing that everyone knows as Internet. (*Hindustan Times*, 1998).

THE PERFECT COMPETITION

Adam Smith himself recognised that the virtues of market mechanism are fully realised when the checks and balances of perfect competition are present (Samuelson, 1992).

Perfect competition refers to a market in which no firm or consumer is effective enough to affect the market price. The firms are usually *price takers*. The buyer is aware of the prevailing prices in the market. The entry and exit of firms have least effect on the market.

Till now, perfect competition was considered to be a myth. But the advent of Internet has made it a reality. The geographical boundaries are eroding rapidly for the purpose of business with the spread of Internet. The implication is that the sellers or buyers which due to their number or capacity were able to affect the price earlier can not do so now. It is not a single country where buyers and firms are spread. They are spread across the globe. Therefore, the number of such firms and buyers are minuscule in proportion which can have impact on globally prevalent prices. The firms are also free to enter and exit from the market place.

Resultantly, Internet growth has led to a host of new developments, such as decreased margins for companies as consumers turn more and more to the Internet to buy goods and demand the best prices, as observed by C.K. Prahalad, Professor, Business School, University of Michigan. The Internet means that traditional businesses will change because "incumbents (in markets) and large firms do not have the advantage" just by virtue of being there first or by being big, he said. The implication of perfectly competitive market as the world will observe is that markets will produce *an efficient allocation of resources.*

In any market with no entry-barriers — the Net is the biggest of them — the continuous influx of competition will, automatically, drive down prices. Add to that the unique economics of Net-based products and services, where the incremental cost of creating additional units is zero and prices also tend to gravitate towards the zero-mark. In such a case, in long-term all firms could only earn normal profits.

Rohan Bulchandani is booking his place in the virtual profit-zone by managing prices. In June, 1998, Annet Communications, the technology solutions company of which he is the CEO, set-up India's first on-line bookstore, IndiaBookShop (www.india bookshop.com). Although it has subsequently expanded has become a part of Indishop (www.indishop.com), which e-retails music, gifts, flowers, etc. alongside books. India Book Shop remains the engine of this e-biz. Its discount of at least 20 per cent on the cover price of the books that it sells. IndiaBookShop does it by positioning itself as wholesaler and not as a retailer in the book-trade. This brings us trade discounts which we pass on to buyer. Also, we own our delivery as well as procurement networks." In other words, its the cost-structure that counts. However, its never-say-no-to-an-order strategy frequently raises sourcing and delivery costs. But Bulchandani's real focus is on increasing the conversion rate, which, at present, stands at 1.20 per cent — or, about 60 sales out of the daily average of 5,000 hits — amounting to an annual turnover of Rs. 73 lakh. After all, he'd love to be India's Amazon *et al.* (1999).

WHAT IS INTERNET COMMERCE?

According to the US-based Aberdeen Group: *Internet Commerce* is a term used to describe the automation, the full range of interactions across corporate borders between companies and people – from marketing to sales, order placement to invoicing and payment, product distribution and customer service – by establishing computer-to-computer service by establishing computer-to-computer communication, utilising the infrastructure and standards of the Internet (*Data Quest*, 1998).

Business over the NET comprises different types of commerce. The first is *business-to-business* commerce, which replaces the classic way of doing business – using telephone calls, purchase orders, faxes, mail messages and so on – with real-time interfacing over the NET. This is expected to be the dominant form of business transaction as we move forward. The second is, perhaps, glamorous and so, gets greater publicity in the press: *home-to-business* or *individual consumer-to-business transactions* – where the individual end-user can buy flowers, books, real estate and automobiles over the Net. The interesting fact about this forecast – which suggests that by 2002, $ 500 billion of business will be transacted on the Net – is that each time this forecast is updated, the figure tends to increase by 30 per cent. IBM transacts business worth approximately $ 5 billion over the NET (Craig Radford Barrett, 1998).

The greatest payoff for corporate IT investments shall come from actually conducting trade on Internet, i.e. selling goods and services over the net. Companies all over the world are only now coming to terms with what it actually means. Among other things, it actually represents the opportunity for companies to reach beyond the boundaries of its limited reach, be it within its country or outside. Clearly, it promises of possibilities that would have been once considered utopian by practical business heads.

There are several estimates floating around about the potential of this medium as a means of facilitating trade. Going by IDC figures, in 1997 alone more than $ 10 billion in transactions were executed over the Internet. Given the size of conventional trade, perhaps the figure is small indeed, as it amounts to a mere 0.05% of the global trade.

But again, it would be indeed shortsighted to ignore its impact. IDC forecasts that by year 2001, Internet commerce will surge over $ 220 billion. Another research study by Forester predicts that by 2002, the value of goods and services traded between companies over the Internet will reach $ 327 billion, just under 1% of global trade (Craig Radford Barrette, 1998).

BENEFITS OF E-COMMERCE

A survey on the status of E-commerce has been conducted by KPMG, covering a sample of 116 companies operating in the country more than two-thirds of which have a turnover of over Rs. 100 crore. The survey evaluates the perceptions, status and triggers of the use of E-commerce in Indian companies. The results of survey done by *KPMG India Electronic Commerce Survey* regarding the benefits the corporates are observing by conducting business through Internet are summarised below:

What Benefits are you Getting from E-commerce?

Improved Productivity
Improved Product Quality
Improved Customer
Reduced Costs
Sortened Supply Chain
New Product Development
Reaching New Customers
Improved Cash-Flows

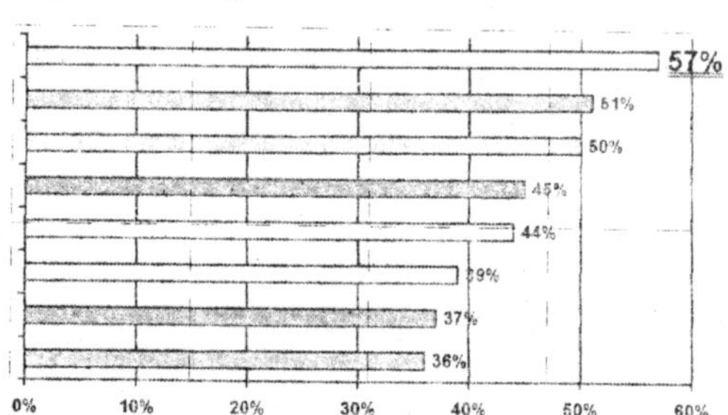

Source: KPMG India Electronic Commerce Survey Report, 1998-99 adapted from *Business Today*, March 22, 1999, pp. 80-83.

It is clear from the above chart that largest benefit to the corporates transacting business through Internet is improved productivity. It is followed by improved product quality, improved customer service, reduced costs, shortened supply chain, etc. It can well be concluded from the array of data that the greatest beneficiary of Internet is consumer. He is going to gain by improved products quality, service, reduced costs, etc. In other words, greater the business transacted on Internet, the more consumer satisfaction shall follow.

NET PROFITS

Drawn irresistibly by the digital economy, where 100 million shoppers will spend an estimated $ 15 billion in 1999, a host of entrepreneurs around the world have planted their start-ups in the marketspace, capitalising on the fact that it only needs a computer and a phone-line to get going so have corporates with deep roots in the physical marketplace, whose entry has been parked off more by the fear of mission out on an opportunity than by the profit motive *et al.* (1999).

Most of them have proved that economics of E-commerce isn't easy to master. Most, but not all, for, a small, but select, set of Net-millionaires are demonstrating that the Net can, indeed, be a theatre for profitable business.

- Bill Gross is millionaire many times over after an e-biz, *shopping.com,* funded by his company, ideala!, was acquired by Compaq Computer for $ 220 million.
- The 39 per cent equity held by Jeff Bezos in *Amazon.com,* which he founded, is worth $ 2.50 million with the company's stock priced at $ 133.
- Brothers Andrew and Thomas Parkinson's stake in America's No. 1 online-retailer, Penpod, is worth $ 64 million.
- Timothy A. Koogle, the CEO of Yahoo!, can value his stock at $ 625 million, with the company being priced by the stockmarkets at $ 2 billion.
- By selling, Junglee to Amazon.com, founders Venky Harinarayan, Rakesh Mathur, Anand Rajaram and Ashish Gupta raked in $ 180 million.

Several genres of such media have emerged: the portal – Yahoo!, MSN, Lycos or Excite are classic examples – in its most generalised form acts as an entry-point to the vast reaches of the Net for surfers, offering them links to the subject of their choice. A more specialised version, the so-called affinity portal, acts as a broad window to a narrow theme – such as ESPN Sportzone to sports, or C-Net to technology. And, in its most focused form, the portal is devoted to specific events – the Academy Awards, for instance.

ON-LINE SHOPPING YET TO TAKE OFF IN INDIA

According to a survey done by Capital Images (Chatterjee, 1999) with a sample of 470 individuals across the four metros of Mumbai, Delhi, Pune and Bangalore only 29 per cent of the respondents have shopped on the Internet. And an overwhelmingly 71 per cent of the respondents have not done so-ever.

This is interesting on two counts. First, considering the fact that

91 per cent of the respondents are users of Internet, the fact that they are 'passive' would come in the way of companies launching E-commerce business.

Second, since the survey was conducted among respondents aged between 25 and 15 years and comprised of corporate executives and professionals (middle-to-high-income-groups), it also proves that the cost of the product is not a hindrance. It is simply the mindset of the respondents.

According to the survey, buying movie tickets on the Net is the most preferred option. Thirty-four per cent of the respondents have bought movie tickets on-line, while 27 per cent have bought audio cassettes/CDs. Another 25 per cent respondents have bought books, while 12 per cent have bought items like flowers and chocolates. The remaining 2 per cent have bought items like cosmetics, garments or booked train tickets.

Bottomline: Low-cost purchases dominate E-commerce in India today, with high-end products yet to make any impact.

There were some other interesting findings in the survey. As 33 per cent of the respondents surf the Net 'very often' and another 25 per cent 'often' surf. Internet surfing in urban India is clearly beginning to emerge as a regular habit, with approximately 58 per cent of the respondents logging on fairly often. However, around 42 per cent of the respondents are infrequent users.

Among the favourite sites and search engines, Yahoo.com emerged as the most widely-used search engine with 49 per cent of the respondents giving it the first choice, followed by Netsape.com with 3 per cent respondents choosing it as the second most preferred search engine.

Excite.com and AOL.com me not very popular, with only 5 per cent and 4 per cent of the respondents using them respectively. Significantly, the most widely used sites are Indiatimes.com, Indiajobs.com, Khoj.com, Khel.com, Infoseek.com and Askjeeves.com.

In terms of users' buying patterns for consumer durables involving a higher budget outlay, consumers would prefer to physically examine product specifications prior to purchase. This refers to computers, TV, properties and cars. Buyers of consumer durables also look at value discount, freebies and financing options.

Interestingly, a significant 52 per cent of the respondents are flexible on buying branded clothes on the Net. The respondents were confident of the consistency of brand value and also the fact that they could choose from a colour range wherein many have a prior disposition.

Moreover, in the readywear market there seems to be a trend to buy instantly on the 'known size'. However, 48 per cent of the respondents are not keen to buy apparel on the Net, as they would like to 'try them on first'.

E-commerce essentially relies on electronic transfer of money involving instruments like credit cards. In India, it could be difficult. Sixty-seven per cent of the respondents do not want to give their credit card details over the Net. This, in fact, is one of the main reasons they are averse to shopping on the Net. The remaining 33 per cent do not mind giving their credit card details, subject to the authenticity and brand perception of the site.

As regards choice of payments, surprisingly 35 per cent of the respondents would still prefer to make their payments *via* cheques, 34 per cent through credit cards, 24 per cent in cash, while the remaining 7 per cent would prefer to make their payments through VPP.

Convenience in shopping, guarantees on product quality and discounts were some of the main reasons that prompted a Net user to buy goods and services over the Net.

While the potential of E-commerce in India is phenomenal, the fact of the matter is that India is way behind developed nations in terms of the Internet and its allied services. Consider this: 72 per cent of the Web sites are still based in the US and 92 per cent of the total volume of E-commerce business is generated through US-based Web sites.

CONCLUSION

It can fairly be concluded that the advent of Internet at last could turn the myth of perfect competition into reality. Though it is the best form of competition but it eluded so far due to imperfections prevailing in the real world. But the introduction of Internet could remove the imperfections from the market. The biggest beneficiary in such a case is the consumer. It will be in the interest of consumers that the Internet be used as a means of transacting business at the earliest. But the scenario in India presently is not very encouraging. It will still take time for the Internet to become a full-fledged tool for transacting business due to low per capita incomes and poor infrastructure.

REFERENCES

Chandrashekar, S., Dabhal Shailesh and Sukumar, R. (1999), "Net Profits or how (finally) to make money on the net", *Business Today*, March 22, p. 77.

Chandrashekar, S., Dabhal Shailesh and Sukumar, R. (1999), "Net Profits or how (finally) to make money on the net", *Business Today*, March 22, pp. 68-79.

Chatterjee, Aditya (1999), *The Times of India*, September 20, p. 12.

Data Quest (1998), "Internet Commerce—Leveraging the Net for Profit", *Internet Commerce Supplement*, September 30, p. 6.

Excerpts from Intel's Business Strategy by its CEO Craig Radford Barrette (1998), "Inside New Millennium Computing", *Business Today*, November 22-December 6, p. 102.

Ibid., p. 7.

Hindustan Times, 18 June, 1998, p. 12.

KPMG India Electronic Commerce Survey Report, 1998-99, adapted from *Business Today*, March 22, 1999, pp. 80-83.

Samuelson, A. Paul and Nordhaus, D. Williams (1992), *Economics*, McGraw-Hill International Ed., p. 40.

Index